Making Good Preaching Better

A Step-by-Step Guide to Scripture-Based, People-Centered Preaching

Alvin C. Rueter

A Liturgical Press Book

THE LITURGICAL PRESS
Collegeville, Minnesota

Cover design by Greg Becker

1   2   3   4   5   6   7   8   9

Library of Congress Cataloging-in-Publication Data

Rueter, Alvin C.
　　Making good preaching better : a step-by-step guide to scripture-based, people-centered preaching / Alvin C. Rueter.
　　　　　p.　cm.
　　Includes bibliographical references and index.
　　ISBN 0-8146-2215-1
　　1. Preaching.　　I. Title.
BV4211.2.R84 1996
251—dc20   96-42563
　　　　　　　　　　　　　　　　　　　　　　　　　　　　　　　　　CIP

Contents

Exercises

Appendix

Preface

With so many other homiletics books available, why this one too? Does this book's content offer anything different? Yes. I have numerous written testimonials from those who have attended my preaching workshops saying things like, "I wish I had learned this in the seminary."

What accounts for this? I lay it to an unexpected turn in my life, leading to my graduate work studying homiletics in the departments of speech communication in two state universities.

In 1963, while serving American Lutheran Church, Lincoln, Nebraska, the Central District of The American Lutheran Church surprised me with a thousand-dollar grant for graduate work. With a wife and four children, I could not see my way to resigning my parish and moving to a theological school. So I searched the catalog of the University of Nebraska-Lincoln and settled upon the speech department. Having had only two hours of speech in college, my professors required me first to complete an undergraduate major. When I later accepted a call to a parish in St. Paul, Minnesota, I applied to the Graduate School of the University of Minnesota. In every course I asked myself, "Is this compatible with Christian theology?" The papers I wrote were usually my response to that question. It took me twenty-five years to complete my doctorate because I was working on it while serving full time as a parish pastor and later as a professor. While this may not be the recommended way to pursue a doctorate, I see an advantage in having had to struggle with theory and practice side by side.

The fruit of this cross-fertilization between speech communication and Christian theology was ripening not only in my pastoral experience but also as I led over thirty preaching workshops in various locations but primarily at Dana College, Blair, Nebraska; St. Olaf College, Northfield, Minnesota; and St. John's University, Collegeville, Minnesota. In these I was working with preaching professionals.

I reaped further insights from working with students who mostly were preaching beginners: in the School of Theology, St. John's University, Collegeville, Minnesota; the Lutheran Theological Seminary, Hong Kong; and in the Diaconate Formation programs of the Archdiocese of St. Paul and Minneapolis and of the Diocese of St. Cloud, Minnesota.

Out of all this comes a work with these qualities:

1. In matters of content and strategy, this book is different from other books, particularly in dealing with such questions as the legitimacy of the appeal to self-interest, the ethics of preaching, and how to handle themes difficult for some listeners to accept.

2. In matters of form and style, this book deals with a topic often overlooked, the ancient rhetorical canon of memory, not necessarily memorizing but learning how to transmit those golden words etched onto the paper by the sweat of so many hours. While not ruling out other methods of memory, this book favors preaching without notes. Not rambling, not impromptu, not memorized, but so well prepared that preachers are freed up to think on their feet. The secret lies in how one goes about preparing; a properly prepared sermon will be alive even when it is read.

One obstacle to memory is the lack of cohesiveness. The only thing holding some sermons together is the paper they are written on. That is why some preachers must read their homilies: even they cannot remember them. This book deals extensively with cohesiveness.

3. Although this book should be useful to Roman Catholic priests and deacons and Protestant pastors—all of whom are already preaching regularly—it is also intended to be a textbook for seminaries, diaconate formation programs, and preaching workshops. Pedagogically, this book may be different from others because it offers readings and exercises both to enhance and to reinforce the theory developed in each chapter.

The exercises are built on a step-by-step plan patterned after the system of teaching used by early rhetoricians. The exercises have been tested in over thirty preaching workshops and ten years of classroom teaching, but there may be instructors using this book who for good reason may decide not to use my suggestions; I believe this book will be useful even without them. In the section entitled "To the Instructor,"

I describe the assumptions on which these exercises are based.

This book does not attack homilists. We are indeed easy targets for criticism.

1. We are compared with some TV personalities.

I marvel at the list of credits at the end of programs; we preachers don't have that kind of support. TV programs also get by with reruns; we have to produce all year long.

2. We are compared with Rotary Club speakers.

These speakers may have only one speech that they recycle for the next audience; we preachers know how hard it is to keep preaching to the same fine people, some of whom—God bless them—come every time the church is open.

Rotary Club audiences are homogeneous; we preachers must address the needs and hopes of people of an assortment of ages and social conditions.

3. In addition to criticism from the general population, we are also taken to task by professionals in theology, literature, and the use of language, all of whom have legitimate complaints, but few of whom grunt in the homiletical trenches week after week after week.

And because I was a parish pastor for thirty-three years, that's why, dear reader, I'm on your side.

Protestants will notice that I usually speak about homilies instead of sermons. That's to avoid confusion. For Roman Catholics the word *sermon* means "a religious talk," whether based on Scripture or not. For them *homily* means "a message growing out of the readings."

Perhaps every reader will notice the oral style in which this book is written. In chapter 7, "Making Homilies Oral," I plead against writing essays for the pulpit. To help me practice writing for the ear, I strive to make all of my writing in oral style. That accounts for the reaction of some who've read this work in manuscript, "When I read this, I hear you speaking."

I gratefully acknowledge the suggestions and the affirmation received from Dr. Bernard Evans and Dr. Maxwell Johnson, School of Theology, St. John's University, Collegeville, Minnesota, who read parts of my manuscript while it was in progress; Bishop Lowell Erdahl, former bishop of the St. Paul Area Synod, Evangelical Lutheran Church in America and former professor of homiletics,

Luther Seminary, St. Paul, Minnesota, who read my entire manuscript while it was in progress; and Dr. Pirkko Lehtiö, Dr. Peter Lee,
and Dr. Andrew Ng, Lutheran Theological Seminary, Hong Kong,
who critiqued my manuscript after it was written.

I dedicate this book to the memory of my wife, Beulah, who
died 8 December 1993. She kept me going during those twenty-five
years when I was often tempted to quit my schooling. She also kept
encouraging me to write this book.

Alvin C. Rueter

(My name is a problem for most people. Say it: not "Royter" but
"Rooter." Spell it: the u before the e—not "Reuter" but "Rueter.")

Acknowledgments

The Scripture quotations contained herein (unless otherwise noted) are from the *New Revised Standard Version* (NRSV), copyright 1989 by the Division of Christian Education of the National Council of the Churches of Christ in the United States of America. Used by permission. All rights reserved.

Much of this book is based on material originally written by the author in columns entitled "People-Centered Preaching," for *Emphasis,* CSS Publishing Company, Lima, Ohio. Chapter 2 is based not only on that column but on articles written for *Lutheran Partners,* Evangelical Lutheran Church in America, Chicago, Illinois. Chapter 12 is also based on the column "People-Centered Preaching" as well as an article in *Word & World,* Luther Seminary, St. Paul, Minnesota.

"Abstraction Ladder" from *Language in Thought and Action,* copyright 1939 and renewed 1967 by S. I. Hayakawa, reproduced by permission of Harcourt Brace & Company.

Two homilies in the appendix, "Do We Need God?" and "Much More," are reprinted from *Augsburg Sermons, Gospels, Series C,* copyright 1973, Augsburg Publishing House. Used by permission of Augsburg Fortress.

Regarding other items in the Appendix:

Numbers 7, 8, 9, and 13, articles by the author, were published first in *The Lutheran Standard,* Augsburg Publishing House, used by permission of Augsburg Fortress.

Numbers 4, 6, and 11 are from Alvin Rueter, *The Freedom to Be Wrong* (Lima, Ohio: CSS Publishing Co., 1985), reprinted by permission. Unpublished homilies not by the author, numbers 10, 12, and 14, are printed by permission of the homilists.

To the Instructor

About the Suggested Exercises

(You probably have a time-tested way of teaching. By disregarding the suggested exercises, I believe the substance of this book will fit any system of pedagogy. The following is an explanation of why and how the suggested exercises were developed.)

In my first years of teaching homiletics, I had sections of ten students, two periods per week. We devoted a period (fifty minutes) twice during the quarter to each student, first to preach and then to receive constructive comments. The philosophy was, "We learn best by doing."

I noticed that the students too often were overwhelmed by the magnitude of the task. They were trying to follow my emphasis on exegesis and hermeneutics, on structure and style, and were coming up short. It was too much to manage all at once, and they felt defeated. They were not looking forward to preaching with the enthusiasm I had hoped they would have. This system of learning by doing was teaching them that "Preaching is a chore."

Learning by Doing: "Elementary Exercises"

During this time I had two experiences that pushed me into another mode of learning by doing: I was learning to swim, and I was studying classical rhetoric.

Where did the swimming coach start? Did she push me off the side into the deep water and then sit calmly in her chair taking notes on all my mistakes as I was thrashing and flailing to stay alive? No, but that is the model used sometimes in homiletics classes. "You stand up and preach and we'll tell you what you did wrong."

I have heard a theory that says, "The student needs such a defeat—to slay the ego, to become teachable." Yet suppose this process does indeed render preachers teachable; then what? Do we continue with the same strategy, still dumping them overboard, still to flap and flounder without guidance? Would it not be better—like the swimming coach—to show them one step at a time? Would that not be more like the gospel? Just as a discouraged sinner does not need more failure, the discouraged preacher needs success. If we analyze what must be known and practiced to achieve the desired outcome and then break up that process into steps that can be managed one at a time, then the preacher can enjoy success at each stage and continue to be enthusiastic about proclaiming good news.

This idea is hardly new: it goes back to the fourth century B.C. An anonymous work, *Rhetorica ad Alexandrum,* refers to *progymnasmata,* elementary exercises in writing and speaking. Suetonius writes that elementary exercises were used in the Roman schools from the first century B.C. Quintilian describes them briefly in the first century A.D. The earliest surviving textbook using *progymnasmata* is from the second century. Elementary exercises were used at least through the seventeenth century.

Elementary exercises presented a graded series of exercises in writing and speaking, proceeding from the easy to the more difficult. They built on what the students had learned, repeating something from the previous exercise, yet always adding something new.[1]

I have been designing and testing *progymnasmata* for homiletics in over thirty preaching workshops for both Protestant and Roman Catholic clergy. If I called them "elementary exercises," I have found they were still appreciated by the professionals, some of whom were in their fifties and sixties. After I had been holding preaching workshops for a while, I taught homiletics in the School of Theology, St. John's University, Collegeville, Minnesota. After retiring, I was invited to teach homiletics to aspiring permanent deacons in the Archdiocese of St. Paul and Minneapolis. After four years of retirement, I was invited to teach again at St. John's University. I was also invited to teach aspiring permanent deacons in the Diocese of St. Cloud, Minnesota. In the spring semester both in 1996 and 1997, I taught in the Lutheran Theological Seminary of Hong Kong. In all four places I have learned that beginners appre-

---

1. More about elementary exercises in Donald Yemen Clark, *Rhetoric in Greco-Roman Education* (New York: Columbia University Press, 1957) esp. pp. 177–261; Donald Yemen Clark, "The Rise and Fall of Progymnasmata in Sixteenth and Seventeenth Century Grammar Schools," *Speech Monographs* 19 (November 1952) 259–63; Ray Nadeau, "The Progymnasmata of Aphthonius," *Speech Monographs* 19 (November 1952) 264–85.

ciate having success as they develop step by step. Even though they may have discovered preaching to be far more work than they had ever imagined, I have been delighted to feel their enthusiasm for the opportunity of bringing good news.

Three-Minute Homiletical Exercises

The compressed preaching workshop format—four days at some places, five at others—pushed me to limit the exercises in front of the VCR to a strictly enforced three minutes. When I began teaching semester-long courses at St. John's University, I retained the three-minute limit, for the most part. I liked the results I'd been getting in preaching workshops; furthermore, this way the students were being critiqued five times instead of only twice: each time they were gaining new confidence, and each time their fellow class members were growing in their critiquing skills. (Being sharper in their awareness of what makes good preaching only helped them become better the next time as well.)

I see another advantage for the three-minute exercise: it enables me to combine theory and practice at a pace that's manageable.

The system with which I began—you preach and we'll tell what was wrong—allowed for no systematic way of developing the theory; there was barely time to cover whatever problems the homily may have had. To overcome this difficulty, other professors who have the luxury of having more time allocated to homiletics may devote the first part of the term to theory, the second to letting students preach one or two complete homilies. The difficulty I see with this is that there is a time-lag between theory and practice and an information deluge hard to take in all at once. The three-minute VCR exercise allows me to present one item of homiletical theory and have the students practice it immediately, in the later exercises not forgetting what was practiced in the previous assignments.

In a setting other than a week-long workshop, the last exercise can be a full-length homily, putting together all that has been practiced in the previous exercises. If you follow the exercises offered in this book, your students will have been preaching without notes three minutes at a time. By the end of the term they will be able to deliver a full-length homily the same way without memorizing.

Within the limits of week-long preaching workshops, I had to find a way that priests and pastors could practice the first VCR exercise without also mastering a Scripture text. Since I am a Lutheran and have been teaching in Lutheran and Roman Catholic settings, it was natural for me to assign materials from our catechisms, something my workshop participants knew backwards and for-wards, as the basis for the content. From time to time I have had clergy from other heritages who still had no difficulty dealing with assignments based on the Commandments, the Creeds, and the Lord's Prayer. Those instructors whose students may not be com-fortable with such components from the catechism will want to find other ways to frame these exercises.

Will Exercises Based on the Catechism Prejudice Students Against Exegesis?

When students have success delivering three-minute homilies on material they already know, does that teach them they don't need to work hard on the Scriptures? That has always worried me, and so I have taken pains to ward against that. Soon after we've gotten started on the VCR exercises, I've devoted a part of each period working as a group on a gospel reading coming soon in the lec-tionary. This too is done step-by-step according to the process de-scribed in the chapters, "Releasing Our Creativity," and "Making Homilies Textual." Because we're working as a group, I put each Scripture verse on a sheet of newsprint and attach the paper to the chalkboard with masking tape. I write our comments and questions on the appropriate sheets. I save the sheets for future sessions. This procedure includes a written exegetical paper on that text.

About Preaching Without Notes in the Three-Minute Exercises

This book is biased towards training homilists to preach without notes. But I try to allow for the fact that there are preachers who are effective with other means. In chapter seven, "Making Homilies Oral," I contend, "It's not the reading but the writing," that the diffi-culty is in trying to read essays instead of adapting to an acoustical medium. In chapter fifteen, "Remembering Your Homily," again I allow that any method of reproducing what we have prepared can be useful so long as the homily is visual, oral, and cohesive.

So why do I still require my students to deliver their three-minute oral exercises without notes? Because I've discovered noth-ing else that so quickly forces them to be visual, oral, and cohesive. I may allow them to do the first oral exercise by reading a manu-script, but when I require the second one to be without notes, the improvement is dramatic. I tell my students, "I'll grant that you're under more pressure than your listeners, but if you can't remember what you're going to say, how can they? You've been working on your homily for hours; they have to get it in one sitting." And how can the homilist remember? When the homilist can see what will be said; when what is said is spoken in oral style, (easier to remember than the complicated sentences of written style), and when the homily hangs together on its own. As I observe in chapter seven, "The only thing holding some homilies together is the paper they're written on." They're not cohesive; the homilist must read them because the homilist can't remember otherwise what comes next. Preaching without notes is the acid test as to whether the homily is cohesive or not. If the homilist always gets stuck in a certain place and can't remember what comes next without looking at the paper, there's something wrong with the structure.

The step-by-step process of practicing cohesiveness, visualness, and oralness, three minutes at a time, helps them grow into this skill. You'll notice that the exercises emphasize not memorizing the order of the words but the flow of the pictures, that we simply remember the sequence of the scenes and how they relate to our purpose, and then we merely report what we see. If we were trying to recall the order of the words and couldn't, we'd be undone. But when we're dealing with pictures assembled in an orderly fashion and talking about them in simple sentences, we can see what we're saying and we can keep going.

If students plan in the future to use notes in the pulpit, my insistence that they preach without notes during the time of instruction will prepare them to be better at reading because they will have composed their homilies so they'll be visual, oral, and cohesive. What they'll read will be easier to deliver and easier to listen to.

So I see this requirement not as an end in itself but as a means to an end—to help train them in producing homilies that are visual, oral, and cohesive no matter what means they might use in the future to deliver the product of their sweat to the people.

About Preaching Without a Pulpit in the Three-Minute Exercises

Nowhere else in this book do I mention that in my classes and workshops, we stand before the video camera with no pulpit, no lectern, no music stand. For various reasons other homiletics professors will have a different policy. I'm only explaining how I got into this.

I've seen many preachers hanging onto the pulpit as though it might otherwise get away from them. I've tried gentle persuasion. This involved explaining what I discuss in chapter thirteen, "Nonverbal Preaching," that through empathy the muscles of the listeners imitate the tensing or relaxing of the preacher's muscles, they don't want to communicate all that tightness to their people. This has worked sometimes. I've tried using a music stand instead of a pulpit or lectern, thinking that if the preacher leans too hard on the music stand, it will lower itself and take away the preacher's support. That also worked–for some. It was during one of our preaching workshops for homilists already in the business that I decided to take away all such props, to let them stand out in the open with nothing to hide behind. It was tough love, and there was some muted grumbling. But it worked, and it keeps on working. When they get back to their own pulpits, they're not fastened down anymore.

Using the VCR

The VCR has been the answer to Robert Burns's prayer for the gift to see ourselves as others see us. Now having that gift, we homiletics professors have been experimenting as to the best way to use it. I have tried various plans.

My comments are colored by a principle I developed from my experiences as a student in public speaking assignments. We had two categories on our critique sheets: compliments and suggestions. In those early days we weren't using the VCR. The pupil/instructor ratio was so high there was no time for oral feedback and no time between speeches for writing our reactions. So that we speakers could have eye contact with at least half the class, we numbered off; the "odds" would write critiques of the first speech, the "evens" would write on the second speech, etc. Whenever I was giving a speech, as soon as I noticed someone writing–even though it might have been a compliment–I still worried, "What was wrong with that?" It distracted me so much I vowed if I should ever have any control over such a situation, the whole room would give the speaker full support; no one–not even the instructor–would be allowed to write anything while the speech or sermon was being delivered.

Here are the various methods I've tried.

> 1. For a full-length homily, play back just a minute for the homilist and the class.
>
> *For:* It gives the homilist at least a brief view of himself/herself and provides more time for oral feedback.
>
> *Against:* The classmates may be so intent on writing that they pay little attention to the playback, not getting maximum learning benefit from the VCR.

2. The students have their own video cassettes; they view their preaching on their own time by themselves.

For: Students may go back at any time and view their earlier efforts, seeing their progress.

Against: Most are too hard on themselves; they see only their defects. Even with the VCR's aid, they still do not see themselves as others see them.

It could happen that precious class time is lost cuing up each student's video cassette, particularly later in the course when there's more than one homily on the cassette.

3. No playback during class; instructor and student view the tape together a few days later.

For: It saves time for oral feedback.

Viewing the tape a few days later provides a little space for students so they may be a bit more calm in reflecting on their preaching.

It provides personal contact between instructor and student.

Against: It deprives classmates of the greater learning that would come as they gave a second look at the homily.

The homilists—not having the support of their peers—may still be too hard on themselves.

It requires a great deal of time from the professor.

4. The plan I use now: with three-minute exercises, the entire class sees the entire playback each time.

For: The homilists do see themselves as others see them, because when they are too hard on themselves, their peers correct them.

Not being allowed to write during the actual preaching, it takes hardly any more time to write during the playback than if the students were writing without a playback.

Letting the whole class see the playback improves their critiquing skills. I believe I can claim this because students sometimes say they observed something during the playback that they missed the first time.

It can help homilists appreciate their strengths. After the class has given its compliments, I ask the homilists, particularly early in the term: "What did you like about this homily?" If they drift into finding fault with their work, I say, "We'll talk about that later. What did you see and hear that you liked?"

Against: It loses the built-in structure of plan 3 for conversation between instructor and homilist. However, at least in the places where I have taught, other ways came up in the natural course of things to foster these personal relationships.

With three-minute exercises, you may have more than one homilist speaking each class session. You could have the playback and feedback immediately following the first preacher and then have the second homilist with playback and feedback, etc. Two problems with that: the preachers down the list are jittery and thinking only about what they're going to preach; and the instructor and class may spend so much time on one homily that there is little left for later speakers. So I prefer to let all homilists preach one after the other before any playbacks occur.

It would seem logical to stop the camera when one homilist is finished and start it when the next one begins. But since there is no space on the tape between preachers, it is harder to cue it up on playbacks. I have found it easier to let the camera run between speakers.

In order for me to give full attention to the preaching, I ask students to run the equipment, even if I first have to show them how.

Helping Students Rehearse

I always took it for granted that preachers would rehearse, but in my preaching workshops I discovered that a few homilists hardly ever practice—especially those who read a manuscript. One of the expectations of this book is that students will rehearse their homilies. Since both students and professional clergy are short of time, they will appreciate being shown how to rehearse more effectively. I have two suggestions on this point.

1. Show them how to store the homily in their heads.
   Before standing up to rehearse, I suggest they recall the purpose of this homily. (In terms of the chapter "Making Homilies Cohesive," the purpose is the destination towards which they and their people are moving in this homily.) Next, I suggest they recall the introduction, the start of the journey. Then they will reflect on how they will get from the start to the destination. (In terms of the chapter "Making Homilies Visual," this means recalling the flow of the pictures that they are drawing for the people.) I emphasize that

they should memorize not the order of the words but the order of the pictures.

2. They should rehearse not only by themselves but, to gain constructive feedback, also with a partner.

This may seem as strange to you as it did to me when I first thought of it. I came upon the idea by accident. Through a series of events I don't mind describing but which takes too long to tell, I found myself in the business world coaching executives in public speaking and meeting the press. Then I was offered a position at St. John's University, half-time in the School of Theology teaching homiletics and half-time in the college teaching an introductory course in public speaking and an upper division course in persuasion. But I had two or three training sessions with business clients still to fulfill in that first year I was to teach at St. John's; I asked the academic vice-president whether she would allow me to meet my commitments to these clients. She said, "Yes; just figure out some way to keep your students occupied profitably."

So I had my students draw for rehearsal partners. They were to use the class time I missed to rehearse their next homily or speech. I designed critique sheets requiring two rehearsals, to be signed by both homilist and rehearsal partner. After I returned from my first absence, I found the students so much improved that I kept the policy of requiring rehearsal partners as a regular feature of my courses. However, after I finished with my business clients, I didn't give students class time for it.

After I retired from St. John's, the Archdiocese of St. Paul and Minneapolis asked me to teach homiletics in its formation program for permanent deacons. Here I found a natural application of this approach to rehearsing with a partner for constructive feedback. The archdiocese encourages spouses to attend with their husbands. Who would be better rehearsal partners than spouses? Would it be the answer to the special burden that Protestant spouses carry? (How and when can they say anything about last Sunday's sermon without putting stress on their marriages?)

It turned out as I had hoped it would. The spouses were partners before the fact. They could take special pride in how their husbands were preaching in class, because they had played a role in making it happen. They could even have post-homily discussions without danger to their marriages because they were talking about what both had produced. It has been a delightful part of my experience in training aspiring deacons to watch how the spouses support their husbands.

I didn't realize it at the time, but my wife, Beulah, had been operating like this already. On Saturday nights in our early years together she would say to me, "Why don't you preach your sermon to me now?" She would give me encouragement and helpful suggestions. Knowing her, now that I reflect on it, I wonder if this wasn't a deliberate plan to avoid having to wait until the following Wednesday before it might be safe to speak up.

Could Roman Catholic priests also have a rehearsal partner—maybe several of them, changing off, one at a time?

Conclusion

Now you know the assumptions on which this book's suggested exercises are built. I hope you will be willing to try them with your classes. But if these exercises don't seem good to you, I believe you could still use this book, whatever system of teaching you employ.

ONE

Preaching Is a Privilege

A Homily[1]

And the Word became flesh and lived among us, and we have seen his glory, the glory as of a father's only son, full of grace and truth. . . . From his fullness we have all received, grace upon grace. The law indeed was given through Moses; grace and truth came through Jesus Christ (John 1:14, 16-17).

As one who is a preacher and glad of it, I wince when I hear someone say, "Now don't preach to me," or when I read a review of a novel or a play where the critic writes, "The author makes his point without preaching."

It's ironic that preaching has become bad news. The message of the angel of the Lord to the shepherds in the field begins: "Do not be afraid; I have good news for you" (Luke 2:10 NEB). That's the Bible's idea of preaching.

I.

Perhaps we should first examine why preaching has become a nasty word.

We'll say that one of you children fools around in school. You bother others as they stand in line. You whisper while the teacher reads a story. You write sloppily, and you make silly mistakes.

---

1. Preached at Bethlehem Lutheran in-the-Midway, St. Paul, Minnesota, then published under the title, "Christmas Makes Preaching a Privilege," *The Lutheran Standard*, 27 December 1966, 3–4, 7. Reprinted by permission of Augsburg Fortress.

Then the teacher asks, "Why aren't you like your brother when he was in this grade?"

This is what has come to be called "preaching," and it's bad news.

Let's think about one of you women. Perhaps your hair isn't always neat, and your car isn't always clean, and your work not always caught up.

Then someone (if you're married, who else but your husband?) points out how well the neighbor woman does it, and why aren't you like her?

This is supposed to be preaching, and it's bad news.

Or let's take one of us men. We have an image of ourselves as being rather witty. So when we get a present, we try to make a humorous remark, and it sounds to the giver as though we're making fun of the gift. Most likely the giver is too gracious to display any hurt, and perhaps no one else will scold us either. But we do it to ourselves. We think of the boss, who is courteous and considerate everywhere she goes. Why can't we be like her?

This is preaching to yourself, and it's also bad news. Does it do any good?

For years there have been football games throughout the country where stars from many teams are selected to play for the benefit of crippled children. Before the event the players fly to a hospital, each to be paired off with a cripple; the athlete is to identify with the cripple and play the game for that child. Now would anyone be so heartless as to say to crippled youngsters as they were being entertained by their very own football stars, "See here, why can't you run like he does?"

But that's what we've made out of preaching, and who wants it?

The part of the text I'm trying to illustrate is this: "The law was given through Moses" (John 1:17a).

The law that came through Moses is real. It's there. The older brother, the neighbor woman, and the boss, being better models, do accuse us. It's appropriate that the Ten Commandments should have been delivered on top a stern and stony mountain, accompanied by the stage effects of smoke, thunder, and lightning. For the law is severe.

Isn't it sad that for some, all that Jesus means is that he was a good example? Perfect he was, to be sure. Not a blemish that even his enemies could detect. But if he were no more than that, then wouldn't it be just as cruel to listen to him say, "Follow me," as it would be to ask the crippled child, "Why can't you run as well as your football star?" If that's what we call preaching, no wonder it's gotten such a bad name.

II.

But I'm here to tell you, "Preaching is a privilege." "The law indeed was given through Moses; grace and truth came through Jesus Christ."

John explains how that happened: "The Word became flesh and lived among us, and we have seen his glory, the glory as of a father's only son, full of grace and truth."

You may have seen a television program years ago that might be called a parable of this. It was a report of a young British woman who spent five years in an African jungle studying chimpanzees. It took her weeks and weeks just to find some chimps to study; they knew she was there, and they hung out of sight. When at last she discovered a few, they were on another mountain. They'd tolerate her only if she'd watch at the limit of her binoculars.

After months of long distance observation, they let Jane Goodall put up a blind 100 yards away, though they were noticeably anxious at first. How much easier it would have been if this young scientist could have turned herself into one of them.

On Christmas "the Word became flesh and lived among us," and during his ministry he explained himself in our language. That's how we discovered what the angels meant, that God showed his good will towards us, that he didn't merely come to be a good example—what a cruel rebuke that would have been—to pair off the brawny halfback with the cripple and command the cripple to measure up. No. We can see how he was full of grace and truth.

The truth that we observe in Jesus, the truth with which he is filled, is there because he is the Word of God. In everyday speech, we might call him "the last Word about God," for what more truth could you expect than that God should come and show us himself?

The truth we see in Jesus is that God is full of grace. I'm sure the devil doesn't want us to understand that. I suspect that Satan is so set against grace he takes care that we don't even remember what the word means, much less experience its power. I'm constantly amazed when I teach a class how few know that grace means "undeserved love." The devil doesn't want us to know; grace is his undoing.

Grace is when you make clumsy jokes about the gift someone gave you, and the giver isn't offended, and he or she even laughs at your peculiar humor. That's grace. You didn't have it coming.

When the Word became flesh and dwelt among us, people like us could observe his glory, that he was full of undeserved love. So full of grace, that when they dragged a woman before him caught in the act of adultery—for which their penalty was stoning to death—and demanded to know how he'd treat such a sinner, he replied, "Let him who is without sin cast the first stone."

When the crowd of accusers melted away, he asked, "Has no one condemned you?" She answered, "No, Lord." He said, "Neither do I condemn you. Don't do it again."

Not one word about how naughty she was. Not a breath wasted in asking why she wasn't like the decent women in town. Just full of grace and truth. Good news. Real preaching.

We aren't told what became of this woman. Yet I have the confidence that the Good News did more good than the bad news would have done.

For that's the way it's worked with us. When we found out that the Perfect Example was not a threat or a rebuke but a Co-worker, we cripples drew on his power and could walk a few steps. For the law is not by itself anymore. (True, God's grace and truth had always been here on earth, but the world couldn't see it bright and clear, until Jesus displayed them in his flesh.)

This Word in the flesh was so full of grace that he met head-on the problem the law causes for us. For we've seen and felt how stern the law can be, and we've seen and felt that it just doesn't go away by wishing it so. Things must be set right, and when we can't set them right, it bothers us. Penalties must be paid, and when we can't pay them, it bothers us.

Preaching is a privilege because it tells the good news that the Perfect One was so full of grace that he met the penalties of the Law, that he measured up to the standards, that he set things right—all for us. So we have received of his fullness, grace upon grace, forgiveness upon forgiveness.

Good news. It's a privilege to preach it. And it's an honor not limited to us who stand in the pulpit. You can preach it to yourself and you can preach it to your neighbor, that "the law indeed was given through Moses; grace and truth came through Jesus Christ."

TWO

The Pursuit of Preaching: Gimmick or Theology?

A few years ago I went to a lecture on Erasmus by Dr. Roland Bainton. It was on a Tuesday evening at Augsburg College in Minneapolis. I recognized some of those present as clergy, but it seemed as though the greater share of the rather large audience consisted of lay people. Among the various statements Bainton quoted from Erasmus was this one: "If elephants can be trained to dance, lions to play, and leopards to hunt, surely preachers can be taught to preach."[1]

The audience laughed and laughed and laughed. I did too, but my heart wasn't in it. Can't I take a joke? After all, people who'd come out on a Tuesday evening to listen to a talk on Erasmus were probably not enemies of the church. This was just a little fun inside the family.

Why am I sensitive about my preaching? Why am I filled with arguments I'd like to fling at those who laugh, such as: "Don't compare me with the speakers at your Rotary Club meetings; all they have is one speech they keep polishing by giving it to different audiences, audiences that are usually homogeneous. Why don't you try preaching to virtually the same people—people of various ages, experience, and interests—week after week? Why don't you try being disciplined in your preparation in spite of all the interruptions week after week?"

After I cool off, I admit I'm being defensive. I realize that preaching is such a personal struggle that if someone attacks my preaching,

1. Roland H. Bainton, *Erasmus of Christendom* (New York: Charles Scribner's Sons, 1969) 168.

5

he appears to be attacking my whole being. I remind myself of professional athletes, top musicians, and fine actors, how they receive coaching constantly without it diminishing their self-esteem, and realize I can accept Erasmus's counsel and still keep my ego intact.

While serving as a parish pastor, I completed a doctoral program at the University of Minnesota. The registrar thought I had been studying speech communication, but whenever possible I wrote my papers on homiletics. I tried to examine rhetoric with the eyes of a theologian, asking always, "Is this concept something I can use as a Christian preacher?" One of the bigger problems I had to wrestle with is whether I should have been doing this at all. No matter what Erasmus said about the possibility of training wild animals, is it legitimate theologically for Christian preachers to study form? Doesn't this deny the power of the Holy Spirit? Homiletics professor Ronald Sleeth describes the dilemma like this: "Theology contends that the transmission of the religious message . . . is a divine action in which God and/or the Holy Spirit is directly at work. . . . Theologians see communications theory as affirming that right techniques rightly learned can put across this message. The theologians believe this is a misunderstanding of the Christian message."[2]

The Church Father Jerome had already sounded the alarm in the fifth century: "We do not wish for the field of rhetorical eloquence, nor the snares of the dialecticians, nor do we seek the subtleties of Aristotle, but the very words of Scripture must be set down."[3]

Pastors have no problem with continuing education in Scripture or systematics. Seminary students and candidates for the permanent diaconate know well the need to learn exegesis and doctrine. But preaching? Well, it's all right if you're studying what to preach, but what about if you're studying how? Don't we resent homilists who are smooth, dramatic, and empty? It is claimed that George Whitefield, evangelist of the Great Awakening and coworker with the Wesley brothers, could move an audience to tears simply by the way he said, "Mesopotamia."

Can we distinguish between gimmickry and concepts of communication that have a theological base?

My starting place on my journey was where I'd been all the time: *content is all-important.* I used to have nightmares that I was stand-

2. Ronald Sleeth, "Theology Versus Communication Theories," *Religion in Life* 32 (1963) 549.

3. *Liber contra Helvidum de perpetua virginitatae Maria*, 12, cited in James J. Murphy, "St. Augustine and the Debate about Christian Rhetoric," *Quarterly Journal of Speech* 46, 405.

ing in the pulpit naked. Instead of a Bible in front of me, there was a Sears Roebuck catalog through which I'd be paging frantically. Others more insightful than I may read other meanings into those dreams, but I interpret them to signify my fear of having nothing to say.

Content is all-important. Karl Barth declared: "Preaching should be an explanation of Scripture; the preacher . . . does not have to invent, but rather to repeat something."[4]

Content is all-important. One of the New Testament words for preaching is *kerusso*, "I proclaim as a herald." The herald had no words of his own. All he needed was a horse, the ability to read, fairly good diction, and a strong voice. The authority of the king made the message compelling. In our calling as heralds, we also know that our content is given, and we are also sure that we need only to proclaim it and without question it will do its job: "For as the rain and the snow come down from heaven, and do not return there until they have watered the earth, making it bring forth and sprout, giving seed to the sower and bread to the eater, so shall my word be that goes out from my mouth; it shall not return to me empty, but it shall accomplish that which I purpose, and succeed in the thing for which I sent it" (Isa 55:10-11).

My next step in my journey was to realize that *form is part of the content.* I based that on the early Church's response to the docetists, to whom all material things were bad. Two very different behaviors came from this outlook. With one group—whom I call "Whoopee-makers"—it worked this way: they figured that since only the spirit was any good, it didn't make any difference what they did with their bodies. With the other group—whom I call "Kill-joys"—it worked the opposite way: they deduced that since only the spirit was any good, they shouldn't enjoy the body in any way whatever. Of course the "Whoopee-makers" didn't care one whit about their neighbors; all they wanted was a good time for themselves. Nor did the "Kill-joys" care for their neighbors; all they wanted was to save their own souls.

In connecting this with a theology of form for homiletics, my reasoning goes like this: If it is vital to the Christian faith that Christ actually took on a body, and if it would have had serious consequences to our outlook and behavior if the Word had not had a material shape, then the form of the Word is part of its content.

4. Karl Barth, *The Preaching of the Gospel,* trans. B. E. Hooke (Philadelphia: The Westminster Press, 1963).

Is my reasoning sound? I think so. Will it also stand up in the world of experience? Are there serious consequences in our pulpit outlook and behavior when the Word is proclaimed without regard to form?

Let's consider the pulpit outlook and behavior of Karl Barth. Barth has a rightful place in Church history for his monumental contribution to theology, reacting to the Church of the nineteenth century. As Barth climbed the stairs to his Swiss pulpit Sunday by Sunday, he trembled at having nothing to proclaim. His seminary professors had tried to accommodate the Word of God to the social and physical sciences of the day. Searching the Scriptures for a message he could preach, Barth discovered in the Letter to the Romans a God who is Wholly-Other and whose Word is autonomous. So Barth restored the office of the herald, the function of the preacher being not to invent but to repeat: "Proclamation is human language in and through which God Himself speaks, like a king through the mouth of a herald."[5]

That led Barth also to say: "We are under orders to 'make no image or likeness.' Since God wills to utter his own truth, his Word, the preacher must not adulterate that truth by adding his own knowledge or art."[6]

We are grateful for Barth's advocacy of the power of the Word of God. Knowing the odds against him, we can appreciate his single-mindedness. But how did this outlook affect his pulpit behavior? In his manual on homiletics, he wrote that sermon introductions are unnecessary unless their content is biblical, since people go to church to hear the Word of God, and introductions should not divert them from that purpose.[7] As for the body of the sermon, no theme, no parts, because that would be imposing human art on the divine message. Just proceed verse by verse. From the same point of view, "a sermon does not require a set conclusion; it comes to an end when it reaches the end of the text. If a conclusion is necessary to sum up what has been said, then the preacher has missed the mark."[8]

The same well-intentioned emphasis on the autonomy of the Word also led Barth to say: "The preacher must not be tedious. . . . Here again the remedy is to preach the authentic truth of Scripture. If preaching is faithful to the Bible, it cannot be tedious. Scripture is

---

5. Karl Barth, *Church Dogmatics*, vol. 1, part 1, *The Doctrine of the Word of God*, trans. G. T. Thomson (Edinburgh: T & T Clark, 1963) 57.

6. Barth, *The Preaching of the Gospel*, 12–13.

7. Ibid., 78–81.

8. Ibid., 82.

in fact so interesting, it has so many new and startling things to tell us, that those who listen cannot possibly be overcome with sleep."[9]

Well, yes, if you're a genius like Karl Barth. But I can show you any number of sermons in print that are biblical to the core and deadening to the spirit. Geniuses do all the right things by intuition and may not know how they do them. The rest of us grow in our skills by analyzing the art of the geniuses and framing that analysis into a system we can manage. This means putting a form on our content. I contend that paying attention to the shape of the message is not heresy, that not to do so could be heresy, because if the Good News comes out as dull, that's false teaching.

No introductions unless they're biblical? No motivation necessary to gain attention? Everyone in the pew is raring to engage in a dialogue with the pulpit? What about Scripture's own doctrine that even we who are reborn have struggles with the good? How is it that someone with such maturity as Paul could confess, "For I do not do the good I want, but the evil I do not want is what I do"? (Rom 7:19) (which suggests that even the most dedicated churchgoer may sometimes have difficulty paying attention).

No conclusions? If the preacher needs to repeat, it means he or she hasn't done the job? I wonder why certain themes keep on rising up in the teaching of Jesus: "He who exalts himself shall be humbled," "For whoever would save his life will lose it," "And he began to teach them that the Son of man must suffer many things."

If the incarnation is crucial to theology and life, then the shape in which the message comes is part of the message. That's the theological underpinning for what we observe in practice.

A Scripture-based, doctrinally correct pronouncement with no connections with the people transmits the signal that the gospel is irrelevant.

A stiff, unbending presence in the pulpit with eyes glued to the notes communicates the notion that the preacher is stand-offish and uncaring. (The preacher is probably anything but that.)

A harsh, hoarse, or strident voice may give the impression of anger or gruffness. A breathy, thin, or weak voice may send the message of immaturity. A nasal voice may be interpreted as representing a whining personality. (The impressions are likely wrong, but the form is coloring the content.)

A booming voice may convey the sense that God Almighty is growling on Mt. Sinai. A rising inflection (which one researcher

9. Ibid., 48.

finds to be characteristic of feminine speech)[10] may signify a feeling of powerlessness.

A friendly tone, with the body at ease and eyes looking at the people, suggests that the preacher likes them, that the Word of grace has become flesh and is dwelling among them.

An attitude of dialogue, showing the homilist not as one thundering from the mansion's porch to the slaves below but as a sinner exploring the treasures of grace with fellow sinners, radiates an aura of mutual respect: the people esteem the homilist for his or her humility; the homilist honors the image of God in the people.

It is frustrating to realize that after all the years we've put into theology and all the hours we've poured into the exegesis of a particular text the two-edged sword of the Word of God can be blunted by some seemingly irrelevant matters of poise, posture, and attitude. Instead of attending to what we are saying, they are wondering, consciously or unconsciously, why are you so superior? Or why are you immobile? Or why are you in perpetual motion, swinging your arms, hunching your shoulders, swaying back and forth, shifting your body weight from one leg to another? Or why don't you go to the optician and get those glasses adjusted? Or if you've done that and the glasses aren't sliding, what does that gesture mean? Or why do you smack your lips so often? (I had a professor who was a prodigy at lip smacking. Several of us used to keep score. As we gained in expertise we were able to rate the various intensities—an 8 or a 9 as distinguished from a 5 or a 6.)

Why do we allow these distractions to creep into our delivery? My guess is that it is because we may be losing our concentration on the people. The golfer preparing to putt—if he or she is going to make this putt—doesn't let an itch or the chirping of a squirrel deter him or her from the challenge at hand. When I stand in front of my class—even when using no podium—I usually don't have problems with my hands. But when beginners ask, "What shall we do with our hands?" suddenly mine become awkward weights. I've lost my concentration on my students, and I'm thinking about myself.

Is there a theology about nonverbal preaching? Am I going too far in connecting this with the words of our Lord that we find ourselves by losing our lives for his sake? Could this be part of the content of our prayer before preaching, that we be freed up to forget self and concentrate on bringing the Good News of Christ to our people?

10. Cited by Robert N. Bostrom, *Communicating in Public: Speaking and Listening* (Edina, Minn.: Burgess Publishing, 1988) 168.

So far I have been dealing with attitude and body language as one aspect of the form of the message. Now I want to show that the way the words are put together—the shape of the verbal message—is also part of the content.

In the early 1930s my dad was pastor of a suburban mission church. The original American Lutheran Church had just been formed and during the Depression it was trying to pay off the debts of the merging synods. Subsidy for missions was on a pay-as-you-go basis. One summer my father's total income was $29. Not $29 a month but $29 for three months. The house was provided, the garden was bountiful, and so we survived. But looking back, I can understand why Dad accepted a call to a congregation of German Russian immigrants, one that levied a certain fee per family. Multiplying the number of families by the levy totaled a sum that in that day was a dream.

Yet Dad stayed there only two years. He spoke German well; his High German was better than their dialect. He was a good preacher and pastor. But he was frustrated because he wanted to bring the Word of God to them in English, and they didn't like that.

Other groups have had their holy tongues: Latin, Norwegian, Swedish, Danish, Polish, French, or even King James English. The practice began with good sense; even the Vulgate was the idiom of the people at the time.

Dad didn't object to conducting German services for the older generation. German was their native speech and his as well. Nor did he despise their ethnic culture. As I interpret his policy, he was getting at a theological principle, that the Word of God is a means of grace, not an end in itself. To spray the Word of God on the second generation in a foreign language is coming close to the practice of magic—as though the Word could work its wonders whether the children understood or not.

Earlier in this chapter we looked at Isaiah's promise that God's Word has the power to accomplish that which God intends (Isa 55:11), which would seem to make homiletic method irrelevant. But the Bible also claims that what God intends is not just that we should have the truth but that the truth should change people: "All Scripture is inspired by God and is useful for teaching, for reproof, for correction, and for training in righteousness, so that everyone who belongs to God may be proficient, equipped for every good work" (2 Tim 3:16-17).

Jesus did say, "Your word is truth." But he led into that by praying, "Sanctify them in the truth" (John 17:17). The Bible itself indicates that it does not exist for its own sake but for the sake of people.

So we part company again with the giant theologian Karl Barth who with his (needed) emphasis on the autonomy of the Word of God may have made it almost an end in itself. In *Theology Today*, F. L. Herzog wrote: "It is well known that, according to Barth, revelation creates its own point of contact. An understandable objection to this point of view asks whether this does not mean to throw the Biblical message at man like a stone."[11]

If churches—including the Roman Catholic Church—have now accepted the logic of translating the Scriptures into words the people understand, then may we not say that good preaching is also a translation? Isn't it the function of good preaching to translate the king's message into a form the people can comprehend? Using ethical methods of persuasion, isn't the work of the preacher to shape his or her proposal into an instrument that will open the ears and move the hearts of the people? As Kenneth Burke observes, "Form is the creation of an appetite in the mind of the auditor, and the adequate satisfying of that appetite."[12] So we don't only plead with ourselves to repent, we see ourselves as persons with feelings, with barriers built up because of problems of ego. That's why we motivate ourselves, to show that it is to our advantage to be abased ("those who humble themselves will be exalted," Luke 14:11). We may use a parable (as Nathan did with David), sneaking by the defenses set up at the front porch and slipping in by the side entrance. Or we may establish common ground (as Jesus did with his accusers who had dragged an adulterous woman before him). In that way the Holy Spirit's inspired Word which is useful for reproof and correction is translated into concepts we homilists (who preach first to ourselves) and our people will pay attention to. For God's Word—even though it is the truth and valuable in itself—is still not an end but a means. To declare that one merely needs to proclaim the autonomous Word of God without knowing how to do it is not consistent with sound theology.

All this struggling with the tension on theological grounds between form and content has led me to develop a principle: *the shape of our preaching wants to be consistent with our message.* Our message is about our sin and God's grace, which means that our content is about relationships: "In Christ God was reconciling the world to himself" (2 Cor 5:19). "You shall love the Lord your God with all

11. F. L. Herzog, "Theologian of the Word of God," *Theology Today* 13 (October 1956) 326.

12. Kenneth Burke, *Counter-Statement* (Los Altos, Calif.: Hermes Publications, 1931) 31.

your heart, and with all your soul, and with all your mind. . . . You shall love your neighbor as yourself" (Matt 22:37, 39).

If it is true that, as the heresy of docetism shows the danger of proclaiming a disembodied Word, so form is part of our content, then the way we say the gospel wants also to be gospel. The tension between rhetoric and theology goes away when I see that our message is relationship and so is our method.

Kenneth Burke focuses our eyes on relationship. His key word in persuasion is *identification*. He claims that we don't persuade people unless they can identify with us. (We will say more about this in chapter 4.) Burke says, "Rhetoric is concerned with the state of Babel after the Fall." Here is the context of that statement:

> Identification is affirmed with earnestness precisely because there is division. Identification is compensatory to division. If men were not apart from each other, there would be no need for the rhetorician to proclaim their unity. If men were wholly and truly of one substance, absolute communication would be of man's very essence. . . . The Rhetoric must lead us through the Scramble, the Wrangle of the Market Place, the flurries and flare-ups of the Human Barnyard, the Give and Take. . . . For one need not scrutinize the concept of "Identification" very sharply to see, implied at every turn, its ironic counterpart: division. Rhetoric is concerned with the state of Babel after the Fall.[13]

Quoting the above may in itself cause division with at least part of my readership since it uses exclusive language. The content is worthwhile: the form is faulty.

Unfortunately, the form of our preaching may also cause division. Lack of an oral mode is one example. There are great preachers who read their scripts, but they're not reading essays. They don't have a stilted style. They employ simple sentences, simple words—like Jesus. They draw pictures—like Jesus. Division comes with using high-level abstractions, pretentious jargon, and syntax that twists with dependent clauses and parenthetical ideas, giving the impression that the pulpiteer is pompous.

A superior attitude is another example of how faulty form brings division. One of the tasks of the communicator is to establish credibility. We need to find ways of doing that without putting people off. Name-dropping could be risky. An illustration that comes from our travels may be apt, but not everyone in the pew can fly to Europe or

---

13. Kenneth Burke, *A Grammar of Motives and a Rhetoric of Motives* (Cleveland: World Publishing Co., 1968) 547.

Israel or China. How do we let the people know the significance of the aorist tense in Greek without seeming to boast? How do we fulfill our calling as prophets without sounding off, as though we were saying, "Listen up, you peasants!"?

The form of our message when we deal with controversial issues also has potential for division. If we don't concede what must be conceded, or avoid biased language, or steer clear of sweeping assertions; if we don't mark out all the common ground we can discover—then not just the content of that preaching but especially the form will separate the homilist from the people. Yet if the form is right, even the harsh content will not push sender and receiver further apart—as we see in Nathan's way of handling his adulterous and murderous king or in Paul's way of persuading slave-owner Philemon to allow runaway Onesimus to live.

Instead of continuing to argue against division, I will put it in the way I really want to say it: the form of our preaching can be almost sacramental. By that I mean what I mentioned before: the way we *say* the gospel can *be* gospel.

Kenneth Burke talks about speaker and audience being consubstantial.[14] That's another way of presenting his concept of identification as the counterpart to division. Other rhetoricians speak of persuasion as the process of reducing the distance between sender and receiver. As I have tested out rhetorical principles against Scripture, one of the things most satisfying to me is discovering that biblical communicators practice what I have found in rhetoric, that to study the Scriptures is profitable not only for what they say but how they say it. This strategy of consubstantiality (or of reducing the distance) is a model case. Just a few examples of wiping out the space between sender and receiver:

> And the Word became flesh and lived among us (John 1:14). [Jesus] emptied himself, taking the form of a slave (Phil 2:7).

> For though I am free with respect to all, I have made myself a slave to all, so that I might win more of them (1 Cor 9:19).

We see how Paul followed this policy when he faced the skeptics on Mars Hill, quoting not his Book but their writings: "As even some of your own poets have said, 'For we too are his offspring'" (Acts 17:28).

Some who don't believe the form of preaching is important have reasoned that Paul repudiated his Mars Hill strategy when he went to Corinth: "When I came to you, brothers and sisters, I did not

14. Ibid., 544–47.

come proclaiming the mystery of God to you in lofty words or wisdom. For I decided to know nothing among you except Jesus Christ, and him crucified" (1 Cor 2:1-2).

But what about 1 Corinthians 9? No matter which scholar we hold with as to how many Corinthian letters there were and which chapter belongs to which letter—as far as I can tell—both chapter 2 and chapter 9 must have been written to the saints in Corinth. Both attest to Paul's earnestness for the gospel, and chapter 9 does not repudiate the Mars Hill strategy; it underscores it: "I have made myself a slave to all, that I might win more of them." That's the form of Paul's communication, and in that form Paul acted out how Jesus described his own mission: "For the Son of man also came not to be served but to serve, and to give his life as a ransom for many" (Mark 10:45).

Another Scripture again shows how the form of our preaching can be almost sacramental:

> As you know and God is our witness, we never came with words of flattery or with a pretext for greed; nor did we seek praise from mortals, whether from you or from others, though we might have made demands as apostles of Christ. But we were gentle among you, like a nurse tenderly caring for her own children. So deeply do we care for you that we are determined to share with you not only the gospel of God but also our own selves, because you have become very dear to us (1 Thess 2:5-8).

Surely that's a picture of wiping out the space between sender and receiver.

One theologian from whom I gain reinforcement for this conviction is Sallie McFague. She simply takes it for granted that form is relevant: "If we believe in the unity of form and content, then I think we must take seriously when we try to spell out the content of Christian faith, the forms in which we have that content."[15]

She recommends the parable as the way to go, especially in our age: "The parable is a genre for sceptics, for it assumes no faith, no theological and ecclesiastical tradition, no sacred language, and for these reasons may be an appropriate genre for our time."[16]

If I interpret her correctly, she avows what I avow: "To say, then, that a New Testament parable is an extended metaphor means not

---

15. Sallie McFague, CSCW Report (Cambridge, Mass.: Church Society for College Work) 33, 3 (July 1975) 8.

16. Ibid., 9.

that the parable 'has a point' or teaches a lesson, but that it is itself what it is talking about."[17]

Why is that? Because the parables of Jesus are in themselves the Word becoming flesh; in themselves they wipe out the space between sender and receiver; in themselves they act out how Jesus stands at the door and knocks: "They assert lightly, calling for but not insisting upon assent. . . . A parable puts the question but puts it lightly."[18]

The Word became flesh not only in Bethlehem but in Nazareth, Capernaum, and Jerusalem as Jesus kept wiping out the space between others and himself, not only by teaching in parables but in his whole form of life. With no place to lay his head, the distance between him and the homeless disappears. In speaking to a woman who was no lady and allowing her to do him a favor, the distance between him and society's refuse fades away.

Back in the 1950s I was visiting with a pastor who told me he was resigning his parish to go back to school. When I asked, "What are you going to study?" he answered, "Homiletics," and I laughed. I am embarrassed to realize how rude I was. My laughter must have been an unconscious betrayal of my attitude that since I had already studied how to preach, I had nothing more to learn. Then somehow I was "converted," only to find others giving me the same treatment with apparent theological support based on doctrines of the Holy Spirit and the power of his Word. What has bolstered me is to study the Scriptures not only for what they say (which is paramount) but also for how they say it. If the Bible is from the Holy Spirit and if biblical communicators used sound rhetorical principles, then it must be all right for me to use them as well. I find no better preaching model than Jesus. The way he communicated is also what he communicated.

In trying to look at rhetoric with the eyes of a theologian and at homiletics with the eyes of a rhetorician:

The rhetorician in me agrees with Erasmus: preachers can be taught to preach, and we can show good ones how to do it better.

The theologian in me asks, "Does this deny the Holy Spirit's function?" But as a theologian I believe I also have the right to connect this with the crucial doctrine that "the Word was made flesh," arguing that although content is all-important, form is part of the content.

17. Ibid., 8.
18. Ibid., 8–9.

The rhetorician in me looks for ways to make my message more attractive to the hearer.

The theologian in me knows that the Word of God is powerful and autonomous, not needing my feeble help. But the theologian in me also knows that since the Word is given to sanctify us in the truth, this means the Word is not an end in itself but the means of grace. Just as we agree that the powerful Word first given in other languages is to be translated into the tongue of the people, we may also agree that effective preaching is an exercise in translation: putting the Word into a form that will open ears and keep them open so that the powerful Word can get in.

The rhetorician in me agrees with Kenneth Burke that the key word in persuasion is *identification,* which means that relationship– reducing the distance between sender and receiver–is crucial in communication.

The theologian in me sees the content of Scripture covered by two concepts: God's reconciling the world to himself in Christ, and our responding by loving God and neighbor. In other words, the content of our preaching is relationship.

The rhetorician-theologian in me sees rhetoric and theology merging in the act of preaching: our method is relationship and so is our content. As we look at Jesus and Paul, we discover that how we say the gospel can be gospel.

A skilled performer could stir the emotions simply by reading a page from the telephone directory; we keep up our guard all the time against gimmickry, emboldened by the knowledge that homiletical method has theological substance.

For Further Reading

Craddock, Fred B. *As One without Authority*. 3d ed. Nashville: Abingdon, 1979, 51–53.
_____. *Overhearing the Gospel*. Nashville: Abingdon, 1978, 9–22.

THREE

The Mood We Want

When I first took homiletics, the mood in my class seemed to be: "Don't say anything during the critiques." Why not? Because we noticed that those who spoke out really got it when it was their turn to preach. Our attitude was certainly not that of people living forgiven.

Now when we have video cameras and instant playbacks, the potential for dread is compounded. At the end of our first day in a preaching workshop, an experienced pastor admitted he had "kicked himself" every day since sending in his registration: "Why am I putting myself through this?" But after having survived the first video session without scars, he was relieved to be able to tell me, "The way you handle it is great. I'm not dreading the rest of the week anymore."

A large part of his relief was due to the living-forgiven atmosphere in that company of preachers. The day before we had reminded ourselves of two lines in the Apostles' Creed: "[I believe] in the communion of saints, the forgiveness of sins."

The glorious thing is, knowing we're already forgiven for Jesus' sake sets us free from needing to prove ourselves. That sets us free to take risks, and that sets us free to improve. And the whole process sublimates our fear.

We had also reminded ourselves that since the people we preach to are forgiven sinners like us and since none of us could make it with God except by his grace, then the communion of saints is the safest place in the world to make mistakes. I had showed them a quotation from *Theology Today:*

> The quality that should mark the Christian Church is not goodness but grace; not merit but mercy; not moralism but forgiveness; not

the enshrinement of success but the acceptance of failure. . . . Lacking the nerve of failure, we have suffered a failure of nerve—to dare to dream dreams, venture visions, and risk getting splinters that come from cutting against the grain.

Armed with the knowledge that Jesus failed, that he expects us to fail, and has provided us with a sacrament of failure, we can shake off the shackles that fetter us to success and be free to fail without guilt, without embarrassment, without timidity.[1]

I had also shared a statement by the renowned concert pianist Vladimir Horowitz:

For me, the intellect is always the guide but not the goal of the performance. Three things have to be coordinated and not one must stick out. Not too much intellect because it can become scholastic. Not too much heart because it can become schmaltz. Not too much technique because you become a mechanic. Always there should be a little mistake here and there—I am for it. The people who don't do mistakes are cold like ice. It takes risk to make a mistake. If you don't take risk, you are boring.[2]

I have heard and seen Horowitz play. If he made any mistakes, I didn't catch them. But I'm not a concert pianist practicing eight hours a day, and so I wouldn't know. I do know that when I heard and saw Horowitz play, I was feeling—in only a small way I'm sure—what Horowitz was feeling because he was more intent about communicating the music than trying to be perfect.

But you're still nervous, you say? You do believe in the communion of saints and the forgiveness of sins, but you're still tense?

Good for you. Nervousness is our friend. It means we care about our message and the people we bring it to.

A veteran pastor was chatting with his bishop. "You know, thirty years ago I was always nervous in the pulpit. Now I can preach and think nothing of it." The bishop replied, "Your people tell me they feel the same way. They don't think much of your preaching either."

I have read of a football coach who chooses his starting line-up just before the game by asking his players to hold out their hands. Those whose hands are dry he doesn't take. Upsets can be traced sometimes to the fact that the favored team had no "butterflies in the stomach." William Jennings Bryan, noted orator of the late nineteenth and early twentieth century, said he had anxiety every time he

1. Leonard I. Sweet, *Theology Today* (July 1977).
2. Quoted in Helen Epstein, "The Grand Eccentric of the Concert Hall," *New York Times Magazine*, 8 January 1978.

spoke but once—and that was the worst speech he ever gave. Harry Emerson Fosdick, former well-known preacher at Riverside Church, New York City, often had to take sedatives on Saturday night to get his rest. In his judgment, anyone not tense before speaking was no good. "Fear is not something to be feared, but something to be sublimated."[3]

Constructive emotional tension triggers a reaction that prepares the body for better effort. It would be wasteful for a 350 horsepower engine to use all its capacity to propel a car at twenty-five miles per hour. Just so, it would be inefficient for the human body to run at top speed all the time. But when there's an emergency, the adrenal gland pumps adrenalin into the system. The liver releases larger quantities of sugar into the blood. Breathing speeds up to inhale more oxygen and exhale more carbon dioxide. The pulse rate quickens to send more fresh blood to the muscles, heart, and brain. The brain can think more clearly, quickly, perceptively. The muscles can exert themselves more intensely. The central nervous system can react more speedily. Being nervous isn't bad.

How do we sublimate our anxiety, so that instead of letting nervousness short-circuit the communication hookup, we get a rapport between homilist and people that crackles with excitement?

Sublimating our anxiety involves three kinds of preparation: spiritual, mental, and physical.

The spiritual preparation includes reminding ourselves of the freedom to take risks that comes from the forgiveness of sins and the communion of saints and in praying that we may be able to lose ourselves for Jesus' sake in the privilege of bringing God's Word to our hearers.

The mental preparation is what we will discuss throughout the rest of this book. If we haven't spent serious time in prayer and study getting ready for a homily, then we can't blame anyone but ourselves for our anxiety. Getting ready to preach is not for the lazy. The apostle's word to Timothy motivates every devoted homilist: "Do your best to present yourself to God as one approved by him, a worker who has no need to be ashamed, rightly explaining the word of truth" (2 Tim 2:15). If we work hard to get ready, we have come a long way in transforming our anxiety into fruitful energy.

But even with fervent spiritual and mental preparation, there may still be tension in our bodies. To relieve such tension a simple exercise may be helpful. Try this: reach for the ceiling and then bend

---

3. Quoted in R. C. McCall, "Harry Emerson Fosdick: Paragon and Paradox," *Quarterly Journal of Speech* 39 (1953) 289.

over and reach for the floor; remain hanging like this for a few moments, and then come back up slowly, one vertebra at a time. (I told the acolytes in the sacristy, "This is a new way to pray.")

A tension reliever for when you're right there in the public gaze: take several deep breaths from the diaphragm. (The diaphragm is the muscle between your chest and your stomach.) Many people when taking a deep breath will raise their shoulders and suck in their stomachs, the opposite of breathing from the diaphragm. They are increasing the tension and reducing the space for taking in air. Breathing from the diaphragm means letting that large muscle go down and out, enlarging the air space. The easiest way I know to explain how to get started doing this is that you put your hand on your stomach and push in to expel the air from the lungs and then just let the air come in by itself. Breathing from the diaphragm is the right way to breathe all the time and especially when preaching: it improves the quality of the voice and enables us to project the voice without straining. If your voice gets tired easily, that may be a sign that you're not breathing from the diaphragm. A voice teacher can show you how to breathe the way you did when you were a baby. (Take good care of your voice: no yelling on Saturdays at football games.)

Now let's put all three together—your spiritual, mental, and physical preparation—and visualize how all of them working in harmony will help channel your nervous energy into productive rapport. See yourself walking to the pulpit, neither timid nor brassy but confident because you know what you're going to say and why it is vital to the people. As you walk, see yourself not rushing. You're not wasting time getting there—that would only call attention to yourself—but you're not speeding to get the ordeal over with. In the pulpit, see yourself standing on both feet because that also declares that you're assured without being arrogant. See yourself letting your hands be at the end of your arms. That's all there is to it. Perhaps one hand (or both) will rest easily on the pulpit. But you're not stuck in this position and you're not hanging on for dear life. That body language would communicate rigidity and fear, making the people uneasy. Your weight is on both your feet, not your hands.

You see yourself not frittering away precious moments while standing there, but you don't start until the people are ready to listen. You look at them and announce the gospel. Then you pause just slightly, to set off the reading. Visualize yourself not rushing as you read. People with destructive nervous energy race pell-mell to get it over with. But you know the characters you're reading about. You're wearing their skin as you read. You visualize yourself pausing just a bit here and there—to react, to emphasize, to group words that belong together. You don't read it flat nor do you "ham it up." You take enough time to let your emotions show in an understated way.

As the people sit down, you wait again for them, this time to get settled. You don't start until they are ready to listen. That in itself gains attention and puts you in control. Then you see yourself as an ambassador for Christ, entering into a heart-to-heart dialogue with every person, pleading, "Be reconciled to God."

As you walk away from the pulpit, you visualize yourself still in the role that has John the Baptizer as its model: "He must increase, but I must decrease," (John 3:30)—not swaggering as though you'd just put on an Oscar-winning performance, but not mouse-like either. Modest, but still the herald of the King.

In a class at the University of Minnesota, my professor, William Howell, remarked that there are three stages in the development of a public speaker: self-centered, content-centered, and people-centered. Self-centered is when we are consumed with ourselves, fretting and wondering if we can survive the ordeal. With practice and experience, most people graduate from this level and arrive at being content-centered, when they worry about what they will say and how they will say it. Dr. Howell observed that most people get stuck on this level. He claimed that being people-centered is the highest achievement, when self is forgotten and content is important because it can reach the people and serve them. I was impressed with how aptly that describes the goal for us preachers.

Summary

So far we have laid out these principles:

1. The form of our preaching should be consistent with our message. Our form is relationship because our message is relationship.

2. In pursuing a method of learning to preach consistent with the gospel, the mood we want involves the permission to fail without being destroyed, the freedom that comes from the forgiveness of failure, the freedom to grow that comes from the freedom to risk.

Further Reading on Nervousness

Bostrom, Robert N. *Communicating in Public: Speaking and Listening*. Edina, Minn.: Burgess Publishing, 1988, 53-61.

Fletcher, Leon. *How to Design and Deliver a Speech.* 4th ed. New York: Harper & Row, 1990, 61-67.

Metcalfe, Sheldon. *Building a Speech.* Fort Worth: Holt, Rinehart and Winston, Inc., 1991, 76-91.

Ross, Raymond S. *Speech Communication: Fundamentals and Practice.* 7th ed. Englewood Cliffs, N.J., 1986, 133-51.

Sprague, Jo, and Douglas Stuart. *The Speaker's Handbook.* 2d ed. San Diego: Harcourt Brace Jovanovich Publishers, 1988, 76-82.

Exercises

Exercise 1

Objectives:

1. To get you started in appearing before a TV camera;

2. To help build the mood we want, the feeling of trust in one another.

Assignment:

Give a talk of at least one minute but no longer than three minutes introducing yourself.

Plan how you'll start. Then organize the rest of your talk in a series of scenes: see yourself where you've been and what you've done. Then just tell us what you see. You may use notes this time, but then again, you may not need them. Try memorizing the sequence of scenes but not the words. As you rehearse, perhaps you'll use some words almost the same way every time, but by thinking about what you're seeing and not about what word comes next, you're not as likely to get stuck.

To sum up:

Make the whole talk something you can see and then simply report what you see.

FOUR

The Risky but Scriptural Appeal
to Self-Interest

When I as a Lutheran pastor began to teach homiletics at St. John's University, a Roman Catholic school operated by the Order of St. Benedict, a question commonly asked me was, "How long do you think a homily should be?" I discovered the expected answer was, "No longer than five minutes." When I asked, "Why?" the reply was often, "Because homilies are boring." I heard of one man who told his priest, "If you ever preach longer than seven minutes, I'm walking out."

I once read an article by an organist (not representative of church musicians as a whole, I know) in which he described the various ways he passes the time while the preacher is in the pulpit, none of them involving paying attention. He ended the paragraph by saying something like, "In due time we'll succeed in eliminating sermons."

We've all experienced homilies that might just as well have been eliminated, making us feel that *homily* and *dull* were synonyms. In this book we'll explore several ways sermons can become arresting and rapport-building. In this chapter we will investigate one of them, a principle of rhetoric: identification.

Identification is basic to capturing and holding attention, but it has given me as a Christian theologian a great deal of trouble, because it recommends that we appeal to our listeners' self-interest. I saw that self-interest doesn't have to mean selfishness, but I still rejected this concept for a long time because self-interest seems to be contrary to *agape*, selfless love, and it could lend itself to unethical practices such as manipulation. I call it risky, but I also find it scriptural. Stay with me, dear reader, as I show you the struggles I went through in grappling with this term.

Kenneth Burke and Identification

Kenneth Burke is the fountainhead of this strategy in rhetoric. To read him is to deal with an encyclopedia. Stanley Edgar Hyman reports that "like Bacon, Burke has set out to do no less than to integrate all man's knowledge into one workable frame."[1] Although he began as an author of poems and novels and also as a critic, Burke also found himself grazing in the pastures of persuasion, becoming recognized as the founder of a "new rhetoric."[2] Marie Hochmuth describes his background like this:

> Years of study and contemplation of the general idea of effectiveness in language have equipped him to deal competently with the subject of rhetoric from its beginning as a specialized discipline to the present time. To his thorough knowledge of classical tradition he has added rich insights gained from serious study of anthropology, sociology, history, psychology, philosophy, and the whole body of humane letters. With such equipment, he has become the most profound student of rhetoric now writing in America.[3]

As Burke searched through all these fields, classical and modern, he found the common element of persuasion to be identification. I understand him to say that identification has two aspects: identifying with the people's ways and identifying with the people's self-interest.

This is how Burke defines identification: "to persuade a man by identifying your cause with his interests."[4] "You persuade a man only insofar as you can talk his language by speech, gesture, tonality, order, image, attitude, idea, *identifying* your ways with his."[5]

> All told, persuasion ranges from the bluntest quest of advantage, as in sales promotion or propaganda, through courtship, social etiquette, education, and the sermon, to a "pure" form that delights in the process of appeal for itself alone, without ulterior purpose. And identification ranges from the politician who, addressing an audience of farmers, says, "I was a farm boy myself," through the mysteries of

1. *The Armed Vision: A Study in the Methods of Modern Literary Criticism* (New York: Alfred A. Knopf, 1952) 375.
2. Marie Hochmuth, "Kenneth Burke and the 'New Rhetoric,'" *Quarterly Journal of Speech* 38, no. 2 (April 1952) 133–44.
3. Ibid., 144.
4. Burke, *A Rhetoric of Motives*, 548.
5. Ibid., 579.

social status, to the mystic's devout identification with the source of all being.[6]

Commenting on a passage from *Hamlet,* Burke observed that "form is the creation of an appetite in the mind of the auditor, and the adequate satisfying of that appetite."[7]

In chapter 2 I quoted Burke as saying that identification is the counterpart of division: "For one need not scrutinize the concept of 'identification' very sharply to see, implied at every turn, its ironic counterpart: division. Rhetoric is concerned with the state of Babel after the Fall."[8]

Burke finds identification in the writings of Augustine. In *De doctrina christiana* the bishop and former teacher of rhetoric notes that a person is persuaded if

> he likes what you promise, fears what you say is imminent, hates what you censure, embraces what you command, regrets what you build up as regrettable, rejoices at what you say is cause for rejoicing, sympathizes with those whose wretchedness your words bring before his eyes, shuns those whom you admonish him to shun . . . and in whatever other ways your high eloquence can affect the minds of your hearers, bringing them not merely to know what should be done, but to do what they know should be done.[9]

Burke finds identification in Aristotle's *Rhetoric:* "It is not hard to praise Athenians among Athenians."[10]

He finds identification in sociology:

> But how would Veblen's *Theory of the Leisure Class* fit into such a distinction? Sometimes the identifications he reveals seem of the more accidental sort. People seem to be bent on doing and acquiring certain things simply because these things happen to have become the signs of an admired status. And one can imagine these same people doing exactly the opposite, if the opposite happened to be the sign of the same status.[11]

Burke finds identification informing the despot in Machiavelli's *The Prince,* advising him how to gain favor with his subjects by ap-

6. Ibid., 522.

7. Kenneth Burke, *Counter-Statement* (Los Altos, Calif.: Hermes Publications, 1931) 31.

8. Burke, *A Rhetoric of Motives,* 546–47.

9. Ibid., 574.

10. Ibid., 579.

11. Ibid., 658.

pearing to be merciful, dependable, humane, devout, upright, but being the opposite in fact whenever the circumstances require it; to leave the "affairs of reproach" to the hands of others but to keep those of "grace" in his own; to be the patron of all the arts, to sponsor festivals and spectacles, and to support all local organizations.[12] In this way, the peasants will identify with the despot as a good man.

Enlarging the borders of rhetoric to include symbolic action and stage effects, Burke finds persuasion as identification in medicine, when the patient participates in the transaction and so identifies with it:

> We could observe that even the medical equipment of a doctor's office is not to be judged purely for its diagnostic usefulness, but also has a function in the *rhetoric* of medicine. Whatever it is as apparatus, it also appeals to imagery; and if a man has been treated to a fulsome series of tappings, scrutinizings, and listenings, with the aid of various scopes, meters, and gauges, he may feel content to have participated as a patient in such histrionic action, though absolutely no material thing has been done for him, whereas he might count himself cheated if he were given a real cure but without the pageantry. A *related* popular term is "bedside manner."[13]

Burke also uncovers identification as a working principle in theology in Luther's commentary on Galatians:

> All the prophets saw that Christ would be the greatest brigand of all, the greatest adulterer, thief, profaner of temples, blasphemer, and so on, that there would never be a greater in all the world. . . . God sent his only begotten Son into the world and laid all sins on him, saying: "You are to be Peter the denier, Paul the persecutor, blasphemer, and wild beast, David the adulterer, you are to be the sinner who ate the apple in the Garden of Eden, you are to be the crucified thief, you are to be the person who commits all the sins in the world."[14]

To show that Kenneth Burke represents a current emphasis in other rhetoricians, here are sample excerpts from college and university textbooks: "Persuasion is more effective, other things being equal, when related to people's wants."[15]

---

12. Ibid., 682.
13. Ibid., 695.
14. Ibid., 852.
15. William Norwood Brigance, *Speech: Its Techniques and Discipline in a Free Society*, 2d ed. (New York: Appleton-Century-Crofts, 1961) 146.

Make your listeners feel that their needs or desires will be satisfied by what you are recommending. . . . As they listen to you, they are asking, "What's in it for me?" But don't assume that everyone acts only for selfish purposes. Every day people are moved by calls to greatness. Every day they make personal sacrifices for the sake of justice, compassion and the common good.

In short, the key to effective motivation is first to identify the needs, interests, wants and desires of your listeners and then to show them how your proposition will help satisfy those needs.[16]

We tell ourselves listeners ought to wait attentively to hear what we have to say. "I know what they need to hear," we tell ourselves; if we then discover "they" didn't listen, we complete the self-delusion by saying, "Well, that's their loss, for I am right and I spoke for their good. They could have caught my meaning had they tried." But the mistake was our own. We spoke to please ourselves, not to influence people as they are. . . . Therefore, if the speaker is to reach the minds of his listeners, he must forget himself enough to fit his thoughts to their preferences, understandings, and interests.[17]

Charles U. Larson shows us how identification works in advertising:

Much of contemporary marketing research attempts to identify those major premises that are held by audiences, so that persuaders can shape their appeals to these. For example, the beer industry knows that a large potential market holds a major premise that might be stated: "Being slim is good." Using this building block, they can design appeals that emphasize that the new low-alcohol beer has fewer calories than does traditional beer—a minor premise that might be stated: "Low-alcohol beer helps keep you slim." The conclusion that the low-alcohol beers are good comes from the audience and not the persuader—there has been a *co-creation of meaning or identification*.[18]

By now, red flags may be springing up: aren't these appeals to identification with the people's self-interest at least dangerous, and maybe unethical? But there's another aspect to Burke's strategy, that of identifying with the people's ways. Before we deal with the red

16. James H. McBurney and Ernest J. Wrage, *Guide to Good Speech*, 3d ed. (Englewood Cliffs, N.J.: Prentice-Hall, 1965) 244.

17. John F. Wilson and Carroll C. Arnold, *Public Speaking as a Liberal Art*, 2d ed. (Boston: Allyn and Bacon, Inc., 1968) 74.

18. Charles U. Larson, *Persuasion: Reception and Responsibility*, 5th ed. (Belmont, Calif.: Wadsworth Publishing Company, 1989) 62.

flags already raised, we may be able to agree that identifying with the people's ways is permissible and even admirable.

Identifying with the People's Ways

Identifying with the people's ways is scriptural, in spite of the fact we worship a transcendent deity who would seem to be the ultimate in aloofness. In chapter 2 we talked about Barth's commendable insistence on the autonomy of the Word of God. His vision of the other-ness of God's revelation of himself was justified simply on the basis of the symbolism of Jahweh's contacts with Moses. There was the call to be his people's deliverer from slavery in Egypt: the voice of the Lord came out of a burning bush, a manifestation so holy that Moses was not to come near nor to leave his shoes on his feet (Exod 3:1-6). There was the period of forty days on Mount Sinai when the prophet received the Ten Commandments. Returning to the bottom of the mountain, Moses' face was so bright—after having been in the presence of the Almighty—that others could not bear to look at him, and he was forced to put a veil on his face (Exod 34:27-35).

Yet Burke's principle of identifying with the people's ways is illustrated already in the symbolism of the tabernacle, a portable temple. When the children of Israel camped, there were to be three tribes to each side—east, west, north, south—of the tabernacle (Num 2:1-34). That this was the token of the presence of Jahweh among his people may be inferred from this passage:

> Then the cloud covered the tent of meeting, and the glory of the LORD filled the tabernacle. Moses was not able to enter the tent of meeting because the cloud settled upon it, and the glory of the LORD filled the tabernacle. Whenever the cloud was taken up from the tabernacle, the Israelites would set out on each stage of their journey; but if the cloud was not taken up, then they did not set out until the day that it was taken up. For the cloud of the LORD was on the tabernacle by day, and fire was in the cloud by night, before the eyes of all the house of Israel at each stage of their journey (Exod 40:34-38).

So transcendent is the Lord that not even his chief servant, Moses, could come into his presence, yet Jahweh still chose to be in the midst of his people, identifying himself with their plight.

The New Testament example of God's desire to be among his people is the incarnation: "And the Word became flesh and lived among us" (John 1:14). The original Greek could be translated: "And the Word became flesh and tabernacled among us." The glory and holiness that sinful human creatures could not tolerate was toned down, as the Christmas hymn "Hark the Herald Angels Sing" pictures it: "Veiled in flesh the Godhead see." If Kenneth Burke could illustrate his theory of persuasion by referring to the "mystic's devout identification with the source of all being,"[19] then we may also go in the opposite direction and find an example in the Word's becoming flesh, God's coming down to identify with our ways. Other Scriptures describe this phenomenon: for example, how Jesus who was rich became poor so that we through his poverty might become rich (2 Cor 8:9) and how Christ did not regard equality with God as something to be exploited but emptied himself, taking the form of a slave (Phil 2:6-7).

Paul also exerted himself to identify with the ways of the people he sought to win. In 1 Corinthians 9 he argues at length (vv. 1-18) that he has every right to receive a salary for his work as an apostle. "But we endure anything rather than put an obstacle in the way of the gospel of Christ" (1 Cor 9:12). His reward was this, "that in my proclamation I may make the gospel free of charge, so as not to make full use of my rights in the gospel" (1 Cor 9:18). What follows is his classic statement of how he took advantage of every opportunity to identify with the ways of the people:

> For though I am free with respect to all, I have made myself a slave to all, so that I might win more of them. To the Jews, I became as a Jew, in order to win Jews. To those under the law I became as one under the law (though I myself am not under the law) so that I might win those under the law. To those outside the law I became as one outside the law (though I am not free from God's law but am under Christ's law) so that I might win those outside the law. To the weak I became weak, so that I might win the weak. I have become all things to all people, that I might by all means save some. I do it all for the sake of the gospel, so that I may share in its blessings (1 Cor 9:19-23).

My Problems with Identifying with the People's Self-Interest

With the examples and counsel of Jesus and Paul, it was no problem for me to accept Kenneth Burke's policy of identifying with the people's ways. What gave me trouble was his insistence that we also want to identify with the people's self-interest: "It is so clearly a matter of rhetoric to persuade a man by identifying your cause with

19. Burke, *A Rhetoric of Motives*, 522.

his interests."[20] I have taken issue with a small part of Karl Barth's theology as it applies to homiletics, but I can't dismiss his warning against making preaching "a service performed for clients."[21] We see this going on in the motion picture and stage play *Mass Appeal,* where the priest rebukes the seminarian for upsetting the people. The seminarian had preached about the lethargy of the well-to-do in facing social issues. The priest was comfortable in his parish and he didn't want any young upstart spoiling his "mass appeal." The priest was coming close to being the kind of person against whom the Apostle warned Timothy: "For the time is coming when people will not put up with sound doctrine, but having itching ears, they will accumulate for themselves teachers to suit their own desires, and will turn away from listening to the truth and wander away to myths" (2 Tim 4:3-4).

I also take seriously the caution of H. Grady Davis: "Any successful appeal to selfish motives, however 'religious' the form it takes, leads my victim away from the lordship of Christ. I cannot sell Christ, I cannot sell the mysteries of Christ, by a skillful appeal to motives of self-interest. I can only sell him short."[22]

Davis further elaborates the dangers in a passage about what he calls "the *in order to* sermon" and "the *it will pay us* sermon":

> Its stock in trade is expediency, profit, gain, either temporal or "spiritual." (It somehow assumes that selfishness becomes sanctified when its object is "spiritual.") Its danger is work-righteousness, an attempt to bargain with God. The conditional mode misleads people into supposing that they secure God's favor by what they are and what they do. . . .
>
> No wonder such preaching is popular. Its good is created by its hearer's desire. Its values are measured by his profit. Its only truth is expediency. It appeals to every person's wish to make God a sort of magical servant to his wishes, and to make religion a formula for getting what he wants.[23]

Is it possible to persuade by identifying with the people's self-interest without resorting to expediency or turning God into our personal giant genie? I found it difficult to accept this strategy, especially when I considered Jesus' teaching against exploiting or manipulating

20. Ibid., 548.

21. Karl Barth, *The Preaching of the Gospel,* trans. B. E. Hooke (Philadelphia: Westminster, 1983) 54.

22. H. Grady Davis, *Design for Preaching* (Philadelphia: Muhlenberg, 1958) 136.

23. Ibid., 215, 217.

any person, human or divine. Jesus taught a kind of love for which we have no English word, requiring us to use its Greek name, *agape*, to describe an affection that extends itself without strings, entirely selfless, turning the other cheek and going the second mile (Matt 5:38-48). With such an outlook, could Jesus identify with the people's self-interest?

Be Selfless: It's in My Self-Interest?

One week I was preparing a homily on Matthew's conclusion to Jesus' Sermon on the Mount. Our Lord recommends that we be like the person who built his house on a rock: "The rain fell, the floods came, and the winds blew and beat on that house, but it did not fall, because it had been founded on rock" (Matt 7:25). We should not be like the foolish man who built his house on sand: "The rain fell, and the floods came, and the winds blew and beat against that house, and it fell—and great was its fall" (Matt 7:27). I asked myself, "What's going on here? Is Jesus actually appealing to my self-interest?" And who are those folks who are like this wise man? "Everyone then who hears these words of mine and acts on them" (Matt 7:24). What words? The Sermon on the Mount, words like, "If anyone strikes you on the right cheek, turn the other also" (Matt 5:39). I had to face the question, Is this a paradox: Be selfless; it's in my self-interest?

As the weeks went by, I began to see Jesus appealing to self-interest all over Palestine. Not only in the ending of the Sermon on the Mount, but in the beginning as well: "Blessed are the poor in spirit. . . . Blessed are those who mourn. . . . Blessed are the meek. . . ." (Matt 5:3-5).

Nor was this something that only Matthew had picked up. According to Mark, our Lord said: "Pay attention to what you hear; the measure you give will be the measure you get, and still more will be given to you" (Mark 4:24). "Those who lose their life for my sake, and for the sake of the gospel, will save it" (Mark 8:35).

In Luke, too, it is in our self-interest to see value in ourselves. Luke doesn't overlook Jesus' assurances of our self-worth: "Rejoice that your names are written in heaven" (Luke 10:20). "Are not five sparrows sold for two pennies? Yet not one of them is forgotten in God's sight. But even the hairs of your head are all counted. Do not be afraid; you are of more value than many sparrows" (Luke 12:6-7).

Luke also records a parable about self-worth. When Jesus noticed how the guests elbowed their way to the places of honor at the table, he said, "Don't be foolish. Who knows if someone who out-ranks you might not show up, and then the host will have to come and demote you, and you'll be embarrassed as you move down. Instead, start at the lowest place, and perhaps the host will come and move you up higher, and then you'll hear murmurs of approval" (Luke 14:7-11). To see myself as so significant in the eyes of God that my very own name was written in heaven: I can rejoice in that. But this parable is not about the hereafter; it deals with the here and now, a social gathering (not even necessarily in a church basement), at which Jesus seems to validate my struggle for esteem.

Then there is this parable's punchline: "For all who exalt themselves will be humbled, and those who humble themselves will be exalted." These same words appear also in two other settings, both concerning show-off piety. In Matthew 23:1-12, it comes after Jesus comments on the pride the scribes and Pharisees had in the signs of their status such as their broad phylacteries and long fringes and being called rabbi. In Luke 18:9-14 it comes after we hear Jesus tell about two men going to the Temple to pray, one a Pharisee, the other a tax collector. Hadn't I noticed this punchline before? Yes. But I must confess I only preached on the first half: "All who exalt themselves will be humbled." (Later I saw that even then I was dealing with self-interest: who wants to be humbled?) I had usually overlooked the rest of it: "All who humble themselves will be exalted."

Going back to Luke 14: after commenting on the elbow-shoving behavior of the guests, our Lord said to the host: "When you give a luncheon or a dinner, do not invite your friends or your brothers or your relatives or rich neighbors, in case they may invite you in return, and you would be repaid. But when you give a banquet, invite the poor, the crippled, the lame, and the blind" (Luke 14:12-13). That's more in line with what I would expect Jesus to say, pure *agape,* anything but self-interest, apparently. But the punchline this time is "And you will be blessed." Why? "Because they cannot repay you." *Agape* again. I expect Jesus to say that. But does he stop there? No. "You will be repaid at the resurrection of the righteous" (Luke 14:14). There's my paradox again: be selfless, it's in my self-interest.

When Jesus said, "It is more blessed to give than to receive" (Acts 20:35), he was directing his followers to a high point in selflessness. Yet at the same time, by declaring that one becomes happier in giving than in receiving, he was presenting the paradox once more: be selfless, it's in my self-interest.

Just Plain Self-Interest

Then there's that strange parable of the unjust steward. A rich man learned that his manager was squandering his property. He gave him due notice that he was being fired. The manager determined to use the authority he still wielded to reduce the accounts of three of his master's debtors, obligating them to help him when he no longer would have a job. Jesus observed: "And his master commended the dishonest manager because he had acted shrewdly; for the children of this age are more shrewd in dealing with their own generation than are the children of light. And I tell you, make friends for yourselves by means of dishonest wealth so that when it is gone, they may welcome you into the eternal homes" (Luke 16:8-9).

This parable has always perplexed the Church. The history of its interpretation could run hundreds of pages. Whenever it came up in the Lectionary, I usually preached on one of the other readings. But somehow I get the impression that it says something about the prudence of converting one's assets into friends and it appears to suggest that somehow this will enhance one's future security. It looks like an appeal to self-interest.

I found identification with self-interest also in John's Gospel. The promise of eternal life is prominent in the Fourth Gospel, and it is an appeal to our desire for security, a matter of legitimate self-interest. It is a prize not to be despised; Paul claimed that he counted everything he had as refuse to gain it (Phil 3:7-11). But just as in the Synoptics, in John I again find Jesus not only promising "pie-in-the-sky-bye-and-bye" but also appealing to my self-interest in the here and now: "You will know the truth, and the truth will make you free" (John 8:32). "I came that they may have life, and have it abundantly" (John 10:10). "I have said these things to you so that my joy may be in you, and that your joy may be complete" (John 15:11).

I discovered that Paul uses this motivation too. Just one example from his treatise on giving, 2 Corinthians 8-9, is enough to make my point. He tells the Christians in Corinth that he has been bragging about them to the Macedonians, how generous they've been in raising an offering for the needy saints in Jerusalem, and that their zeal has stirred up most of the Macedonians. Then he appeals to their pride, no less: "But I am sending the brothers in order that our boasting about you may not prove to have been empty in this case, so that you may be ready, as I said you would be; otherwise, if some Macedonians come with me and find that you are not ready, we would be humiliated—to say nothing of you—in this undertaking" (2 Cor 9:3-4).

The Hebrew Scriptures also do not lack for examples in identifying with self-interest. On almost every page in Deuteronomy Moses promises that if the Israelites will obey the Lord's commandments, they will prosper. In the Psalms David promises that those who delight in the law of the Lord shall be like trees planted by streams of water (Ps 1) and that those who confess their sins are happy (Ps 32).

How Do We Avoid Misusing the Appeal to Self-Interest?

If Jesus and Paul and others in Scripture identified with the people's self-interest, how do we avoid using it as a tool of manipulation? In 2 Corinthians 9 Paul says what it seems H. Grady Davis says we shouldn't say: "The one who sows sparingly will also reap sparingly, and the one who sows bountifully will also reap bountifully" (2 Cor 9:6), implying that a generous gift will pay off. How is that different from what Davis rejects, "the *it will pay us* sermon"?

I'm still exploring the ins and outs of the ethics of preaching. I don't have a finished system, but I have found two general principles that will protect us against the misuse of the appeal to self-interest.

The first principle comes from the first century A.D., from the Roman rhetorician Quintilian. Aware of the power of the persuasive word, Quintilian said, "The orator must be a good person." (He actually said, "The orator must be a good man," but in those days the orator never was a woman.) For the destructive potential of persuasion gone awry, we need only look at the havoc Hitler wrought with his mouth. In the same breath in which Jesus said, "Be wise as serpents," he also said, "Be harmless as doves" (Matt 10:16). In judging the ethics of appealing to self-interest, our assumption will be that the homilist is a good person, always praying, "In framing my appeal in this way, am I loving my neighbor as I love myself?"

I find the other guiding principle in what we Lutherans call "the theology of the cross." Nothing we do or promise in identifying with the people's self-interest shall be contrary to what Jesus laid out as primary for his disciples: "If any want to become my followers, let them deny themselves and take up their cross and follow me" (Mark 8:34). For example, if I'm preaching on the commandment, "You shall not bear false witness," I could in good conscience try to show that it's in our self-interest to be honest (as in the proverb, "Honesty is the best policy"). But I'd also have to allow that there could be times when telling the truth would mean denying my self-interest and taking up my cross.

The abuse of the appeal to self-interest comes in those who are addicted to "the theology of glory," those who promise the sky. It's these exploiters Davis is warning against, those who preach "the *it will pay you* sermon." I am glad that there are rich, famous, and beautiful people who believe in Christ, but why are these virtually the only persons some TV evangelists interview on their programs?

An Ethical Question in Not Using It

Although the scriptural appeal to self-interest is risky, there is also an ethical problem in not using it, in treating people as objects, assuming they need no motivation. Rhetoricians would call such pulpit discourse "monologue," and they regard monologue as inherently unethical because it is one-way and the one-way is top-down, superior to inferior. Barth's critics have said: "It is well known that, according to Barth, revelation creates its own point of contact. An understandable objection to this view asks whether this does not mean to throw the Biblical message at man like a stone."[24] "There was a lack of emphasis on man's personal existence and responsibility in the first years. Barth so strongly emphasized the divine, transcendent aspect that the human aspect was almost neglected. . . . Later on, Barth admitted that this approach was one-sided and tried to correct it, but the damage had been done."[25]

Barth never intended that damage. A man who on his own time went Sunday after Sunday to the prison in Basel, Switzerland, to preach the gospel to the inmates, he certainly didn't regard people as things. We can understand that while he was reacting against rationalism he would go way over to the other side. I fully agree that God's Word needs no human help. My point is that one must translate God's Word into a form the people can hear.

Identification and Homily Construction

Bishop Fulton Sheen was one of the earliest stars on television. His weekly program was on prime time with a commercial sponsor, competing successfully for viewers with comedian Milton Berle. What did he do on TV? He preached. And not just for five minutes—except for commercials, he preached for the full half-hour. The title of his program, "Life Is Worth Living," wasn't the only reason he commanded a national audience, but the title did sound the tenor of his speaking. His theme identified with the ways and self-interest of his hearers.

Examples of homily themes that grab me where I live: "Do We Need God?"; "How To Fail By Succeeding"; "To Your Advantage."

24. F. L. Herzog, "Theologian of the Word of God," *Theology Today* 13 (October 1956) 326.

25. Klaas Runia, "Why So Much Influence?" *Christianity Today*, 5 (December 1969) 9.

There are preachers who gain attention at the start of a sermon by telling a good story. Everyone in the pew is alert. But then they start "preaching." We need more than a good title and a good opener. How about identification with the hearers all the way through?

We can observe an example of this in a sermon by Augustine on almsgiving. With his standing he just could have said, "Give to the poor; our Lord commands it." Instead, he shows first how we have a problem, and he develops that problem at some length. He observes that when we are in difficulty, we consult a prudent person. He asks, "What counselor is more prudent than Christ?" Then he describes a common difficulty: What shall we do with our possessions? For whom are we laying them up? For our children? What will they do with them? Squander them? or will they also store them up for their children? Then what will our children's children do with them? Or will thieves take them from us? To solve this problem, let us take the counsel of Christ who said, "Lay up for yourselves treasures in heaven." But how do we transfer our wealth to heaven? It's easy: let the poor be our porters.[26]

From Bishop Sheen we learn that our homily titles or themes should reflect not only the biblical text but also the people's ways and self-interest.

From Bishop Augustine we learn that our entire homily will not only develop the biblical text but will connect with the people's ways and self-interest from beginning to end.

Adjusting Our Homily-Making Accordingly

Take for example one pattern of developing a sermon or a class session:

1. Exposition
2. Application

The application bids fair to be people-centered, identifying with the listeners' ways and self-interest. The exposition—even though it might be the best in all Christendom—stands a good chance of being content-centered, with the people seeing no connection between the fine exposition and their daily concerns. Who's to know if they'll still be awake when the application finally comes?

Suppose there is a sermon for Maundy Thursday called "The New Passover." People who come for the sacrament during Holy

---

26. Augustine, *Sermon* 60.

Week may well be interested in their spiritual roots and would appreciate an exposition of the Passover. But if the pew-sitters are honest, I'm afraid some would have to confess they feel like saying, "So what? What good is the 'New Passover' to me?" The homilist may eventually get around to that, drawing the parallel between Israel's slavery in Egypt and our own, showing how "The New Passover" redeems us from our misery. But why couldn't the preacher have started with our problem? He or she could have drawn various scenes of the agonies we suffer in our enslavement by sin today. Then he or she could have gone into the exposition, showing what the original passover did for Israel, next demonstrating how "The New Passover" rescues us today. That way, even during the exposition the people could have been making some of the applications themselves.

When I was first adjusting my homily-making to the principle of identification, I remember how it affected my approach to Jesus' parable of the four soils. I had studied the commentaries and read other homilies on this text. The sermons I was looking at usually had four parts, one for each kind of soil. I found them interesting expositions of farming practices in the Holy Land two thousand years ago. But so what? Then the preachers took it for granted that the people wanted to be good soil. How could they be so sure? Doesn't Scripture describe how the human spirit resists God? Didn't the preachers' own experience agree? I would bet that they might secretly want to enjoy some of the "cares and pleasures of this life," the thorns that choke out the Word.

In trying to find a way to identify with the people's ways and self-interest, I rejected the four-part structure and came up with this outline:

The Secret of Growing As a Person

1. How we all wish to be better.
2. Becoming good soil, we bear fruit.

In part 1, I used several examples of people we admire—examples from Scripture and the life of the Church—and I asked, "What was their secret? How did they grow so well?" That led to part 2, how in them God had broken up the hard path and given them some depth and rooted out the thorns—so they could grow as persons.

We strive to construct our homily themes not only to reflect the biblical text but also to connect with the people. We strive to connect our proposal with the people's motives from the very first of the homily and we strive to keep their ways and self-interest in mind throughout.

When I got to this point in one of my preaching workshops, one pastor suggested this format:

1. Bait the hook.
2. Set the hook.
3. Keep tension on the line.

Identification and Analysis

There is a serious theological objection to audience analysis. Isn't adapting your message to fit the audience questioning the power of the Holy Spirit and prostituting the pulpit? Doesn't the caution to Timothy belong here, about those who have "itching ears . . . accumulate for themselves teachers to suit their own likings" (2 Tim 4:3)? Doesn't audience analysis smack of marketing and politics where pollsters sample the public's taste, with the merchant and the vote-seeker then cooking up to order what will tempt and please? Did John the Baptist take a poll before he rebuked King Herod?

Of course, we reject all of this outright. What I'm trying to master is the audience analysis and adaptation demonstrated by Paul. When he addressed a Jewish audience, he started with God's promise to Abraham. When he addressed Greeks, he didn't mention Abraham. Was he tickling ears or wandering into myths? No, he was adapting to his listeners' way of seeing the world, translating the good news into a language they could hear.

Paul even used audience analysis to get himself out of a scrape. Recall the time he came to Jerusalem to deliver the offering for the poor he had gathered from his converts. The zealots mobbed him. So the Roman army took him into protective custody. But the tribune became flustered because he had bound Paul and was about to flog him without a trial before he discovered that Paul was a Roman citizen. Perhaps to shift responsibility, he put Paul before the chief priests and the council. Luke reports that when Paul perceived that some were Sadducees and some Pharisees (i.e., when he analyzed his audience), he cried out in the council, "Brethren, I am a Pharisee, a son of Pharisees; with respect to the hope and the resurrection of the dead I am on trial." If that indeed was the issue, Luke hadn't let us know it beforehand. At any rate, this maneuver caused a clamor in the house since Sadducees didn't believe in the resurrection while the Pharisees did. The Pharisees stood up for Paul, and the tribune, "fearing that they would tear Paul to pieces, ordered the soldiers to go down, take him by force, and bring him to the barracks" (Acts 23:10). A narrow escape by the strategy of audience analysis.

I believe I can also support adjusting to the people by an inference from C. F. W. Walther, patriarch of the Lutheran Church–Missouri Synod. Walther was an expert in two theological categories beloved by Lutherans, Law (God's diagnosis of our plight caused by sin) and Gospel (God's offer of rescue from our plight through Christ). If we Lutherans know nothing else about preaching, we're sure that a sermon will be measured by the standard, "Does it distinguish properly between Law and Gospel?"

Walther implies our need for audience analysis and adaptation in his eighth thesis: "The Word of God is not rightly divided when the Law is preached to those who are already in terror on account of their sins or the Gospel to those who live securely in their sins."[27] If we thunder God's judgment at those who are already bludgeoned by their guilt, or if we croon "Sweet Jesus" into the ears of those who have no conscience, we haven't analyzed our audience nor adapted ourselves thereto, and we have been derelict in our duty.

When Jesus said, "Do not give what is holy to dogs; and do not throw your pearls before swine, or they will trample them underfoot and turn and maul you" (Matt 7:6), I suspect that he was directing us to be aware of who is in our audience and to react appropriately.

Analysis through a "Panel of Diversity"

One year at St. John's University, we had a French Canadian priest doing graduate work who told me that when he went back home, he wouldn't get an associate until his parish became larger than five thousand families. How could he know everyone and adapt to their needs and interests? What about pastors with far smaller congregations who also lament that they can't get around to become acquainted with everyone? Or how can a homilist serving vacationers make adjustments for the strangers coming every week? How do we handle those occasions when we are in a guest pulpit? And even if we do know our listeners fairly well, how do we go about analyzing their motives and framing our appeal appropriately? What about the differences in temperament between those who come on Saturday night and those who worship at 8:00 Sunday morning, both different from those who come at 11:00?

One of my professors at the University of Minnesota, Dr. William Howell, gave me a strategy for audience analysis. He sug-

27. C.F.W. Walther, *The Proper Distinction between Law and Gospel,* trans. W.H.T. Dau (St. Louis: Concordia, 1928) 2 (thesis VIII).

gests a "panel of diversity": four, five, or six people who represent various categories of people in your pews. He recommends that as you prepare to speak, you interact with these individuals. Knowing what you know about them, ask yourself, "How would Jim react to this? How would Joann feel about it? Howard? Charlie? Gladys? Bob? Omar? How do I connect this with their lives? How do I overcome their objections, if any? What hope can I bring them?" Some pastors take this one step further: they actually meet with a representative group before the sermon is preached, to get their "feedforward" in person.

For the sake of variety, I change the personnel of my panel every little while: sometimes choosing them by age, other times by vocation, still other times by station in life.

If the panel of diversity reflects the various kinds of people in the parish, it gives the homilist who doesn't know everyone a chance still of identifying with their needs and hopes.

Even the homilist who knows everyone can benefit greatly by this approach. After interacting in my mind and heart with numerous panels of diversity, I discovered that my exegesis was taking on a new dimension. I was praying through the Scriptures not only with my eyes but also trying to see them with the eyes of others. The Bible came alive in new ways, giving new excitement to the homily. On the basis of my experience, I recommend communing with a panel of diversity every time.

A System to Assist My Intuition

Dealing with a panel of diversity takes time. We pastors don't usually have time. Besides, don't we usually adapt to the needs and hopes of our people by intuition?

I was invited to be a guest preacher for a midweek Lenten service in a large downtown church. The pastors were developing a series on the Ten Commandments. They assigned me, "You shall not steal." I had been attending on Wednesday nights, so I had some sense of the congregation. I noticed hardly any senior citizens. I developed a sermon making applications to honesty in the workplace.

There was also a noontime service on Thursdays. I assumed that since this sanctuary was planted in the vicinity of skyscrapers, those attending would be taking their lunch-breaks from their offices and stores. As I came into the nave, my heart sank. I saw that for most of those in the pews, their work history was in the past. For them my homily would be largely irrelevant. I did what I could to adapt on the spot, but I wasn't happy with my work. Intuition had failed me, and I had been careless.

What I need is a system to assist my intuition. I see something comparable in the checklist that airplane pilots use as they get ready to take off. One could argue that veteran pilots with their practiced eyes could simply look over their dials and controls and be able to spot any trouble immediately. But when I'm sitting behind them, I want them to go through every last item on their list. Granted that an oversight in the study may not be as life-threatening as a mistake in the cockpit, I do think it is serious when I waste golden minutes for the people of God because my sermon misses the mark.

What kind of checklist can we use as we try to get into the skins of the people on our panel of diversity? One possibility: "Maslow's Ladder."[28] Abraham Maslow has five rungs on this scale of human needs:

5. Self-fulfillment
4. Esteem
3. Social
2. Safety
1. Physiological

On a ladder one usually starts at the bottom and goes up a step at a time. That suggests that, usually, one set of needs must be satisfied before the next set appears. Basic to all is the physiological. Gandhi is reported to have said, "To a starving person, God himself would have to come first as a piece of bread." A confirmation class that's been sitting too long can't handle much more of the catechism.

The next rung is safety. If I had been using this system to analyze the congregation for that guest Lenten homily, I could have realized why I hadn't seen many retired people at the evening services and I might have seen that I could expect them during the day— for safety reasons.

After safety needs are filled comes the need to belong, to be loved. Some congregations pride themselves on being "family churches." We are learning that they may be unintentionally cutting off singles of all ages.

The next rung is esteem. It explains why those who "have everything" still keep driving. They are thirsty for acclaim, so they keep grabbing for money, influence, the front page.

28. Abraham H. Maslow, *Motivation and Personality* (New York: Harper & Row, 1954) 80–92.

At the top of Maslow's ladder is self-fulfillment. The people standing here aspire to live up to their potential. The U.S. Army's recruiting slogan, "Be all that you can be," aims at satisfying this desire. Peter Drucker notices that there are those who are moved by a "commitment to contribution."

Climbing the ladder in this way is typical, but not inevitable. Some recent studies indicate that just because someone is loved doesn't necessarily mean he or she will now be aching for esteem or that having food, water, and shelter one will automatically look next for safety.[29] Furthermore, we know people who are self-fulfilled, who are standing on the top rung having skipped some or most of the other rungs, disciples who have lost their lives and thereby found them. We know of people who have defied their need for safety to rescue someone from a burning building or a hole in the ice, people of a nobility born from being made in the image of God. It's thrilling to frame our gospel appeal to such persons and to challenge the rest of us to go and do likewise. So I don't use Maslow's ladder as a hierarchy, as though one rung must lead to another. Besides, we know how quickly things can change: a household may have everything going for it when someone has an accident or a catastrophic illness or someone loses a spouse or a child or a job, and then where are they? I rather see Maslow's ladder as a checklist to assist my intuition, a useful description of the various situations my people might find themselves in, helping me better to identify with their ways and connect with their needs and hopes.

Summary

It is risky to appeal to self-interest, but we may avoid the risks by measuring every appeal against the standards of loving our neighbor as ourselves and the "theology of the cross" (i.e., whether it contradicts Jesus' demand that we deny ourselves, take up his cross and follow him).

Risky as it is, identifying with people's self-interest is scriptural, following the examples of Jesus, Paul, the Deuteronomist, and David. (Notice that I have been saying "self-interest," not "selfishness.") I contend that though we must avoid the risks of this appeal, we must also avoid the neglect of it, that while it is unethical to manipulate the people, it is also unethical to disregard their divine

---

29. Frank J. Landy, *Psychology of Work Behavior* (Homewood, Ill.: Dorsey Press, 1985) 318–24.

image and treat them as inferiors as though all we have to do is to give them their orders, one-way, top-down.

Identifying with the people's ways and self-interest is one factor in changing the perception that *homily* and *dull* are synonyms. When the homily theme and structure from start to finish connect the Word of God to the lives of the people, boredom vanishes. The rapport in the sanctuary begins in the study where we commune with the people as together we dialogue with the Scriptures.

For Further Reading

Fulfilled in Your Hearing. Washington, D.C.: United States Catholic Conference, The Bishops' Committee on Priestly Life and Ministry, 1982, 1–8.

Marshall, Paul V. *Preaching for the Church Today.* New York: The Church Hymnal Corporation, 1990, 15–30.

Exercises

Exercise 2

On the matter of identifying with the people's ways:

1. If you're not preaching this weekend, observe how much you can learn about the people in the parish just from listening to the homily.

2. If you are preaching this weekend, look at your notes (or listen to the cassette) of your latest homily to see what one could have learned about the people in your parish from your homily.

Exercise 3

Jot down the names of five or six people from your parish who represent groups of others. Commune in spirit with this panel of diversity as you work on your next homily.

Exercise 4

Examine two homilies in the Appendix, numbers 1 (page 203) and 2 (page 209). Criticize them in two ways:

1. How the homilist did or did not identify with the people's ways and self-interest

2. To what degree the homilist was aware of the people: list all the things you can discover about the congregation the homilist was addressing

EXERCISE 5

Objective:

To practice identification, identifying with the people's ways and self-interest.

Assignment:

A three-minute homily on one of the Ten Commandments, identifying with the people's ways and self-interest. You may use notes if necessary.

Your hearers: those in your group.

You may find yourself admitting that because we follow Christ and carry our cross, there could be times when it looks as though it's against our self-interest to obey this commandment.

Show that it is not only to our advantage to keep the commandment you've chosen but our privilege. We love God because God first loved us. We love our neighbors because God's love has been shed abroad in our hearts. Being redeemed, it is not a burden but a joy to try to do God's will. So we preachers would rather not say, "We ought to," "We need to," or "We should," but "We want to," "We get to," or "It is our privilege to."

In making your critiques of your fellow homilists not only this time but also in the future, please observe these guidelines:

1. So as not to distract the homilist, no writing while he or she is speaking

2. Write only during the playback

3. Organize your comments under the two headings of compliments and suggestions

4. On the theory that we may learn more from observing what is commendable than from observing what is not, please give more attention to what is worth imitating

5. When making oral comments, stick to the subject. When your group is dealing with compliments, don't wander into suggestions. Don't say, "I liked . . . , but . . ."

FIVE

Making Homilies Cohesive

Once my wife and I were guests on a farm in Iowa. One morning, while we were waiting for breakfast, the farmer and I were standing in the living room looking out the window. A ditch-digging machine went by, going west. Ed said, "I wonder where that ditch-digging machine is going. Oh! My neighbor's son must be getting married." I said, "Ed, this is remarkable. You see a ditch-digging machine going west early in the morning, and you deduce that your neighbor's son is getting married!" Ed didn't say, "It's elementary, my dear Watson," but something like that. He explained that his neighbor and son had just gone into partnership that spring, that they'd rented a farm down the road to the west, that there was no one living on that place, that he had seen the neighbor's son keeping company with a young woman, and that he figured she probably wouldn't live in a house without inside plumbing. So: ditch-digging machine going west adds up to neighbor's son is getting married. Some months later, I saw Ed again and asked, "Did your neighbor's son get married?" "Oh, yes."

Ed was exhibiting a drive that comes from being created in the image of God, the urge to organize, the impulse to make sense out of our environment. Adam's naming the animals is a picture of this compulsion: to sort out, to define, and to classify. I know little about Einstein's unified field theory except its name and that it was Einstein's effort to unify everything we know about the universe. *Uni-verse* says it all: turning into one. The Gestalt school of psychology builds on this: people are driven to put a *Gestalt*—a form or shape—on everything. This is what Archie Bunker did in the TV series "All in the Family." Archie classified his neighbors into "hebes" and "wops" and "pinkos" and "fags" and "four-eyes." He had a big picture, and he could fit everything into it. I'm not arguing the rightness or wrongness of how he sorted things out; I'm just pointing to the fact that he did it. Liberals do it too.

When you or I stand up to preach, people may be courteous and give us their attention to begin with, but what happens if we start riding off in all directions? That sight may amuse them for a moment, but if they can't put a shape on what we offer them, they will soon give up and pursue other lines of thought. They want to see the big picture and how what we're talking about at the moment fits into it.

Now just putting your ideas down on paper with Roman numerals and subtitles doesn't necessarily make your homily cohesive. It could be nothing more than a stream of consciousness. I have heard homilies like that, where apparently the preacher had his or her desk covered with books and notes, finding something here and saying, "That looks good," and copying it down, leading to another idea, writing that into the sermon, coming up against a mental block, going to another book, finding something else, writing that down, going off on another idea, and so on. The only thing holding these sermons together is the paper they are written on. No wonder these preachers must read their homilies: even they can't remember them.

Lack of cohesiveness is also a problem with some homilies that are simply collections of stories. They may have come from a file, the file may have a topic heading (e.g., "Repentance"), and the text may have that topic in it. But when you see that sermon in print and try to outline it, you will find that it's a collage, with the preacher zigzagging to get from one story to the next.

A number of adjectives describe the cohesive homily. One is *unity*, which is what we have been discussing so far. A related adjective is *relevance*, meaning that a cohesive homily contains only those ideas that fit into the Big Picture. If you bring up something that doesn't sound as though it fits—and you think it does—you owe it to your people sooner or later to explain why it does fit. Still another adjective is *clustering*. You bring everything together under the point to which it belongs. If part 1 is the problem and part 2 the solution, you put everything that belongs to the problem in part 1—and only there—and everything that belongs in the solution in part 2—and only there. You keep your categories clean. Still another adjective is *textual*. The outline—being the structure holding the homily together—will naturally be built from materials in the text. (What other materials could there be?)

Cohesive Homilies Have a Purpose

"If you don't know where you're going, any road will take you there." *Alice in Wonderland*

At one stage in my career, I coached business executives in public speaking and meeting the press. Once I was working with a chief executive officer to help him get ready for his annual meeting. The first thing I asked was, "What's the purpose of this meeting?" He said, "Well, the law says we have to have it." I said, "That's certainly a good reason but is it the only one? Who will be there?" He thought about it and replied, "Some shareholders, some stock analysts, some brokers, some reporters, and a few employees." Then I asked, "Isn't this an opportunity to build good will with each of these audiences?" Afterwards the CEO told me, "That question about the purpose was worth your whole fee."

Earlier in my ministry if anyone had asked me, "What's the purpose of the celebration you're holding this Sunday?" I might have answered, "Well, the law says, 'Remember the Sabbath Day to keep it holy.'" If the questioner had gone on to ask, "Why are you preaching this sermon?" I might have responded, "That's what I'm paid to do." If the person had persisted, "What difference would it make if you didn't preach that sermon?" I could have replied, "I suppose the people could have gone home twelve minutes earlier."

I'm putting words in my mouth. Like you I have always had a higher vision of the pulpit than that. Surely there must have been times when I had a specific purpose for a certain sermon such as when I was encouraging people to read the Bible or to try to discover the mind of Christ in their dealings with minorities or to search their hearts and examine their priorities at pledging time. But I admit it was relatively late in my preaching career before I began to plan a purpose for every homily. I'm afraid I have delivered too many sermons where the line from *Alice in Wonderland* could apply.

There is nothing in Scripture or canon law or, as far as I know, the confessional statements of any other denomination that require the preacher to draft a specific purpose for every homily, but I do find biblical examples of it. According to Mark, when Jesus came into Galilee preaching, he had a specific purpose for that campaign: "The time is fulfilled, and the kingdom of God has come near; repent, and believe in the good news" (Mark 1:15). According to Luke, when the crowds on Pentecost "were cut to the heart and said to Peter and to the other apostles, 'Brothers, what should we do?' Peter said to them, 'Repent, and be baptized every one of you in the name of Jesus Christ so that your sins may be forgiven; and you will receive the gift of the Holy Spirit'" (Acts 2:37-38).

This is not to say that every homily to every gathering will always aim at a decision for Christ. Paul had quite a different purpose when writing to Philemon than when addressing the skeptics on Mars Hill. Just so, the homily's purpose will vary according to the make-up of the assembly and the content of the Scripture text. Among the various aims we might have: to inspire our people to stand in greater awe of God's majesty and grace, to pray more persistently, or to "rejoice with those who rejoice, weep with those who weep" (Rom 12:15).

After we have to stop working on our exegesis, the first thing we do is start working on our conclusion. We want to know where we are going so we can find the road to take us there. As I understand it, the conclusion has two functions: (1) to summarize; (2) to call for a response. The reason for the summary is to allow the impact of the entire message to undergird the call for a response. We are not ready to write the summary until the body of the homily is composed. But we do want to frame the call to a response because that is our destination. We know where we're going because we have a specific purpose for this specific homily.

While I was serving a parish in St. Paul, I served part-time as a critic in preaching labs at Luther Seminary. It was early in my development as a teacher of preaching, and so I share the blame for what I'm going to describe next. When the seminarian had been laboring in his or her preaching and we in our seats had been laboring in our listening, I sometimes would ask the homilist, "What was your purpose today?" I generally got an answer that lasted three or four minutes, ironic when the whole sermon may have been less than ten minutes. That usually made it clear that the homilist didn't have a purpose.

The accumulated wisdom of the ages tells us we should be able to state our purpose in one simple sentence. If we can't do that, it probably means we don't have our purpose clearly in mind yet.

I find support in Herbert Farmer:

> A sermon . . . should have something of the quality of a knock on the door. A knock . . . is a call for attention . . . but it is more than that, it is a call for an answer. . . . Yet how many sermons I have heard which lack this summoning note almost entirely. They begin, they trickle on, they stop, like the turning on and turning off of a tap.
>
> I am not suggesting that every sermon should be a continuous nagging at people, or should end with an impassioned evangelical appeal for that final decision for Christ. . . . There are many types of sermons, and some will rightly be for the instruction, edification and confirming of the saints, rather than be directly intended for the conversion of sinners. Yet even in the instruction, edification,

and confirming of the saints the note of claim and summons should not be absent.[1]

At the end of this chapter under "For Further Reading" I suggest some pages from David Buttrick's *Homiletic* in which he styles this emphasis on having a purpose as belonging to an older homiletic. I deem his "intending to do" to be not much different from my "having a purpose." His viewpoint is worth considering in helping us stay out of a rut.

The Difference between Purpose, Theme, and Title

I have discovered that often the one-sentence purpose is the same or almost the same as the theme. However, when preaching on a hard topic (more on this in chapter 10), the homilist won't want to reveal the purpose until the end when all the scriptural evidence has been laid out. Otherwise the homilist runs the risk of closing ears before he or she has a chance to make a case. Still, the homilist owes the people an organizing principle to aid them in their part of the dialogue, to help them fit everything into the Big Picture. In chapter 10 I advocate that when preaching on hard topics, we have an initial theme and a concluding theme, the latter containing the homily's purpose, the former containing a neutral statement or a question that arouses interest and does not shut off dialogue.

The initial theme/concluding theme strategy also works in other types of homilies. It can be useful in inductive preaching: the initial theme to arouse interest without giving away the punch line; the concluding theme—either stated or unstated—to provide the destination towards which this homily is headed.

I believe this pattern is also helpful in deductive preaching. I agree with advocates of inductive preaching such as Fred Craddock[2] and advocates of narrative preaching such as Eugene Lowry[3] who have decried deductive preaching as boring because there's no suspense: you give away every reason to listen by stating your purpose upfront; you also demean your listeners by giving them answers, not letting them work things out for themselves. But I don't think de-

---

1. Herbert H. Farmer, *The Servant of the Word* (Philadelphia: Fortress, 1942) 44–45.

2. Fred B. Craddock, *As One without Authority* (Nashville: Abingdon, 1979).

3. Eugene L. Lowry, *The Homiletical Plot* (Atlanta: John Knox Press, 1980).

ductive preaching has to be boring, not if we use the risky but scriptural appeal to self-interest (chap. 4), not if we make our homilies visual (chap. 6), not if we make them oral (chap. 7). Nor does deductive preaching need to be demeaning, not if we are ethical, avoiding monologue, all semblance of talking down (chap. 12). As for a strategy that would make it more likely that the deductive homily would not be boring, I didn't realize I was using the initial theme/concluding theme policy until I'd read Craddock and Lowry and others. I see that my initial theme has often been a question: "Is This Life All There Is?" "Is Christianity an Escape?"

Looking back I see that sometimes the initial theme was a question that led to a deductive homily, but having asked the initial question in my study, I didn't ask it in the pulpit. "The Freedom to Be Wrong," homily number 5 in the Appendix, is an example. Jesus said that the tax collector went down to his house justified. Communing with my panel of diversity, I asked, "Who cares about being justified?" Unlike Luther in the sixteenth century, many today aren't afraid of God, so what's the problem? Wrestling with this, I saw that whether or not we worry about hell, we are concerned about "face," so we are prone to make alibis, to be defensive, trying to justify ourselves. Out of this came a homily with the title, "The Freedom to Be Wrong": a deductive sermon in which I had the experience of rapport with the people throughout.

The issue of homily titles may be foreign to Roman Catholic priests and permanent deacons. To them I explain that Protestant preachers frequently publish their sermon titles in their service bulletins and newsletters and newspaper advertisements and may post them outside their church buildings. The aim is to draw people in. Sometimes the sermon title is the concluding theme. If the sermon title gives away the punchline, then the criticism of Craddock and Lowry is justified: why should anyone come to listen; we already know how it's going to turn out. "The Freedom to Be Wrong" is a homily title. It suggests the theme but doesn't give it away.

In either case—whether the homily is inductive or deductive—the observation from *Alice in Wonderland* still applies: "If you don't know where you're going, any road will take you there."

Outlines: Not Preacher-Centered but People-Centered

Here is an example of what I mean by "preacher-centered." It was produced by a seminary student and is typical of others I've seen:

On Luke 21:25-36, Advent 1, Year C
The Night after Christmas

1. The Scripture message
2. Bethlehem
3. Back to reality

There's nothing immoral about this outline. I can quote no Scripture against it. And if it helps the preacher remember the homily, who can quarrel with it?

Yet if the homily is for the sake of the people, shouldn't it be built so the people can remember it too? Shouldn't it help them to see how everything fits into the Big Picture? If the homily exists not in the manuscript but in the dialogue between homilist and people, shouldn't the preacher help the people take part in the dialogue more effectively?

I took the student's manuscript home and reworked the outline:

1. The Gospel goes beyond the tinsel of Christmas.
2. The Gospel brings the tinsel of Christmas back to reality.

Whether or not this was the best development of this text is not my argument here. I was just taking what the preacher had in the manuscript and reshaping it into a people-centered structure—not only to jog the homilist's memory but also to give the people a package by which they could carry the entire homily home.

In chapter 4 I looked at Jesus' parable of the four soils. I was dealing with identification, the "so what" factor: what difference does it make to know the farming practices of Jesus' time unless I see how this concerns me? And I'd better see it from the very beginning or I might not be awake when you do get around to it. Now I want to say something about this parable in terms of preacher-centered vs. people-centered outlining.

I commented before on looking at some sermons in print that took each kind of soil in turn:

1. Hard path
2. Rocky ground
3. Thorns
4. Good soil

No doubt this skeleton could flesh out into a text-based, people-centered homily; that is, it could foster dialogue because it is orderly, cohesive, and textual. Just to say "hard path" could stimulate pictures in the people's minds because the parable is well known. I am sure many effective proclamations of the gospel have been made with outlines with these four parts.

Nevertheless, this orderly, cohesive, and textual outline doesn't say what the homily says. It only indicates that it is about these four soils. Then too, there's no identification with the ways and self-interest of the people. If those are human beings in the pews and not robots, shouldn't there be some motivation to help them want to be good soil? (And doesn't the preacher also need the same kind of encouragement?)

Trying to make a people-centered outline with identification produced the sermon outline on this parable I gave in chapter 4:

The Secret of Growing As a Person

1. How we all wish to be better!
2. Becoming good soil, we bear fruit.

A people-centered outline states everything from the people's point of view. It uses complete sentences or implied sentences. For the sake of ease in remembering, its wording is as brief and memorable as possible.

How Difficult It Is!

I think this is the hardest part of homily making: making cohesive homilies with a structure that not only covers the whole text and the homily and also identifies with the people's ways and self-interest but is stated from the people's point of view.

Here is an outline that has much to commend it, on the story of Martha's conversation with Jesus at the death of her brother Lazarus, John 11:20-27:

The Hour of Need in Bethany

1. The need at its worst
2. The help at its best

It identifies with the people's ways and self-interest. It is people-centered. It is brief, rhythmic, and balanced, making it easy for both homilist and people to remember. Parts 1 and 2 cover the whole text. I like it, except for one thing: the theme and part 1 are the same; that means the theme covers only the first half of the homily. To find a theme that would also include part 2 is a challenge. (One of the exercises at the end of this chapter offers that challenge to you.) Yet I suspect that if I had been the preacher who developed this outline, after having spent a minimum of twelve hours of preparation squeezed out of a normally hectic pastor's workweek, I would have gone with this outline, and I think it would have been a helpful message, even with this defect.

Many times have I experienced the difficulty of making a cohesive, textual homily outline, identifying with the people, with its structure stated from the people's point of view—even in a homily deemed acceptable for publication in the journal of the former American Lutheran Church, *The Lutheran Standard*. It had been preached at my parish in St. Paul, Bethlehem Lutheran In-The-Midway. It was in the 1970s during the stress in our country over the Vietnam War. The clash between the generations was right there in our congregation: the senior citizens who had bought their homes fifty years before and the young adults who found the Midway area a convenient point of entry to the Twin Cities, because rent was relatively cheap and it was located at the center of the entire metropolitan area. So as one of the ways I tried to bring these two generations together, I prepared a sermon with this structure:

What Beards and Gray Hairs Have in Common

1. Both groups have a sense of being ridiculed.
2. Both groups are victims of the system.
3. Both groups are hungering for personal worth.

I believe I could see positive results in the congregation from this sermon. *The Lutheran Standard* editors accepted it for publication because they felt it was useful for their readers. But they saw my theme as not having enough identification with the people; it wasn't attractive enough to draw readers in. So they changed it to *Victims of the System,* putting my theme below in smaller print as a subtitle. I think the editors were probably right. But as a homiletician, I didn't like the fact that their theme was the same as my part 2. It only illustrated again the difficulty of framing a theme that covers the whole sermon, in an outline stated from the people's point of view that identifies with the people's ways and self-interest. How hard it is to get it all right! Knowing this from hard-won experience is one reason I go to church as a worshiper who needs to be nourished, not as a professional critic who's looking for something to nit-pick.

How Many Points?

I read somewhere that the Puritans of New England had deacons with poles to poke the people awake as their preachers would intone, "And twenty-thirdly . . . ."

Today, preachers joke about the fact they always seem to have three points. The truth seems to be, if we will not resort to the tactics of the Puritan meeting house, we don't have many choices except three points, two points, and one point. If we start with four points, we can probably condense them into two. If we have five points, it's too many for the people—and us—to remember unless we resort to the device of counting off the five points on our fingers. If we have six points, we can probably condense them into three or two. There is one other possibility, the one-point homily: the theme supported by one illustration after another.

Summary

To summarize this chapter, I will take a student's outline and show how it could have been made better.

I. Introduction
   A. The letdown
   B. Christmas, New Year
   C. But this is life
   D. The continuing gifts of God

II. Body
   A. Text: Rom 5:2
   B. We ignore God's gifts: dollar story
   C. Look at it or live it?
      1. Library
      2. Fishing
      3. Christmas
   D. Gifts
      1. Forgiveness
      2. The church
      3. Prayer
      4. Redemption

III. Conclusion
   Christmas: an example of the life of grace

One commendable thing about this outline is that it has a clearly defined purpose: "Christmas: an example of the life of grace." The homilist doesn't specify what we should do about that, but he does imply a call to a response, something like "Appreciate Christmas: an example of the life of grace."

The outline does also identify with the people's ways. The Introduction recognizes the letdown after the holidays. The Body offers gifts we all want.

The rest of the outline has problems. It says that the text is Romans 5:2: "Through whom [our Lord Jesus Christ] we have obtained access to this grace in which we stand; and we boast in our hope of sharing the glory of God." If this is to be a homily on those words, how would I know that from looking at the outline? It isn't textual.

Another thing: it isn't people-centered. Only the preacher can look at it and know what it means because not many lines are complete thoughts. So it doesn't help the people take part in the dialogue; it doesn't help them fit each piece into the Big Picture; it doesn't help them know how well they are proceeding towards the destination.

As for its unity, there seems to be an emphasis on God's gifts. But in the Introduction, how does "The letdown" proceed through "Christmas, New Year" and "But this is life" and arrive at "The continuing gifts of God"?

I took this outline and the manuscript home for an overhaul. I sympathized with a difficulty I'd had many times: the manuscript didn't always follow the outline. (The student would have been wise to have altered the outline to fit before handing it in.) I discovered in the manuscript a number of items that weren't relevant (things that belonged under part C were in parts B and/or D). There were items that didn't cluster (things in a paragraph that didn't belong together.)

It seemed the crucial line was part B of the Body: "We ignore God's gifts: dollar story." "Dollar story" was a preacher-centered, memory-jogging phrase to bring to the mind of the homilist the tale of a character who turns up now and then on a street corner, offering to hand out dollar bills to any who will take them. Most people passing by either draw back or simply look straight ahead, ignoring the weirdo.

Trying to reflect the text, having a clear purpose—with the outline constructed from the people's point of view—having identification with them, and being cohesive in putting all the parts together that belonged together and taking out all the parts that didn't fit, I came up with an outline easier to preach and easier for the people to catch and retain. Some of my readers may have seen my original revision in my preaching workshop manual; I confess that I've revised the theme still again, the better to reflect the text and the season:

Text: Rom 5:2
Purpose and Theme:
   Christmas: Appreciating Our Access to Grace through Our
   Lord Jesus Christ

1. People are skeptical of a free lunch.
2. God's gifts–though free–are priceless.

May the grace of God continue to nourish us with the strength
to persevere in the crafting of cohesive homilies.

For Further Reading

Buttrick, David. *Homiletic: Moves and Structures*. Philadelphia: Fortress
   Press, 1987, 100, 297–303.
Craddock, Fred B. *As One without Authority*. 3d ed. Nashville: Abingdon,
   1979, 51–97.
Lowry, Eugene L. *The Homiletical Plot*. Atlanta: John Knox Press, 1980,
   28–73.

Exercises

Exercise 6

Earlier in the chapter we looked at the following outline and
saw that the theme is virtually the same as part 1. Develop a theme
that's easy to remember, reflects the text, identifies with the people,
and includes part 2 as well.

The Hour of Need in Bethany
John 11:20-27

1. The need at its worst
2. The help at its best

Exercise 7

1. Identify the main parts of "Do We Need God?," the first homily
in the Appendix (page 203). Assume that the title is the theme.

2. Where does the introduction end?

3. Where do each of its main parts begin?

4. Where does the conclusion begin?

5. What do you perceive to be the purpose of this homily? Is that purpose reflected in the conclusion in a call to action?

6. Does the outline identify with the people's ways?

7. Does the outline identify with the people's self-interest?

8. Is the outline people-centered?

9. Does the outline develop the text?

EXERCISE 8

Make a bare-bones homily outline on Psalm 1 in writing. (Just the theme and its two or three main points.)

1. What is your purpose?

2. Is your theme people-centered and does it appeal to the people's self-interest?

3. Are your points people-centered, stated from the people's point of view?

EXERCISE 9

For an example of aural underlining, read "Third Word from the Cross," homily number 3 in the Appendix (page 214).

1. Is it deductive or inductive?

2. Any suggestions for improvement?

Read homily number 5, "The Freedom to Be Wrong," in the Appendix.

1. This is a deductive sermon. Does it give away the ending at the start?

2. "The Freedom to Be Wrong" is the title. Is it also the theme? If not, what is the concluding theme?

3. Any suggestions for improvement?

EXERCISE 10

For an example of a one-point homily, read "Did I Give up Praying Too Soon?," homily number 4 in the Appendix (page 220).

1. Is it deductive or inductive?

2. Any suggestions for improvement?

SIX

Making Homilies Visual

I remember a performance by Victor Borge where he stopped in the middle of his playing and said, "Most people cough when they hear this piece." He played a few more bars and stopped again and said, "They cough even if they don't have a cold."

Borge was commenting on the nature of attention. *Voluntary attention* is an act of the will, a conscious effort. It is hard work, so it comes in spurts. *Involuntary attention* happens when people are so caught up in whatever is being communicated that they can't help listening. No one is getting tired. There may be some coughing but not because of boredom.

We preachers have discovered this too. We have experienced times when there has been a plexiglass wall between us and the people. They could see us and we could see them, but nothing was getting through (except the coughing). But there have been other times when this plexiglass wall has disappeared and we were in communion with one another. The rapport was electrifying. It was an emotional "high." We wished it could have lasted forever.

We've felt this when we've told a good story. It had a plot. We could see every detail. If up till then we were reading a manuscript, when we got to the story, we left the paper and looked at the people full time. We didn't need to memorize the story except maybe the punchline. The rest of it came out easily because we could see the action in our heads and simply report what we were seeing. Best of all, we could feel that the people were listening. They could see the action too. They were with us as we established the characters and developed the plot. They were as pleased as we were with the surprise ending. There wasn't much coughing.

That is why some homilists keep files of stories. They catalog them under topics: repentance, sanctification, Christmas, stewardship, spirituality, and so on. Perhaps they cross-reference those illustrations that might go under more than one heading. They are constantly on the lookout, among other things subscribing to homily services and journals that feature illustrations. Then, when they prepare their homilies, they look at the readings for the day, pull out the file under the topic that most closely matches, dump the cards from that category on the desk, and start reading. "This one won't work; throw it aside." "This one I just used last month; throw it aside." "Here's one—maybe I can make it fit; throw it over here." When the pile of possibilities is high enough, they arrange them into a sequence and figure out how to bridge from one story to the next. When that homily is given, they can report that their people were listening. As they make visits the following week, the people will comment favorably on those stories, even retelling them with enthusiasm.

The trouble is, there aren't enough good stories to fill up the whole homily. We could spin one tale after another and the people would be listening, and they might remember the stories but not why we told them. Interesting? Perhaps. Textual? Cohesive? Edifying? Perhaps not.

Some homilists who keep such a file are sensitive to the question "Does the story fit?" So they work all the harder to collect more stories. I salute their diligence. It takes a lot of work to accumulate and classify an abundance of visual materials. But I'm afraid these same pastors will confess that the problem of trying to rasp a square story to fit a round hole still exists. I was discussing this with one of the speakers at a pastors' conference who told me, "You just have to have a large enough file." That evening he preached to the group, one illustration after another. He kept our attention; it was clear that his file was large. He had taken the precaution of choosing a short text—which meant the text didn't confine him to a certain train of thought. I won't say the Holy Spirit couldn't use that sermon; at least we were still awake. But he rambled.

Seeking involuntary attention by pasting together a collage of illustrations may seduce us into telling stories for the sake of telling stories. To avoid that, we could discipline ourselves to use only stories that do fit even if that means we can find only one per homily. (Don't throw your file away; if you find something that actually fits a text, use it.) But that also presents a problem. Where shall we set this jewel? Open with it? We would gain attention, but by starting high we'd have no place to go but down. End with it? We would have a strong finish but all the while we were just putting in time until we got to this powerful illustration, how would we prevent the coughing?

Is there any way to make the entire homily visual even when our supply of appropriate stories is insufficient? I think there is. We find our model in the Scriptures.

Preach Like a Hebrew

With our Western ways, our theologians say such things as "God is the ground of my being." A profound statement rendered simply. It's even a metaphor, but I can't *see* it. How does the Hebrew Bible handle it? "The LORD is my shepherd." I have never been a shepherd, I have never met a shepherd, and except in Christmas pageants I have never seen a shepherd, but I prefer *shepherd* to *ground*.

With our Western mind, we would say it's too bad children have to suffer the sins of their parents. How does the Hebrew preacher put it? "The parents have eaten sour grapes, and the children's teeth are set on edge" (Jer 31:29).

With our Greek heritage, we indoctrinate children and adult candidates with a catechism, dogma organized in logical abstractions. What is the Hebrew style? To transmit an entire theology of sin and grace by means of stories: Abraham and Sarah, Jacob and Esau, Jacob and the ladder, Jacob and Laban, Jacob wrestling with Yahweh, Joseph and his brothers, God hearing the cries of his people in Egypt, Moses the prince, Moses the murderer, outcast, shepherd, prophet, Israel a nation of whiners in the wilderness.

With our Western outlook, we might define *neighbor* as "someone who lives near you." That's clear and fairly concrete. But when Jesus was asked, "Who is my neighbor?" he replied, "A man was going down from Jerusalem to Jericho, and fell into the hands of robbers. . . ." (Luke 10:30).

Suppose somebody asked us Westerners to describe the difference between grace and legalism. We might write a term paper with footnotes referring to the Fathers of the Church or German or Scandinavian or American scholars. How did Jesus do it? "There was a man who had two sons . . . ." (Luke 15:32).

C. H. Dodd observes: "Instead of saying, 'Beneficence should not be ostentatious,' Jesus says, 'When you give alms, do not blow a trumpet.' Instead of saying, 'Wealth is a grave hindrance to true religion,' Jesus says, 'It is easier for a camel . . . .'"[1]

We're not putting down abstractions. The semanticist, S. I. Hayakawa, comments:

---

1. C. H. Dodd, *The Parables of the Kingdom* (London: Nisbet & Co. Ltd., 1935, 1946) 16.

It is to be regretted, although it is understandable, that there exists a tendency in our times to speak contemptuously of "mere abstractions." The ability to climb to higher and higher levels of abstraction is a distinctively human trait, without which none of our philosophical or scientific insights would be possible. In order to have a science of chemistry, one *has* to be able to think of "H_2O," leaving out of consideration for the time being the wetness of water, the hardness of ice, the pearliness of dew, and the other extensional characteristics of H_2O at the objective level. In order to have a study called "ethics," one has to be able to think of what ethical behavior has in common under different conditions and in different civilizations; one has to abstract that which is common to the behavior of the ethical carpenter, the ethical politician, the ethical businessman, the ethical soldier, and that which is common to the laws of conduct of the Buddhist, the Judaist, the Confucian, and the Christian. Thinking that is most abstract can also be that which is most generally useful. The famous injunction of Jesus, "And as ye would that men should do to you, do ye also to them likewise," is, from this point of view, a brilliant generalization at so high a level of abstraction that it appears to be applicable to all men of all cultures.[2]

Hayakawa also observes that we need abstractions to organize our thinking. He laments the kind of communication that is only concrete—where the speaker or writer relates one instance after another without pausing to reflect on how these specifics fit together. Hayakawa calls it "persistent low-level abstracting" and illustrates with a quotation from Professor Wendell Johnson, State University of Iowa, in his book *People in Quandaries:*

Probably all of us know certain people who seem able to talk on and on without ever drawing any very general conclusions. For example, there is the back-fence chatter that is made up of he said and then I said and then she said and I said and then he said, far into the afternoon, ending with, "Well, that's *just* what I told him!" Letters describing vacation trips frequently illustrate this sort of language, detailing places seen, times of arrival and departure, the foods eaten and the prices paid, whether the beds were hard or soft, etc.[3]

Other speakers float perpetually in the clouds: "Experimental analysis of the memory of forms insusceptible of symbolic schemati-

2. S. I. Hayakawa, *Language in Thought and Action* (New York: Harcourt Brace & Co., 1964) 186–87.
3. Ibid., 188.

zation has convinced me of the great importance of ocular kinaesthesia and the small part played by visualization in nearly all individuals, with the general illusion of really visual representations, a very strong illusion, especially when symbolic and verbal schematization is possible."[4]

Big words, easy to ridicule. We preachers use small words, don't we? But there have been small words coming from the pulpit that have been high-level abstractions: "The Holy Spirit is God active today. He is God our contemporary. He is God in and with us now to continue the teaching, illuminating work of the Son. He is the God of the horizons—horizons that 'move forever and forever as we move.' He is the God of Christian growth. The Father's unexpended resources and unrecognized glory become ours through him."[5]

Hayakawa quotes Wendell Johnson again: "The low-level speaker frustrates you because he leaves you with no directions as to what to do with the basketful of information he has given you. The high-level speaker frustrates you because he simply doesn't tell you what he is talking about."[6]

The speaker who commands involuntary attention is one who combines high-level and low-level abstractions, general usefulness and specific illustration. The homily theme and its supporting points (high-level abstractions) are both necessary and desirable. So are the pictures we draw. The theme and its supporting points organize the specifics of the homily and help both preacher and listeners to reflect on what it all means. The pictures help preacher and listener see how the theme and its supporting points fit our daily lives.

So our challenge as homilists is to understand the various levels of abstraction and how to make them serve our purpose in announcing the good news. To that end we may use another concept from Hayakawa, his "Abstraction Ladder" *(see page 64)*.

In preaching like a Hebrew, we strive always to be at least on level four, "cow," the word, and preferably on level three, "Bessie, the Cow." *C-o-w* stands for all manner of bovines: the Jersey, not giving much milk but what it does produce being rich in butterfat; the Holstein, giving tubfuls of milk but with a lower percentage of cream; the Hereford, used more for steaks and roasts than milk and

4. Henri Pieron, cited by Alfred Korzybbski, "On the Structural Differential," *Science and Sanity* (New York: The Science Press Printing Co., 1941) 386.

5. *Augsburg Sermons, Gospels, Series C* (Minneapolis: Augsburg Publishing House, 1973) 165.

6. Hayakawa, *Language*, 189.

ABSTRACTION LADDER[7]

Start reading from the bottom UP

8. "wealth"

8. The word "wealth" is at an extremely high level of abstraction, omitting *almost* all reference to the characteristics of Bessie.

7. "asset"

7. When Bessie is referred to as an "asset," still more of her characteristics are left out.

6. "farm assets"

6. When Bessie is included among "farm assets," reference is made only to what she has in common with all other salable items on the farm.

5. "livestock"

5. When Bessie is referred to as "livestock," only those characteristics she has in common with pigs, chickens, goats, etc., are referred to.

4. "cow"

4. The word "cow" stands for the characteristics we have abstracted as common to cow_1, cow_2, cow_3 . . . cow_n. Characteristics peculiar to specific cows are left out.

3. "Bessie"

3. The word "Bessie" (cow_1) is the *name* we give to the object of perception of level 2. The name *is not* the object; it merely *stands for* the object and omits reference to many of the characteristics of the object.

2.

2. The cow we perceive is not the word, but the object of experience, that which our nervous system abstracts (selects) from the totality that constitutes the process-cow. Many of the characteristics of the process-cow are left out.

1. The cow known to science ultimately consists of atoms, electrons, etc., according to present-day scientific inference. Characteristics (represented by circles) are infinite at this level and everchanging. This is the *process level*.

---

7. Ibid., 179. Reprinted with permission.

cream. Some *c-o-w*s are red, others white, some black; some are red and white; others black and white; some are male, others female, still others are steers; some are calves, some are yearlings, others are older; some roam on the range and exist on grass, some are penned in and munch on hay or silage. *C-o-w* is a file-drawer holding all these concepts.

Cow is on level four on Hayakawa's abstraction ladder. That's pretty good. But why not go just one rung lower? Why not take out just one of the folders in the drawer labeled *cow* and draw a picture of just one of the specific cows? Then we would have "Bessie, the cow."

When you say "Bessie," I think of Susie, the cow I milked my last two years of high school when we lived in Rosalie, Nebraska. Preachers and professors may assume that since we know so much about our topic, we should speak in universals; let the people make their own connections. Not so. You tell me about farm assets, I go to sleep. You tell me about Bessie, I see Susie.

I wrote about Susie in a class in creative writing in my senior year in college. I described our pasture, which was about one hundred yards from the barn, and how, when it was time to milk, I would merely stand at the door of the barn and holler "Susie!" She'd look up from her grazing and start walking toward the lane that led to the gallon of oats that would be in her feedbox as I milked her. Among other things, I also described the birth of one of her calves: how, when the calf was ready to come, Susie got up on her legs so the calf would drop, breaking the umbilical cord, how she licked the sac off the calf, and how the calf immediately tried to get up on its legs, falling repeatedly, but finally mastering the art of standing. Then I pictured the calf testing out its legs, darting first in one direction, then another, always returning to Susie for safety. I wrote, "And it always kept its tail in the air like the antenna on the back fender of a car." Professor Langland wrote in the margin, "Why don't you say, 'On the back fender of a Chevy?'"

Indeed, why not? Why not imitate the Master? He did not say, "A man was going down the road" and leave it there. He did say, "A man was going down from Jerusalem to Jericho . . . ." (Luke 10:30). And his first listeners were thinking to themselves, "I know just the spot where those thieves pounced on him."

"But I have so much ground to cover! Give me some credit for at least saying *cow* instead of *livestock*. I don't have time to draw a picture of Bessie." Why do you want to cover all that ground in one homily? Think of flying from New York to San Francisco. You span a continent, but what do you see? Clouds. Maybe an inflight movie.

Go by train or bus or car, and it will take you quite a bit longer, but you'll have a better notion of what the country looks like. As you map out the destination you want to reach in this homily, why do you need to go all the way across the country in one sitting? Wouldn't it be smarter to leave some of your material for another homily?

Look again at the following paragraph, how every sentence covers a lot of ground, and how when the homilist heaps all six statements together, your eyes glaze over. See how every sentence could be a homily in itself. Instead of flying all the way from New York City to San Francisco in one hop, why not go just one-sixth of the way and see what there is to be seen, and have something left to preach the next five times you preach on this text? "The Holy Spirit is God active today. He is God our contemporary. He is God in and with us now to continue the teaching, illuminating work of the Son. He is the God of the horizons—horizons that 'move forever and forever as we move.' He is the God of Christian growth. The Father's unexpended resources and unrecognized glory become ours through him."

When we soar in the clouds and never land, people go off on their own flights of fancy. Great novelists and poets and playwrights know that people make their connections not when we deal only with universals but when we take time to describe particulars.

My preaching workshops at Dana College (Blair, Nebraska) were scheduled to coincide with Dana's annual Staley Lectures. One year the Staley Lecturer was Elizabeth Achtemeier. Unlike lecturers in other years who attracted almost exclusively faculty and pastors, Dr. Achtemeier filled the auditorium with students as well. One morning we who were in the preaching workshop happened to find Dr. Achtemeier sitting by herself at breakfast; we invited ourselves to sit with her. The pastors asked, "Why do you think so many students are coming to your lectures? What's your secret? Is it because you're a woman?" That she wouldn't grant. Then we asked, "Is it because you're also a professor of Old Testament?" That she would allow. Numerous professors of Old Testament are so immersed in the thought patterns of Israel they can't help preaching like a Hebrew— and we can't help listening to them. Here are a few things Elizabeth Achtemeier has learned about preaching like a Hebrew:

> Suppose we ask, Who is God? We do not know who he is in himself, but from the Bible's similes and metaphors, we do know that in relation to his people he is like a shepherd, a father, a husband, a king, a lover, a bridegroom, a warrior, a master, a vineyard owner,

a lord, a consuming fire, a redeemer of a slave, a savior, never-failing stream, a rock, a fortress, a lion, a bear robbed of her cubs, a moth, a fountain of living water, a way, a light, bread from heaven, a shield, a potter, a mother, a sword-wielder, an axwielder, a judge, a plaintiff, a witness in court. . . .

Or let us ask, What is sin? In the language of the Bible, sin is like becoming a harlot when one is married, or rebelling against a father's love and leaving home, or attempting to storm heaven, or forgetting the past, or wandering away like sheep, or becoming a subversive in a nation, or not being dressed when one is supposed to be ready for a wedding, or becoming like a rotten bunch of grapes in a well-tended vineyard, or trying to drink from an empty cistern when an ever-flowing stream is nearby, or breaking into a house by stealth, or leaning against a feeble reed, or thinking that one is divorced when one is really married, or making empty promises, or failing to release a neighbor from a debt, or grumbling over a neighbor's good fortune, or being blind, or being imprisoned, or being enslaved, or never being born, or being lame, or being deaf, or not knowing what time it is, or distorting the laws of nature, or being like a bird in a snare or a prey for wild beasts.[8]

It profits us preachers to study the Scriptures diligently, above all for what they say but also for how they say it. In pursuing our goal of gaining involuntary attention, instead of pasting together a collage of stories, we strive to preach like a Hebrew.

Learn from the African-American Preacher

In making homilies visual, our next model is the African-American preacher. There is a growing appreciation of black preaching. Those of us who come out of different cultures should not try to be something other than what we are, but we may observe what's going on in the black pulpit and imitate what is appropriate for us.

Part of the power of the black preacher comes from the vocal responsiveness of the people. Those of us preachers who are not black rightly envy that advantage. We may also envy the political orator who doesn't mind at all being interrupted by applause or the stand-up comedian who doesn't mind at all being laughed at. Can we who speak in more solemn assemblies also hope for responsive listeners? Yes. Our listeners may not be exclaiming "Amen!" out loud, but when they are caught up in involuntary attention, we homilists can feel it. There is an energy from them coming back to us that gives us

8. Elizabeth Achtemeier, *Creative Preaching: Finding the Words* (Nashville: Abingdon Press, 1980) 99–100.

still more energy. The assembly is one with us and itself. It is as though time had stopped and we were living in eternity already. This is what happens when the homily identifies with the ways and self-interest of the people, has the cohesion that enables them to participate in the dialogue, and enables them to see what we are saying.

Preaching like an African-American is related to preaching like a Hebrew. The added element is that the black preacher shows us how to take the Hebrew stories from two to four thousand years ago and help people identify with them. See how it's done in this excerpt from a sermon by Evans Crawford, Dean of the Howard University Chapel, at the 1969 session of the Progressive National Baptist Convention:

> You remember Moses . . . after he had committed his act of self-defense on the Egyptian taskmaster down by the brick house. You know he went away. And he went up there and he had to try to get his mind together. This is the first point, really. The responsibility of the Black church for a theology of renewal and relevance is to work on the mind. It's in the Bible there about renewing of what? . . . the renewing of your mind! You have to get this intellectual problem all straightened out.
>
> Now what was his problem? Don't forget. Moses was reared in the Big House. He was with the establishment, Brothers . . . But what happened out there was that something human got him. And when they were mistreating his brother . . . he committed—just to use the language of the day—this act of self-defense. Now what happened to him? Here's what happened to him. Here was a man who had been reared in all the values of the Egyptian culture. But yet he doesn't know what happened to him with that sudden act of identification. It's almost like some of you feel. . . . You don't burn, you don't loot, but you have known of so much commercial stealing that even though you will not advocate it, there's something in you that says, "Something has got to be torn up." And so this was the kind of thing that was happening to Moses, I think. . . .
>
> Now I'm keeping aware of the fact that this has got to be a serious discussion. And I mean it quite seriously. Moses was considering the problem of the nature of God. . . . And he was trying to get it straight, that sudden act of identification. That's what happens to people when they identify. Their whole value system gets all shaken up. Now I didn't say, when you "rationalize." I didn't say that. I said when you *identify*, the whole thing changes.[9]

Henry Mitchell calls this an example of "imaginative elaboration":

9. Henry H. Mitchell, *Black Preaching: The Recovery of a Powerful Art* (Nashville: Abingdon Press, 1990) 65–66.

The imaginative use of the helpful insights of scholars is only a small part of a much broader use of imagination to put flesh on the often skeletal narratives of the Bible—to breathe life into both the story and the truth it teaches. In addition to the scholar's details, there is a great need for more vivid but not less valid details, often not given in the Bible or anywhere else. These details help the hearer to be caught up in the experience being narrated and, as a result, to understand better and be moved to change. Black preaching, at its best, is rich in the imaginative supply of these details and in their dramatic use in telling the Gospel stories.[10]

Before I began looking at black preaching, I had already stumbled onto this way of making homilies visual: "the imaginative use of the helpful insights of the scholars." Back in the days when we were still using the King James Version in Protestant worship, I was dealing with John 12:1-15, the Palm Sunday story preceded by Mary's reckless act of anointing Jesus' feet with a pound of what recent translations call "costly perfume" but which the King James Version called "spikenard." What was spikenard? The narrative told me it was precious and had a fragrant aroma. Matthew and Mark told me it came in an alabaster box. I had heard the word *spikenard* many times, but I didn't know where it came from or why it cost so much. So I got out my Bible dictionaries and learned it was made from the roots of a plant growing in the Himalayan mountains and that it is found at an elevation of eleven thousand to seventeen thousand feet and only there. I also learned that alabaster comes from a place called Alabastron in Egypt (near Thebes), that alabaster is a translucent rock, that alabaster jars for spikenard were one-way containers with no stopper or lid because spikenard was so volatile it had to be sealed up tight, the neck having to be broken to get at the ointment. I took out my Bible atlas and measured the distance between the Himalayas and Bethany, thirty-seven hundred miles, and the distance between Alabastron and Bethany, seven hundred miles. I tried to imagine the men who climbed up the craggy peaks to eleven thousand feet. I read that they could only harvest a little at a time, no more than they could put into a leather bag hanging from their necks, because they had to keep their hands free for climbing up and down. I tried to imagine the traders going thirty-seven hundred miles on their camels to Bethany. I tried to imagine how Mary accumulated the money, a year's salary (three hundred denarii, Judas said: a denarius was a day's wage, so three hundred days—a long time in itself but how long does it take to save a year's salary?). Why did Mary

10. Ibid., 63.

even buy that spikenard? What woman in Bethany would ever keep a pound of spikenard on hand? Was it perhaps to catch a man? If she broke the neck of the jar—expensive in itself but worthless when broken—there would be no sense in trying to put just part of the spikenard on Jesus and keep the rest for another occasion because it would all evaporate anyway. All this wrapped up in that pound of spikenard as Mary broke the neck of the alabaster jar in an extravagant act of devotion to Jesus. It was a thrill to preach that sermon on the theme, "What Does It Cost to Be a Christian?"

Once I was exegeting Ephesians 5, looking at the verse where it says that Christ is like a bridegroom who washes the bridal dress of the Church. In all my years of witnessing weddings, I had never seen a bride with a dirty, wrinkled gown. What a picture that made when I described a wedding where by tradition everybody else marches to the altar with every eyelash in place and standing at attention, waiting for the bride to enter—and here she comes, reeking with mothballs, her hair stringy and disheveled, her dress blotched with gravy and beer. That led me to find a lot of pictures of what our Lord has to put up with in forgiving and sanctifying the Church, all from taking an embarrassed look at just a few stains on her bridal dress. "Imaginative elaboration" based on exegesis, one of the secrets of the African-American preacher.

Once I was preparing a stewardship homily on 2 Corinthians 9. The chapter ends with Paul's exclamation, "Thanks be to God for his inexpressible gift!" I've heard several preachers expound on that verse, often with fine biblical content but not related to that chapter. Usually they've talked about God's grace in Christ, what an unspeakable gift that is. Who can find fault with that? I do, because that's not the main idea of that chapter. When I look at it carefully, I think I see that it's about God's fun in giving. When Paul exclaims, "Thanks be to God for his inexpressible gift," the context shows that he means God's gift of sharing his fun, the gift of being able to give hilariously. Then it was fun for me to invent word pictures to illustrate first what the unspeakable gift is not and then to show what it is. I don't know how it was I happened to think of the little fellow who shared his lunch with Jesus when our Lord fed five thousand people out in the sticks. I was just looking for ways to make visual what was in the text. It takes a while for ideas to simmer in the subconscious. Anyway, somehow it came to me: imagine that little fellow that evening rushing into the house and as soon as he gets into shouting range, yelling at the top of his voice, "Hey Mom! Guess what me and Jesus did today!" Fifty years later I can see his grandchildren running up to him in the evening and saying, "Hey

Grandpa, tell us again about the time when you and Jesus fed five thousand people with your lunch!" The hilarity of being able to give—refreshing him his whole life long. That's the inexpressible gift God shares with us.

I gave that sermon at a conference for pastors on stewardship. One pastor was dubious. He asked me, "What you said about that little boy—where did you find that in the Bible?" This was before I began looking at Black preaching, so I didn't know then I was imitating a characteristic of African-American preachers: using "more vivid but not less valid details." It is true that although the story of the feeding of the five thousand is in all four Gospels, not one of them says anything about that little boy's running home to tell his mother. This homily appears in the Appendix. Those interested may examine it to see whether the details are valid, whether the details from outside Scripture are unscriptural.

Imitate Playwrights and Novelists

In making homilies visual, we preach like Hebrews and we learn from African-Americans. We may also imitate playwrights and novelists.

Whenever you see a play on the stage or on television or on the movie screen, or whenever you're watching a TV commercial, observe how the author is bringing high-level abstractions on Hayakawa's ladder down to level three, "Bessie, the cow." Take the abstraction "parents and teenagers don't understand each other." In a play that line might never be uttered, but the actions will leave no doubt. It's not "Show and Tell," but "Show, Don't Tell." Or take the abstraction "hatred destroys." You don't need a TV drama to tell you that, although television will give you plenty of material. Just go back to Genesis: Cain and Abel, Jacob and Esau, Joseph and his brothers, and you'll have an abundance of pictures to show your people. In your homily you can develop whole scenes. Have a plot. Have the characters talking to each other. Have a punch line, just as you would when telling a story from your file of illustrations. Or take a scene from secular history or the newspaper. Or invent a scene that reflects the realities of the people in your pews: what it's like to live forgiven in a family when a youngster doesn't come home until sixty minutes after the curfew, or when a husband hardly ever picks up his dirty socks from the bedroom floor, or when a co-worker doesn't hold up his or her end of the job. Draw pictures of what sin does to people, and then don't forget to draw pictures of what living under grace does for people.

I think of this as drawing word pictures of scenes that could be shot with a TV camera. I picked this up from a seminar for TV and radio. The instructor wasn't talking about preaching, but I saw possibilities for the pulpit. I really wasn't interested in television; I had just started doing a weekly radio program (now called "Sing for Joy"), vocal music of the Church related to the readings for the day. But what stuck with me was how a TV script is put together. On the left hand side of the page, the planners plot what the viewers will see. On the right hand side, they lay out what they will hear. *They plan the video side first.* I took this course in the 1950s, long before video tape, when TV shows were broadcast live. Our instructor explained how a TV announcer would prepare to give a commercial. He said, "First the announcer will go through all the motions he'll make—that is, first he'll practice what you're going to see; then when he knows what you'll see, he can remember what he's going to say." That turned on a light for me. Here was a device that could both push me to make homilies visual and help me remember what I was going to say. With luck, maybe even my people could both see and remember. So from then on, I began to lay out my homilies as though they were TV scripts. After I needed to stop doing my exegesis and after I had worked out a purpose and a tentative outline, I would write *Video* on the left hand side of the paper and *Audio* on the right. I would try to lay out scenes. I would say to myself, "If I were shooting this with a TV camera, how would I make this point visual?"

Will this work for you? Who knows? It must be all right to make homilies visual because the Bible abounds in examples of going way down the abstraction ladder to level three, "Bessie, the Cow." We don't want to try to accomplish this by hauling in illustrations to impose upon the text; rather, we do want to pray and study the text through to find out what's there and then search for ways to make what's there see-able. If the system of creating a TV script can make this happen for you, you're welcome to it.

Object Lessons for Children

Roman Catholic priests and permanent deacons may have occasion to preach at Masses where children dominate the gathering. Many Protestant pastors have a few minutes in the Sunday service directed to the children, often asking the youngsters to come to the front and sit with them on the chancel steps while they talk. Often the homilist shows an object and then makes applications from it.

Who is the audience? The children, supposedly. But when you look around, who's listening? Who's smiling? Who's chuckling?

Who are the ones who are reinforcing the pastor at the door saying, "I really enjoyed that object lesson"? The adults. It may be that some of the most creative work in making homilies visual is done when the target is children but grownups are the ones who are struck.

Often the kids just don't get it. If one of them answers a question, sometimes it's way off base, and that only makes the adults chuckle all the more. (That raises an ethical question, whether the children aren't being used. I'm embarrassed to admit that I was enjoying my image as an entertainer until I heard by the grapevine that a certain darling had told her parents, "I'm not going up there with Pastor Rueter any more; he just makes the people laugh at me.")

What's going on? Again we ask, who's the audience? The Roman Catholic Mass for children is probably for students in the school, kindergarten through grade 8, with teachers, staff, and perhaps some parents also present. The Protestant gathering of children on the chancel steps usually finds tots no younger than about two and no older than about ten (two at the low end because those younger than that can't handle it and ten at the high end because those older than that see it as "kid stuff").

What's the message? If it's an object lesson, it's a metaphor. But children are literalists. Some of our comic strips make us smile when they picture how youngsters take metaphors literally. (Dennis the Menace, talking to his dad, pointing to their neighbor, Mr. Wilson: "See? His nose isn't outa joint! It always looks that way!") It's not until children are in sixth, seventh, or eighth grade that they begin to think in figures of speech. Before then, a stone is a stone, not a symbol of a hard heart (and "hard heart" is itself a metaphor). So when a pastor uses a flashlight without batteries to represent a person without the Holy Spirit's power, the adults get a message they can visualize but the tots see only the flashlight that won't work. That children are literalists doesn't mean they don't have imagination. Tell them about a tree that can fly and they have no problem. But tell them what Psalm 1 says, that a tree planted by streams of water is a picture of the happiness we enjoy when we meditate on the Word of God . . . .

If we use objects with children, let the objects be what they are. One Palm Sunday I saw a pastor use a small stone as he told the story of people singing praise to Jesus as he rode his donkey; when Jesus' enemies told our Lord to make the people shut up, he observed, "I tell you, if these were silent, the stones would shout out" (Luke 19:40). Here the pastor was using the stone for what it was, a stone that could have shouted the praise of Christ.

The Story Homily

In recent years a new body of homiletical literature has been growing about narrative preaching. I see this as an aspect of "Imitate Playwrights and Novelists." The emphasis is not on stringing together a collection of stories but on telling one story as the framework for the entire homily. In Jesus' preaching, the parable was the homily. In story homilies, the story is the homily.

A story has to do with setting, conflict, and resolution. Its pattern is beginning, middle, and end. The setting, conflict, and resolution may come in various sequences:

1. Beginning   Setting
   Middle   Conflict
   End   Resolution

2. Beginning   Conflict
   Middle   Setting
   End   Resolution

3. Beginning   Resolution
   Middle/End   Setting/Conflict

Sequence 1 is straightforward and useful. It's often the way to go. Sequence 2 is what the Romans used to call "in medias res," starting "in the middle of things." Movies, television, newspapers, and magazines often do this, capturing interest by picturing the conflict first, then filling in the setting, following with the resolution. Sequence 3 is illustrated in the movie *Amadeus:* the film opens by showing us Salieri's throat with a bandage around it–apparently as the result of a suicide attempt–and flashbacks give us the setting and the conflict arising from Salieri's envy of Mozart's genius.

A story homily has to do with God's story and our story. The secret is to let both run in a parallel pattern of setting-conflict-resolution. A common mistake is to tell the story (high rapport with the people) and then to make the application (dullsville). The proper pattern is:

1. Beginning of the story
   Beginning of God's story/our story

2. Middle of the story
   Middle of God's story/our story

3. End of the story
   End of God's story/our story

In the Appendix the homily entitled "The Fool" is one example of running a story in parallel with God's story/our story.

Often the story homily is inductive. That's in contrast to the deductive pattern—stating your case and proving it. The story homily lays out the case as a narrative and then induces the theme from the evidence.

The Book of Jonah is a story homily. The prophet was running away from preaching repentance to Nineveh, because he knew that if Nineveh repented God would show mercy, and that's the last thing he wanted to have happen to Israel's worst enemy. For three chapters, the author develops the setting and the conflict between God and Jonah. Not until chapter 4 do we know why this book was written. Jonah was sitting outside the city to the east to watch what would happen to Nineveh, hoping God would still destroy it even though the people had repented. The sun was hot. God appointed a bush to grow and give shade to the prophet. Jonah was happy about the bush. But the next day God appointed a worm to attack the bush so that it withered. With the sun beating on him, Jonah was faint and asked to die. The Book of Jonah ends with the Lord's saying:

> You are concerned about the bush, for which you did not labor and which you did not grow; it came into being in a night and perished in a night. And should I not be concerned about Nineveh, that great city, in which there are more than a hundred and twenty thousand persons who do not know their right hand from their left, and also many animals?

Jonah's theme is never stated. From the evidence laid out in the narrative, we induce a theme, something like: "Israel's Merciful God Is the Merciful God of All Nations."

Although the story homily and the inductive pattern go well together, the story homily can also be constructed deductively. I see Luke 15 as a story homily with the theme given in verses 1 and 2: "Now all the tax collectors and sinners were coming near to listen to him. And the Pharisees and scribes were grumbling and saying, 'This fellow welcomes sinners and eats with them.'" Luke then shows Jesus telling three stories, the lost sheep, the lost coin, and the lost son and his elder brother.

In the Appendix, "To Be Somebody" is an example of a story homily laid out deductively, with the theme and its supporting points clearly identified. (It is also an example of "imaginative elaboration" based on exegesis.)

Being visual by whatever means is effective. It may be also the way to bring men to church. Lyle Schaller links the right and left brain theory to the reason why some men drop out. The right brain is joined to visual communication. Schaller says: "For sermons to appeal to men, the majority of them being right brain, visual persons, the minister has to use more word pictures. Women, who are more left brain, verbal persons, are more understanding of the verbal skill. That's why churches are attracting more women than men."[11]

My experience and that of many others: whenever we help people to see what we're saying, women like it too.

Summary

In preaching we dream of gaining involuntary attention, the assembly and homilist having palpable rapport. Preachers have discovered that this emotional "high" may be gained when telling stories. Some have been seduced into telling stories for the sake of telling stories, pasting together a collage that may be interesting but perhaps not edifying, not cohesive, not textual. Some preachers discipline themselves to use only stories that fit, even if it means just one story in the whole homily. But how can we overcome the coughing that erupts during the rest of the homily? How can we make the entire discourse visual?

We strive to preach like Hebrews. Our model is in the Scriptures. We study the Bible primarily for its content, but we profit when we also study it for its style. We learn from African-American preachers. We imitate playwrights and novelists. When we can identify with the ways and self-interest of the people, when the homily is cohesive and visual, our listeners may finally be caught up in involuntary attention, united to us and each other and energizing us.

For Further Reading

Achtemeier, Elizabeth. *Creative Preaching: Finding the Words*. Nashville: Abingdon Press, 1980, 97-103.
Mitchell, Henry H. *Black Preaching: The Recovery of a Powerful Art*. Nashville: Abingdon Press, 1990, 56-87.

11. *Your Church*, May/June 1985, 10.

Exercises

EXERCISE 11

In the Appendix, read number 6 (page 228), "Grateful for the Giver." Observe how high-level abstractions are brought down to a lower rung on the abstraction ladder.

> 1. Make an outline of this homily. Discover its theme and its two or three supporting points. These are the high-level abstractions that help homilist and listeners organize their dialogue. Then list the TV scenes that make these high-level abstractions visual.
>
> 2. Is this homily deductive or inductive?
>
> 3. Any suggestions for improvements?

EXERCISE 12

In the Appendix, read number 7 (page 232), "The Uglier She Gets," and number 8 (page 235), "Hey Mom! Guess What Me and Jesus Did Today!" Observe how high-level abstractions are brought down lower on the abstraction ladder by "imaginative elaboration" based on exegesis, in the style of the African-American preacher.

> 1. For one of these homilies, list the TV scenes based on details not given in the specific text for that homily—details "more vivid but not less valid," some coming from other Scriptures, some from research into the customs of Bible people, some from the experiences of people today.
>
> 2. Are these homilies deductive or inductive?
>
> 3. Any suggestions for improvement?

EXERCISE 13

In the Appendix, read number 9 (page 239), "Turn on the Light for Children." In the second last paragraph, the editor changed one paragraph slightly. In so doing, the editor violated the principle this article is advocating. Where is that inconsistency? (After you've looked for this, check out the author's comment at the end of the exercises for this chapter.)

Exercise 14

In the Appendix, read number 10 (page 241), "The Fool."

1. Make an outline showing how the homilist runs the story and God's story/our story in parallel.

2. Is this deductive or inductive?

3. Any suggestions for improvement?

Exercise 15

In the Appendix read number 11 (page 243), "To Be Somebody." Contrary to the usual format of a story homily (inductive, no aural underlining), this one is deductive and also underlines for the ear the theme and its supporting points.

1. Write the theme and its supporting points.

2. Make a list of details not in the biblical text but that have gained "imaginative elaboration" based on exegesis.

3. Any suggestions for improvement?

Exercise 16

Compose a three-minute homily on a line from the Lord's Prayer.

Your hearers: those present in the room with you.

Your purpose: to practice making pictures as though doing a TV script.

One possibility: discover a problem relating to your line from the Lord's Prayer and relating to your listeners' self-interest; construct scenes picturing that problem. Then discover a solution in the good news of Christ relating to the line you've chosen and draw scenes of people experiencing that solution.

To be given without notes. As you rehearse, some lines will come out as they appear in your manuscript but don't try to memorize the words, and especially, don't try to remember which *words* come next. Instead, memorize which *scene* comes next and then simply tell us what you see as it's happening.

Author's Comment on Exercise 13

The inconsistency is in this sentence: "When considering the text, 'Your body is a temple of the Holy Spirit,' and applying that to the care of our bodies, we might show them a toothbrush." Our bodies as temples of the Holy Spirit—that's a metaphor, something that children ages two to ten (being literalists) can't comprehend. My manuscript said, "When considering the commandment, 'You shall not kill,' and talking about the positive side of that, caring for our bodies, we might show them a toothbrush."

If you had difficulty in discovering this inconsistency, I'm not surprised. I've used this exercise in my preaching workshops and have discovered that hardly anyone has been able to find the problem. I see this as an indication of how thoroughly we adults are immersed in metaphors—so thoroughly that we don't always recognize that we're using them. To me this is a sign that I want to use extra care in choosing my words when speaking to our precious youngsters.

I wrote a letter to the editors complimenting them for the attractive way they had set up the page on which this article was printed and then pointing out how their editing had violated my intent. They were good enough to publish my letter, but they still had the last word. Over my letter they put the heading, "Thanks, but No Thanks."

SEVEN

Making Homilies Oral

David Preus, the presiding bishop of the former American Lutheran Church, told of a seminary professor who had a series of meetings with members of various congregations. The professor gave out questions to which people responded with written answers. One of his questions was, "If you could speak to a room full of preachers about preaching, what would you say?" The most frequent response: "Don't read your sermon."[1]

The title of an article implies the same message: "Is a Read Sermon a Dead Sermon?"[2]

Once I received a hand-written nine-page letter from a lay person who had heard that I conduct preaching workshops. He loves his pastors and their families as people but "rarely do they in worship ever look at the congregation. They are always reading to us, even announcements. . . . When they do look at us it is only briefly—and it comes across that the reading is absolutely correct . . . but something from the heart is missing. . . . Why not have the pastors type out the sermon on a word processor and just pass them out and we would read them for ourselves?"

There are preachers who read their manuscripts who make it a lively interchange. Phillips Brooks, author of "O Little Town of Bethlehem," a nineteenth-century American clergyman of the Episcopal Church, was renowned as a preacher; he read every word of his sermons. The act of reading in itself need not kill the rapport, as anyone who's read *Goldilocks and the Three Bears* to a three-

---

1. *Acts: Resources & Ideas for Parish Leadership* (Minneapolis: The American Lutheran Church, October 1986) 3.

2. Norman V. Hope, *Christianity Today,* 28 April 1967, 30–31.

year-old can testify. What counts is what's being read: "The big bed was too hard. . . . The middle-sized bed was too soft. . . . The little bed was just right." Reading that is an oral event. Contrast with: "Goldilocks tested all three beds and found there was a difference in composition and texture, the first two being extremes in hardness and softness, the third one being more to her liking."

It is good to know that there is a rising interest in preaching as an oral event. For evidence I need only to point to the article "Toward An Oral/Aural Homiletic."[3] The author is Michael Williams, Director of Preaching Ministries, General Board of Discipleship, The United Methodist Church. He quotes substantial authorities—Fred Craddock, Richard Lischer, and Walter Ong—to the effect that we need to redefine preaching in terms of acoustics instead of words in print. He suggests that preaching as an oral event affects how we relate to our people and that that relationship affects how we perform. That is why those parishioners told that seminary professor, "Tell them not to read their sermons"—because in the reading something unpleasant was happening both to the relationship and to the performance.

One connection between relationship and performance has to do with whether the homilist is thinking while preaching. When a preacher stands up to preach, he or she is asking the listeners to think. Yet they can sense whether the preacher is thinking with them or is merely reciting (as with a memorized sermon) or is merely voicing words from a page (as when reading a manuscript). A rhetorician explains that vital and personal public speaking involves the speaker's "conscious awareness of the content of the words as they are uttered."[4] Memorizing or reading need not block rapport; the preacher can be a thinking performer while delivering a memorized message or reading a script, though it takes work to make it come off alive.

Another connection between relationship and performance has to do with the eyes. When the preacher looks at the manuscript instead of the people, he or she loses contact. A mid-nineteenth century Methodist circuit rider, William Henry Milburn, described the difference between the style of the frontier preacher and that of the Puritan divine:

3. *Homiletic: A Review of Publications in Religious Communication,* 11, no. 1 (1986) 1–4.
4. James C. McCroskey, *An Introduction to Rhetorical Communication* (Englewood Cliffs, N.J.: Prentice-Hall, 1968) 213.

> The spoken eloquence of New England is for the most part from manuscript. . . . Preachers were set at an appalling distance from their congregations. Between the pulpit, perched far up toward the ceiling, and the seats, was an abysmal depth. . . . [The speaker's] eye was averted and fastened downward upon his manuscript, and his discourse . . . delivered in a monotonous, regular cadence.[5]

How would such speaking be received in the Wild West? Milburn suggested putting the manuscript-reading and learned New England preacher on a stump and surrounding him with people pressing in on every side with no chasm between him and the audience. The listeners would have "eyes intently perusing his to see if he be in real interest—'dead in earnest'—and where, as with a thousand darts, their contemptuous scorn would pierce him through if he were playing a false game."[6]

To see the connection between relationship and performance and to see also that using a manuscript bids fair to make us lose contact, imagine Paul before King Agrippa saying, "If you'll excuse me, O King, I'll first have to take out my notes. I've worked out this humdinger of an appeal and I want to get every word just as I've written it out. You'll enjoy the rhythm and the imagery, and I'm pretty sure you'll be almost persuaded to become a Christian."

Or imagine John the Baptist before the Pharisees and Sadducees. "Just a minute. I have some notes I've been saving just for you under this rock. Let me see now, I say here, 'You brood of vipers! Who warned you to flee from the wrath to come?'"

Or imagine Peter on Pentecost—when the crowds were cut to the heart asking, "Brethren, what shall we do?"—first taking out his spectacles and fumbling in his briefcase for his notebook and finding the place and reading, "Repent, and be baptized every one of you in the name of Jesus Christ for the forgiveness of your sins."

The rhetorician William Norwood Brigance wrote, "As some wit has put it, 'Using a manuscript in making a speech is like courting a girl through a picket fence. Everything you say can be heard, but there's not much contact.'"[7]

---

5. William Henry Milburn, *The Pioneers, Preachers, and People of the Mississippi Valley* (New York: Derby & Jackson, 1860) 414–15, cited in Ernest G. Bormann, *The Force of Fantasy: Restoring the American Dream* (Carbondale and Edwardsville: Southern Illinois University Press, 1985) 125.

6. Ibid.

7. William Norwood Brigance, *Speech: Its Techniques and Disciplines in a Free Society*, 2d ed. (New York: Appleton-Century-Crofts, 1961) 273.

It's Not the Reading but the Writing

In defense of all good preachers who use a manuscript, I say, since reading your homily can be an oral event, it's not necessarily the reading that's the problem—it's the writing. I point again to our Lord as our model. We know of nothing he wrote except something on the ground (John 8:8), but when the evangelists recorded what he said, they preserved his oral style. Whenever we hear a parable of Jesus read aloud in church—even when the reading could have been better—it is still usually an oral event.

In one of my homiletics classes, after we had been working on oral style, a student brought in this example of what's wrong with some pulpits:

> And Jesus said, "But who do you say that I am?"
> And Peter answered: "You are the eschatological manifestation of the Ground of Being, the kerygma in which we find the ultimate meaning of all our interpersonal relationships."
> And Jesus said, "What?"

If we homilists compose a manuscript, we want to write as though we were speaking. To make sure our homilies will be oral, we will practice the oral style whenever possible and strive to make writing in oral style habitual. There is even empirical evidence that oral style is more intelligible than essay style. In a certain experiment, a speech in essay style was read aloud on tape to various audiences. To control the variables, the same speaker read a speech written in oral style to these same audiences. Then the listeners took tests to see how well they comprehended the two kinds of speeches. Using caution and understating the results, it appears that the "oral" speeches were at least 10 percent more intelligible.[8]

John O'Hayre, an employee of the Office of Land Management's Western Information Office, Denver, Colorado, was so distressed with the poor writing of the Department of the Interior employees that he wrote a booklet, *Gobbledygook Has Gotta Go*.[9] Here's an excerpt:

> During Franklin's day a great battle raged over man's right to vote [long before the Constitution was amended giving women the franchise]. Many of the Federalists insisted that before a man could

8. This experiment reported in: Gordon L. Thomas, "Effect of Oral Style on Intelligibility of Speech," *Speech Monographs*, XXIII, 1956, 46–54.

9. John O'Hayre, *Gobbledygook Has Gotta Go* (Washington, D.C.: Supt. of Documents, U.S. Govt. Printing Office, no date given).

vote, he had to own property. The Franklinites opposed this; they explained their philosophical opposition something like this:

> It cannot be adhered to with any reasonable degree of intellectual or moral certainty that the inalienable right man possesses to exercise his political preferences by employing his vote in referendums is rooted in anything other than man's own nature, and is, therefore, called a natural right. To hold, for instance, that this natural right can be limited externally by making its exercise dependent on a prior condition of ownership of property, is to wrongly suppose that man's natural right to vote is somehow more inherent in and more dependent on the property of man than it is on the nature of man. It is obvious that such belief is unreasonable, for it reverses the order of rights intended by nature.

Franklin believed this, all right, but he saw right off that kind of abstract language wouldn't make many converts, simply because ordinary folk wouldn't wallow their way through it to get at clean meaning. So he set about pulling this concept out of the abstract and explained it something like this:

> To require property of voters leads us to this dilemma: I own a jackass; I can vote. The jackass dies; I cannot vote. Therefore the vote represents not me but the jackass.[10]

My observations:

1. Benjamin Franklin's oral style is better *writing*–clearer by far–than that of the Franklinites.

2. This story could just as well have appeared in the previous chapter where we were thinking about making homilies visual–showing the close connection between being visual and being oral.

3. This story illustrates that it is not the reading but the writing that's the problem. Even if you read Franklin's story aloud, it would still be an oral event. But if this story were in your manuscript, would you need to read it?

4. On the other hand, if the Franklinites' version were in your manuscript, wouldn't you have to read it? Who can remember it? Not even you, the author. Can you blame the people for crying, "Don't read your sermons"?

---

10. Ibid., 45–46.

Differences between Oral and Written Language

How do we break out of the stuffy box into which writing essays has gotten us?

We may begin by analyzing the differences between oral and written language. The contrast is easy to recognize; it's harder to describe. My best effort so far has brought me to define these differences under six categories: I say that oral style is immediate, direct, in talking rhythm, lean, profuse, and focused.

ORAL LANGUAGE IS IMMEDIATE

Oral style has to be immediate, because the listener must get it the first time. The reader may go back and plow through it again, but not the listener. That means the sentences must go straight. When we homilists insert parenthetical ideas, we're asking our listeners to suspend the main thrust of the sentence in midair, go off on a tangent, and then when the side trip is finished, pick up the idea where we left off. We who are reading the manuscript can handle the interruption because we can sneak a glance back at the subject and the predicate, but the hearer deals only with sound waves and so is lost. Henry Ward Beecher observed, "Sentences should be straight as a lance. . . . Long sentences may be good, but not twisting ones."[11] I did a small study once of the rhetoric of Robert Ingersoll, the apostle of agnosticism of the nineteenth century. In the speech he gave again and again attacking the Christian faith, he had a sentence that went on for 296 words. But it didn't twist.[12] Our Lord lived in an oral culture with no tape recorders. He framed his epigrams in a form the people could catch and hold on to. He did not say, "The merciful, since they shall obtain mercy, are blessed."

But his chief apostle often zigzagged: "Paul, a servant of Jesus Christ, called to be an apostle, set apart for the gospel of God, which he promised beforehand through his prophets in the holy scriptures, the gospel concerning his Son, who was descended from David according to the flesh . . . ." (That's just the first three verses of the first sentence in Romans 1; he keeps going and going and doesn't reach a period until the end of verse 7.)

It puzzles me why Paul should have written in a way so different from the oral style distinctive of the Hebrew Scriptures. Any place you look in Genesis, you see sentences going straight: "After

11. Brigance, *Speech*, 305.

12. C. P. Farrell, *The Works of Robert G. Ingersoll in Twelve Volumes*, vol. 1, *Lectures* (New York, N.Y.: The Ingersoll Publishers, Inc., 1900) 393–95.

these things God tested Abraham. He said to him, 'Abraham!' And he said, 'Here I am.' He said, 'Take your son, your only son Isaac, whom you love, and go to the land of Moriah, and offer him there as a burnt offering on one of the mountains that I shall show you'" (Gen 22:1-2). The storyteller does pause to add two descriptive phrases after saying, "Take your son." But "Take your son" is a complete thought, so that the listener doesn't have to suspend part of an idea over here while the speaker tacks on another line or two over there.

Reading aloud any part of the Book of Genesis bids fair to be an oral event. But notice what a problem the preacher presents the listener in this homily for Maundy Thursday on Luke 22:7-20:

> Now it is quite possible that, when you have come across this verse in your Bible, you have assumed that our Lord at this point was beginning his institution of Holy Communion, and that St. Luke, for some strange reason, has things turned around, speaking of the wine before the bread instead of the sequence to which we are accustomed. But these words and this action have nothing to do with Holy Communion. The New Testament sacramental use of wine does not come until later, until the third cup, the "cup of blessing." We are concerned here with the first two, of which our Lord says that he will not drink of it, which seems to be an announcement that he does not intend to eat and drink of the Passover meal, even though he wants to and will be present throughout.[13]

If I were preaching this homily, I would try to say the above paragraph something like this:

> Have you ever wondered what's going on here? Luke says Jesus gave the wine first, then the bread. Is Luke telling us here about the Lord's Supper? No. This was the first cup. Jesus didn't institute the Sacrament until the third cup, "the cup of blessing." It's the first cup Jesus says he wasn't drinking.

I wouldn't have to read it, and I wouldn't have to memorize it word-for-word. I can see it, so I can say it, and I will say it the way people speak.

In oral style the sentences go straight. That means a minimum of subordinate clauses. Here's how one homily begins: "When Dale Wasserman was writing 'Man of La Mancha,' which has become a famous musical, he intended it as a mildly cynical commentary on

---

13. *Augsburg Sermons, Gospels, Series C* (Minneapolis: Augsburg Publishing House, 1973) 115.

the human capacity for self-deception."[14] It is a mark of intelligence to distinguish between thoughts and make one idea subordinate to another. This is tolerable in essays and even commendable. But oral style has to be immediate. Here the homilist begins with a subordinate clause and follows with a parenthetical thought before he gets to the subject and the predicate. He's speaking in written style. I wouldn't be surprised if he had to read it in the pulpit.

Two pieces of information come together to give me an insight about this matter of subordinate clauses. One is a quotation from Rudolph Flesch: "It is well known, for instance, that an abstract style contains relatively more descriptive adjectives, indefinite pronouns, and subordinating conjunctions."[15] The other was the memory from my Hebrew class that the Hebrew language has almost no other conjunctions than *waw (and)*. I checked this out later with another professor of Hebrew; he verified it. He went on to point out that *waw* had carried its influence over into the New Testament where we see the Greek conjunction *kai (and)* all over the page. Is this one reason for the immediacy of the Hebrew style?

Oral Language Is Direct

Oral language is more friendly than the language used in many essays. It is aware of other persons in the room and so is more likely to use *I/me/my, you/your, we/us/our,* or some specific person(s) as the subject or object instead of an abstract noun. It prefers the active voice to the passive. It often uses questions.

During World War II someone in the federal bureaucracy wrote a memo on what federal workers were to do in case of an air raid: "Such preparations shall be made as will completely obscure all Federal buildings and non-Federal buildings occupied by the Federal Government during an air raid for any period of time from visibility by reason of internal or external illumination. Such obscuration may be obtained either by blackout construction or by termination of the illumination."

President Franklin Roosevelt happened to see this. It rankled him so much he rewrote it himself: "Tell them that in buildings where they have to keep the work going to put something over the windows; and in buildings where they can let the work stop for a while, to turn out the lights."[16]

14. Ibid., 229.
15. "Measuring the Level of Abstraction," *Journal of Applied Psychology* 34 (Dec. 1950) 384.
16. O'Hayre, *Gobbledygook Has Gotta Go,* 39.

The rhetorician Walker Gibson calls writing that resembles the bureaucrat's style "stuffy." He lays the cause of stuffy rhetoric to the loss of personality: "Stuffiness may imply, by way of the stuffed shirt, that the speaker has no insides, no humanity. It is scarecrow prose."[17] He analyzes the problem thus:

> A key characteristic of stuffy rhetoric is just this refusal to assume personal responsibility. It is accomplished by at least two stylistic techniques. . . . One is the use of the passive verb. (Military prose, among others, is full of this gambit: it is ordered that. . . . It is desired that. . . . Who ordered? Who desired? . . .) The other technique is a preference for abstract nouns as the subject of active verbs. The doer of the action is not a human somebody, certainly not the speaker himself. . . .[18]

The bureaucrat's memo above exhibits both characteristics: (1) the passive verb: "shall be made," "may be obtained"; (2) abstract nouns: "Such preparation," "Such obscuration."

As I have said several times already, I like to study the words of Jesus not only for their content but also for their form. Look at the Sermon on the Mount and notice how few passive verbs there are. There are some, just enough for spice, such as "grass . . . is thrown into the oven." But more often Jesus uses the active verb: "You are the light of the world." Not: "The world is lit by you."

Oral language is direct, aware of the other people in the room. So the homilist using oral language is also likely to ask questions, either to set up the next point or as a rhetorical device to invite the listeners to answer yes or no. Here is an example of directness exhibited by questions: "How could these brothers have met again? Should the elder have left home to meet his brother at a brothel where they could have wasted their lives together? Should the younger have come home to strive to excel his brother in self-righteousness and conceit?"[19]

ORAL LANGUAGE IS IN TALKING RHYTHM

The differences between the written and oral forms of expression are hard to pin down. We know oral style when we hear it, but we're hard put to describe what it is. Talking rhythm is one of its more elusive qualities.

17. Walker Gibson, *Tough, Sweet and Stuffy* (Bloomington: Indiana University Press, 1969) 91.

18. Ibid., 94.

19. *Augsburg Sermons, Gospels, Series C,* 102.

For example, we can say that one of the marks of talking rhythm is that it uses contractions: "That's straight talk, isn't it? It's not pleasant. It's not comforting, and it's nobody's favorite. . . . If you are not comfortable with that, don't feel alone. I don't like it either. To be honest, I'd prefer a gentle pat on the back. I'd rather hear him speak of still waters and green pastures. . . ."[20]

And yet in the same homily, we find sentences that could have used contractions and didn't and yet still are in talking rhythm: "The tree was not chopped down, remember; it was fertilized and given another chance. So there is hope! There is opportunity! The future is open! We are not shackled by the past or imprisoned by the present. We are instead given another chance."[21]

Talking rhythm speaks in shorter, earthy, homespun words, not pompous ones. Here's a case where the preacher isn't using oral language: "That is why the section of Scripture from which our text is taken, the words of Jesus as reported in Luke 12:32-40, themselves admit of various constructions."[22] That sentence is at fault for two reasons. It's not immediate because it zigzags with a parenthetical remark. It also uses heavy language: "admit of various constructions." Does anyone talk like that? If so, does it sound right?

Those sentences come from a homily whose theme I like: "No Need to Panic in the Crises." It's a complete thought, tersely put, and it identifies with my self-interest, but I don't care for the homily's lack of talking rhythm.

Here's another example from the same homily: "Today the pull of involvement in the human problems such professionals encounter in their clients, pupils, or patients is seen to be far more justifiable than formerly. It is even felt that often a really salutary change is better accomplished when personal involvement is present than when professional detachment is strictly maintained."[23] This is at fault for three reasons. First, it's way up on rung number eight on Hayakawa's abstraction ladder; why doesn't he put me on rung number three, "Bessie the Cow," and show me a professional who has a name who lives and works in "the pull of involvement"? Why doesn't he paint a scene showing me just one event illustrating the stress this character-with-a-name feels in "the pull of involvement"? Another problem: the use of the passive—stuffy rhetoric due to the loss of personality, the speaker having no insides, like a scarecrow.

20. Ibid., 98.
21. Ibid., 99.
22. Ibid., 213.
23. Ibid., 214.

"It is even felt . . ."; who felt? And then there's the heavy language: "such professionals encounter . . . ." Talking rhythm wouldn't use "encounter," but "see" or "meet" or "find."

I offer a list of a few pompous words with their plain equivalents. You may not agree with my classification. I won't lay down my life to defend it, because as I have remarked already, the difference between written and oral language is subtle. I offer the list to stimulate discussion on a matter I think is sometimes overlooked.

Pompous	*Talking Rhythm*
nevertheless, notwithstanding	but
moreover, furthermore	and, also
thereupon, consequently, thus, accordingly	so, therefore
to illustrate, to take a case, more specifically	for example
endeavor to ascertain	try to find out
in the event that	if
as regards	about
at this point in time	now
to make reference to	to refer to
to have under consideration	to consider
pursuant to	according to
parameters	limits, boundaries
quantify	measure
I would share with you	I'm going to tell you
that is to say	in other words

One more thing about talking rhythm. In oral language we don't usually say "which" and we may not even say "that." Here's a sentence from no less a wordsmith than Archibald MacLeish: "Do you think it strange they should have heard this?" Winston Churchill was no slouch with the tongue; he said, "We read in the Bible, 'Jeshurun waxed fat and wicked.'"

ORAL LANGUAGE IS LEAN

"We find that the experience of God's forgiveness is absolutely perfect. When we receive his free gift of reconciliation, we get power to seek out those we've wronged and try to make amends."

That's not a quotation from anyone in particular. I pieced it together from fragments I've picked up. What's wrong with it? It's not lean. It has unnecessary modifiers. If something is already perfect, what do we gain by declaring it "absolutely" perfect? If something is a gift, do we also need to say, "It's a free gift"? (The King James Version, the Revised Standard Version, and the New Revised Standard Version are usually good models of English, but in Romans 5:15-16 they translate *charisma* as "free gift" while the lexicon says it means "a gift [freely and graciously given]." That suggests to me that *charisma* refers to the attitude of the giver, rather than implying that some gifts are not free.)

Preaching the way we speak ordinarily does not mean being careless with words in the pulpit. Here are some more examples of oral language that is not lean:

> true facts
> as a usual rule
> very necessary
> cooperate together
> most unique
> important essentials
> definitely harmful
> circulated around
> most complete
> if and when
> at 9:00 A.M. in the morning
> each and every one
>
> Yet there are modifiers we can't do without:
> younger son
> hired servants
> far country
> best robe
> loose living
> fatted calf
> great famine

Seven modifiers are all I can find in the parable of the two sons in Luke 15. Lean as his narration is, our Lord couldn't have told the story without those adjectives. What's his secret? His modifiers don't comment; they define. Good oral style uses modifiers to make meaning exact and shies away from those that try to make meaning emphatic.

Notice also the lean oral style of the Old Testament storyteller. These are the only modifiers in all of Genesis 1:

without form and void
living creatures
good
great sea monsters
dry land
winged bird
two great lights
creeping things
the greater light
green plants
the lesser light
very good

All define except one, "very good." We may excuse that for when "God saw everything that he had made," how could the storyteller hold back from exclaiming, "And behold, it was very good." Observe how this one outburst takes on all the more impact coming at the end of a chapter of restraint. If with each day's accomplishments there would have been the comment "And God saw that it was very good," by the time we came to verse 31, "very good" would have lost its punch. So we use modifiers to define; we hesitate to use them to comment.

Then there's that simple word *is*. How much leaner can you get? Yet it may also mess up our language:

He is a man who likes to fish.
This church is in need of a dynamic stewardship program.

Many of us speak like this (I do), so if this is a piece on preaching in oral style, what's the complaint? Look again at the way Jesus spoke. He didn't say the words in parentheses: "(There was) a man (who) was going down from Jerusalem to Jericho." In the same pattern we could rather say:

He likes to fish.
This church needs a dynamic stewardship program.

Another way to strip the fat: use verbs instead of noun substitutes. Jesus didn't say, "Consider the *growth* of the lilies." Some sermons in print have an occasional noun substitute:

The Christmas story is an *announcement* of the real historical event.
Adam exercised his capacity for *defiance*.

How would we say these in lean oral style?

> Christmas announces an historical event.
> Adam defied God.

Oral Language Is Profuse

If oral language is lean, how does that square with my next description of oral style, that it's profuse? Is this a paradox? I don't think so. In oral discourse we repeat because the listener needs help. Think of the baseball announcer. He knows you could have just gotten into your car wondering, "How's my team doing?" So he tells you: "The Twins are leading 5-3. It's the bottom of the fifth. The Royals scored first in the top of the first inning, and it was 1-0. The Twins came back in their half of the first inning with 3 runs and have led ever since."

If you were reading a newspaper account of the game and you happened to open to the middle of the story on page 3, you could turn to the beginning of the report on page 1. The written story isn't profuse because it doesn't need to be.

But you say, "The people in my church don't come during the middle of the homily. There may be a few latecomers but none that late." Maybe not. At least not so that you could see them moving in and out. Yet consider this: the fastest you can speak is probably no more than 125 words a minute. But your listeners can think up to 400 words a minute. Plenty of time in between to leave the room, maybe even on a trip you generated: something you said stimulated an edifying excursion. In a short time your listener is ready to join you again. Will he or she get back into the dialogue? If you don't give some help, probably not. What kind of help? The kind the baseball announcer gives the listener who went to the kitchen for a beer.

When I hear sermons and homilies, both Roman Catholic and Protestant, I often fail to get this kind of help. I wonder why. I suspect it may be because most of us read homilies and sermons but have little opportunity to hear them. Our models are written discourses where profuseness is out of place. If the homily were in good oral form when delivered in church, either the homilist or the editor may have deleted the profuseness before it appeared in print. Again we have the homily imitating the essay. But the homily is an oral event.

Oral Language Is Focused

Closely related to the profuseness that oral discourse begs for is the quality of being focused: the speaker focuses the hearers' attention on the main ideas. It's the oral equivalent of bold face and white space on the printed page highlighting the headings. It's aural underlining.

Once when President Calvin Coolidge came home from church, someone asked, "Well, what did the preacher preach about today?" Coolidge answered, "He didn't say."

I've had the same experience. I've come away from a Roman Catholic Mass or a Protestant service where the presider was reverent and human and the message was biblical and thoughtful, but when the celebration was over, I couldn't remember the homily. Where was the fault?

I believe I can say I was listening. So am I blaming the preacher? Yes. What was wrong? The homily wasn't focused. The preacher didn't highlight the important points. I've seen and heard student homilies where the written manuscript had headings and subheadings set off with capital letters, italics, and white space, but where the equivalent in sound waves in the oral delivery had been absent.

On the other hand, to focus on points in story homilies is pointless. The story is the structure; the story has the power to evoke its point without our belaboring it.

I recognize that I am contending against important homileticians who decry underlining for the ear as an outdated practice. Why give everything away? Why spoon feed the people? Why not let them make up their own minds? I myself was like-minded for years. I used to object, "Preaching is an art. I refuse to resort to such wooden devices as saying, 'In the first place,' 'In the second place,' and so on. My preaching is good enough that the people can tell when I've finished one point and started the next. My people aren't stupid. They don't need kindergarten aids."

Then I started taking courses in speech. When I began graduate studies at the University of Nebraska I had taken only two hours of speech in college. The rules required me first to fill out an undergraduate major. I took courses with freshmen and sophomores and endured the indignity of being criticized by teaching assistants hardly older than my children. I was forced to go through "Mickey Mouse" stuff such as at the end of the introduction clearly stating, "Today I want to talk about . . . ." Nor was that all. The professor explained two possible formats, the forecasting and the unfolding. By *forecasting* he meant that at the end of the introduction and after you'd announced your topic, you then would state your two or three points that would develop your topic. By *unfolding* he meant you wouldn't reveal your two or three main points at first; you'd lay them out one at a time as you came to them. He also explained the function of transitions: to re-state the point just covered and reiterate how it supports your proposal and then to announce the next point. He also defined the purpose of the conclusion: to summarize the discourse by reaffirming the proposal and its supporting points and then to call for the appropriate action. When I did my speeches in front of a teaching assistant, I had to conform to these standards.

Somehow I allowed myself to try this out in the pulpit. I was dumbfounded when some of the more sophisticated people would comment, "I liked the way you brought out your main points; it made it easier to follow." Or, "I liked it when you summed up your sermon at the end; it brought it all back to me and I could see how everything fit together." Or on a Sunday when I hadn't taken pains to make the handles on the sermon visible, these same sharp people might tell me, "You know, I couldn't follow you as well today." I tried to satisfy my aesthetic sense by inventing different ways of underlining for the ear—with some success. But when I became so creative that the structure was all but submerged, there would be that reaction at the door again, "I liked it better when you let us know what you were preaching about."

Ernest and Nancy Bormann explain what I experienced:

> Over the years, experts have learned how audiences respond to oral messages and have evolved ways of organization that meet the various requirements of the context. Organization of an oral statement is not like the organization of a written statement on the same subject matter. . . . Listeners . . . must participate in a public speech as it unfolds, and if they try to recall something that a speaker has just said to see if it relates to something the speaker has said earlier, they may miss something important that the speaker is saying right at that moment. As speakers have practiced communicating in such clearly-defined circumstances, the public speaking style has developed certain detailed rules about proper organization to guide speakers and critics.[24]

The key in focusing is transitions. According to one author, "A transition is a type of bridge whereby the speaker moves from one idea to another."[25] The transition is the re-entry point for the listener who has gone off on his or her own excursion while we were speaking slower than he or she was thinking.

I'll illustrate how transitions work in oral communication in one of my sermons for the festival of Christ the King, Year C, John

24. Ernest G. Bormann and Nancy R. Bormann, *Speech Communication: A Comprehensive Approach*, 2d ed. (New York: Harper & Row, 1972) 180.

25. James R. Andrews, *Public Speaking: Principles into Practice* (New York: MacMillan Publishing Co., 1987) 170.

12:9-19.[26] The introduction sketched the history of some tyrants like Henry VIII, George III, and others. Here's the transition that signals the listener that the preacher will give the theme: "History abounds with kings who were villains and despots. . . . We don't care for these fellows. In utter contrast, the Gospel for the Festival of Christ the King brings us 'A King Worth Having.'"

Having highlighted the theme, the homily then moves to the first main idea and connects that to the theme: "In the first place, Jesus Christ is a king worth having because he has the courage to sacrifice himself."

After the homily has developed this section, another transition lets the listener know this point has now been made: "If we've had some misgivings about other rulers, then let's cheer ourselves with the knowledge that here's a king worth having, because he has the courage to sacrifice himself."

Immediately follows the aural underlining of the second argument and once more the linking of the argument to the theme: "Another reason he's worth having is because he's a king who's approachable."

At the end of the second section, this transition: "Again we're amazed to find still another sign that there is not any person in all the world nor in all history who can't identify with our king. The most miserable wretch will never feel our king has put himself out of reach. The poorest of the poor can never say our king isn't on their level. Our king doesn't put himself above us, although he'd have every right. With nearly every other king, I'd be out of place. This one is worth having because he's approachable."

Then the homily focuses the attention of the people on the final argument: "He's a king worth having for a third reason too: although he deserves our allegiance, he doesn't force us to give it."

The conclusion should use the power of the whole text to back up the call to action, and so it helps the listeners to recall the entire message: "On this Festival of Christ the King, my only objective is to exalt the king worth having, the one with courage enough to sacrifice himself for us, the one whose dignity doesn't get in his way so that the lowest and poorest among us can still feel he's approachable, the one who deserves our allegiance but doesn't force us to give it. My aim today is simply to move us to yield him our hearts more freely and more gladly than ever before. God help us for that."

26. Alvin C. Rueter, *The Freedom to Be Wrong* (Lima, Ohio: CSS Publishing Co., 1985) 67–71.

Oral language's qualities of profuseness and focusing require a certain amount of repetition. Rhetoricians have conducted experiments to try to discover the ideal amount of repetition. Their results lead them to believe that three repetitions are about right, that saying it twice may not quite do it, and that saying it four times probably causes no better retention than three.[27] In my homily just quoted, I state my points at the beginning and end of each section and again in the conclusion, each point being stated three times. This homily is an example of the unfolding format, where you reveal each point only as you come to it. The forecasting format allows you to state each point four times. In this plan you preview the main ideas at the end of the introduction. Here's an example of forecasting: "How can I make it clear that the Gospel doesn't stifle us? How can I bring it home that Christ is not a wet blanket but a liberator? I'll attempt it by saying forthrightly that I'm here to preach on the topic, "Christ Has Set Us Free," and that I'll support that contention by arguing, first, the devil promises liberty and delivers slavery; second, Christ offers discipleship and delivers freedom."[28]

The oral language attribute of focusing underscores the importance of composing people-centered outlines (described in chapter 5). The preacher-centered outline has only memory-jogging words and phrases. To focus the people's attention on these scraps satisfies no one's hunger. To focus the people's attention on a people-centered outline—where all the ideas are stated from the people's point of view—makes sense. My students have told me, "When I think about what I want to focus the people's attention on, that helps me remember my homily."

The homily "Much More" (number 2 in the Appendix) is well-focused. It follows the rules on underlining for the ear. It's biblical. It develops the text. But I find it boring. Its chief faults are the lack of identification with the people's ways and self-interest, its high-level abstractions, and its essay style. Perhaps sermons like this are why some homileticians decry aural underlining.

Deductive sermons, "State your case and prove it," if they are in oral style, will focus the hearers' attention on the main ideas with underlining for the ear. Inductive sermons, "Here's the evidence; you

---

27. Raymond Ehrensberger, "An Experimental Study of Relative Effectiveness of Certain Forms of Emphasis in Public Speaking," *Speech Monographs* 12, no. 2 (1945) 94–111. See also J. T. Cacioppo and R. E. Petty, "Effects of Message Repetition and Position on Cognitive Responses, Recall, and Persuasion," *Journal of Personality and Social Psychology* 37 (1979) 97–109.

28. Rueter, *The Freedom to Be Wrong*, 39.

figure it out," will also want to focus the hearers' attention on the issues and thus will underline for the ear—not the answers already worked out but the questions.

Summary

I began this chapter by reacting to a finding by a seminary professor that the people in the pew want to tell us preachers, "Don't read your sermons." I have been contending that one reason we may feel compelled to read is because we've constructed our homilies in such a way that no one can remember them, not even we, and so we must read them. That's a strong statement, but I say it out of personal experience. It didn't change for me until I stopped composing essays and began trying to think in oral language.

For Further Reading

Achtemeier, Elizabeth. *Creative Preaching: Finding the Words.* Nashville: Abingdon Press, 1980, 87–96.

Exercises

Exercise 17

Read homily number 12 (page 247), "Beautiful Sinners," in the Appendix. It illustrates the principle, "It's not the reading but the writing." I heard this sermon while teaching one semester at Lutheran Theological Seminary, Hong Kong. The preacher, Dr. Pirkko Lehtiö, a woman professor from Finland, read the entire manuscript at morning prayers. There were two handicaps: someone had forgotten to turn on the public address system, and she speaks with an accent. Yet even so, we could feel that all of us were giving involuntary attention. Note the visual and oral style and how she identifies both with our ways and our legitimate self-interest. "It's not the reading but the writing."

Exercise 18

Rewrite one or more of the following paragraphs into oral style. Remember that oral style is both lean and profuse. Your "rewrite" may be shorter, but then again, it may be longer.

1. Within the texture of this common cry for mercy lies a common faith—a faith that this Nazarene, whose fame had spread even into the isolated communities of the mortally ill, possessed the power to heal their disease.[29]

2. Jesus is speaking to all of us who would assume the master role in the matter of granting forgiveness particularly if we are asked by those we in some way consider inferior. If we are asked seven times in one day to forgive, then to forgive seven times is not some deed that would elevate us to a pedestal before God, but on the contrary is that which is expected of us as servants.[30]

3. Paul, a servant of Jesus Christ, called to be an apostle, set apart for the gospel of God, which he promised beforehand through his prophets in the holy scriptures, the gospel concerning his Son, who was descended from David according to the flesh and was declared to be the Son of God with power according to the spirit of holiness by resurrection from the dead, Jesus Christ our Lord, through whom we have received grace and apostleship to bring about the obedience of faith among all the Gentiles for the sake of his name, including yourselves who are called to belong to Jesus Christ, to all God's beloved in Rome, who are called to be saints, Grace to you and peace from God our Father and the Lord Jesus Christ (Rom 1:1-7).

EXERCISE 19

Examine homily number 3 (page 214), "Third Word from the Cross," in the Appendix. Observe the transitions between introduction and theme and between the parts of the body, as well as the recapitulation in the conclusion.

1. Is this deductive or inductive?

2. Any suggestions for improvement?

EXERCISE 20

Examine homily number 1 (page 203), "Do We Need God?" and number 2 (page 209), "Much More," in the Appendix. Notice their underlining for the ear or any lack of it.

29. *Augsburg Sermons, Gospels, Series C,* 253.
30. Ibid., 249.

EXERCISE 21

Examine a recent homily manuscript of your own in these ways:

1. Rewrite any twisting sentences.

2. Are the pronouns mostly first and second person? If not, rewrite the pertinent sentences.

3. List any pompous expressions and find homespun replacements.

4. List the modifiers that comment and could be eliminated–if any–in contrast to modifiers that define and are necessary.

5. List the passive verbs. Separate those that may give spice from those that could have been better transformed into active verbs, eliminating "scarecrow prose" (no insides).

6. List any noun substitutes. Rewrite the sentences they were in, replacing the noun substitutes with verbs.

7. Note whether you had internal summaries or transitions that would have allowed your hearers to get back in if they'd happened to have left you for a moment. Write such transitions for the places in your homily where they might be missing.

EIGHT

Making Homilies Christian

What distinguishes preaching from the many other forms of comment on the human condition?

News magazines occasionally publish well-researched cover stories such as "The Problem of Evil," giving excellent analysis. Daily newspapers have insightful editorials and columns describing what is wrong with the world. Movies and plays, novels and poems often comment on our foibles and our plight. Harriet Beecher Stowe's *Uncle Tom's Cabin* played a role in the abolition of slavery in the United States. Cartoons and comedians hold up mirrors so we can see our absurdities. Country Western music also has an eye for folly: "You Can't Have Your Kate and Edith Too"; "Would Jesus Wear a Rolex on His Television Show?"

Then there are all those who scold. And there are those who respond: "Don't preach to me." (And we who know what *euangelizo* means—I preach good news—wince.)

We Christian homilists do hold up a mirror. In so doing, we are somewhat like all the other commentators; in fact, we do well to learn from them. But we Christian homilists interpret the human condition from the viewpoint of Scripture: "The Christian interprets the world not as a hostile and evil place, but as a creation of a loving God who did not allow it to destroy itself, but sent his Son to rescue it. The Christian response to the world, then, is one of acceptance and affirmation—along with the recognition that it is still awaiting its full redemption."[1]

We Christian homilists sometimes also scold. I've been wary of using this mode of pulpiteering regularly because I see in myself a temptation to misuse it. When I start pounding on the people,

1. *Fulfilled in Your Hearing* (Washington, D.C.: The Bishop's Committee on Priestly Life and Ministry, United States Catholic Conference, 1982) 18.

sometimes I get a feeling of sadistic satisfaction. It feels too good. I'm afraid of my motives. So I caution myself, "When Scripture says, 'Thus says the Lord,' remember, 'The Lord is saying it also to me.'" But we do follow in the train of Jeremiah and Amos. The Word of God is not only a mirror of our existence but also a hammer of judgment. As prophets of God we dare not shrink from that calling.

When is a homily Christian? When it brings hope in Christ.

Since the Second Vatican Council, the Roman Catholic homily is seen as a discourse growing out of the readings for the day, a vital part of the liturgy that prepares for the Eucharist. Pointing to the Eucharist means that the homily points to hope in Christ.

My Lutheran heritage also defines a homily as Christian when it brings hope in Christ, but it uses different language. Lutherans say a Christian homily proclaims Law and Gospel. If I understand correctly, to Roman Catholics the word *Law* means *Torah,* the Law of Moses, while *Gospel* means the story of Jesus, all that he said and did. In the sense in which Lutherans use these words, *Law* is every Word of God that describes our plight and declares God's judgment and shows us his will; *Gospel* is every Word of God that announces how God has delivered us in Christ. With this understanding, we find both Law and Gospel in both Testaments.

Some Lutherans speak of three uses of the Law:

> 1. As a fence
>   This is for society as a whole, keeping us out of danger, so as to establish order, justice, and peace.
>
> 2. As a hammer or as a mirror
>   This is for us sinners, leading us to repentance and bringing us to Christ.
>
> 3. For some Lutherans, the Law also functions as a guide
>   This is for us forgiven sinners, to show us where to walk after receiving grace.

Although Roman Catholics don't use the terms *Law* and *Gospel* the way we Lutherans do, I see the same concepts in *Fulfilled In Your Hearing,* published by the Bishops' Committee on Priestly Life and Ministry, United States Catholic Conference. On *Law* in the Lutheran sense, it says, "The preacher does not so much attempt to explain the Scriptures as to interpret the human situation through the Scriptures."[2] On *Gospel* in the Lutheran sense, it says, "The preacher is a Christian specially charged with sharing the Christian

---

2. Ibid., 20.

vision of the world as the creation of a loving God. Into this world human beings unleashed the powers of sin and death. These powers have been met, however, by God through his son Jesus Christ, in whom he is at work not only to restore creation but to transform it into a new heaven and a new earth."[3]

To find a common language, I shall use *diagnosis* instead of *Law* and *redemption* or *hope in Christ* instead of *Gospel*.

Making Sure the Homily Is Christian

First of all, we want to know how to distinguish between diagnosis and redemption.

Herman Stuempfle observes:

> If the Law is robbed of its power to expose our utter bankruptcy before God, then our predicament is not extreme and the Word of grace unnecessary. If, on the other hand, the Gospel is presented as in any sense a new demand laid upon us, then our situation is indeed hopeless for there remains no other Word to release us from our already impossible burden. The first error leads people into the false security of self-righteousness; the second plunges them into the abyss of despair. Either way, the result is detrimental to the possibility of a right relationship with God in which his grace and our faith live in dynamic interaction.[4]

There's a common practice of turning the word of redemption into a burden. When some preachers are straining to evoke a response, they may say, "We must believe . . . ." In Stuempfle's terms, that's presenting the Gospel—a gift—as "a new demand."

Even when the hoped-for response is not believing but doing, we want to show how loving our neighbor is not only our duty but also our delight. Because God has loved us in Christ, we respond not because we have to but because we get to. Preachers of the gospel will do well to shy away from "We must," "We ought to," "We need to," "We should." (We were discussing this in one of my classes in the Formation Program for the Permanent Diaconate, Archdiocese of St. Paul and Minneapolis. One of the spouses in the group laughed and said that a friend—a nun—would respond to this kind of preaching by saying, "Don't *should* on me.")

The other factor in composing a homily in such a way that it will actually be a Christian discourse has to do with its structure. In my

3. Ibid., 18–19.
4. Herman G. Stuempfle, Jr., *Preaching Law and Gospel* (Philadelphia: Fortress, 1978) 17–18.

studies of both rhetoric and homiletics, I have been looking for formats that, if they do not guarantee the offer of hope in Christ, will at least make it likely to happen.

There's the *State-Your-Case-and-Prove-It* format, long in use in public speaking courses. This is valid and useful if the Scripture text brings hope in Christ and if the outline reflects the text. But what if the gospel for the day is Mark 7:1-8, in which Pharisees and scribes found fault with Jesus' disciples for eating with defiled hands and Jesus rebukes them with a scorching word from Isaiah? That's all there is: diagnosis aplenty but not a glimmer of hope. With a text like this, state-your-case-and-prove-it won't work.

There's the *Problem-Solution* format. The first point states what's wrong (diagnosis of our plight, the mirror of our existence or the hammer of judgment); the second point shows how to deal with the difficulty (redemption through hope in Christ). This approach has possibilities.

If the problem is the need to repent, we may preach the mirror of existence or the hammer of judgment. But we could also preach redemption: "Do you not realize that God's kindness is meant to lead you to repentance?" (Rom 2:4).

Isaac Watts understood this:

> When I survey the wondrous cross
> On which the prince of glory died,
> My richest gain I count but loss
> And pour contempt on all my pride.

John Newton understood this. He began his second stanza of "Amazing Grace" by declaring, "'Twas grace that taught my heart to fear."

And I've begun to understand it too—through the kindness of my wife, Beulah. The last thing I wanted to do was to hurt her, but I did. Did she browbeat me into a change of heart? No; when she needed to scold me, she began by calling me "Sweetheart." I learned more about my sin from her kindness than from any other source.

So our format might be:

1. Redemption in Christ moving us to repentance
2. Gratitude moving us to obedience

There are variations on the Problem-Solution format. I find two of them in Stuempfle's *Preaching Law and Gospel:* one from Kyle Haselden, the other from Heinrich Ott.[5]

---

5. Ibid., 12–16.

Kyle Haselden examined sermons from centuries of preaching and discovered three elements he describes as indispensable to the Christian sermon:

1. Our peril
2. God's promise
3. God's agent, Christ

When confronted by a text like Mark 7:1-8, Haselden's format can guide us to a Christian proclamation. "Our peril" is easy to find in this passage: the temptation to hypocrisy. It's true, "God's promise" and "God's agent, Christ," aren't in this text, but they are in the context. We remember God's promise that Jesus came to make all things new. We recall how God's agent, Christ, was constantly upsetting human traditions that get in the way of our relationship with God, that he makes that relationship possible by his atonement.

Heinrich Ott based his sermon format on the Heidelberg Catechism which in its three main parts covers:

1. Our sin and wretchedness
2. Our redemption in Christ
3. Our grateful response

Ott explains: "In principle the sermon as a whole has just these three things to say. Its centre lies in the middle point, in the proclamation of God's action. But in order to be intelligible and effective, this proclamation needs the other two parts, the disclosure of the true situation and the emphasis on the resulting obligation."[6]

Some Lutheran theologians have difficulty with Ott's third part. We Lutherans pride ourselves on exalting God's grace, and we're quick to pronounce anathemas on any preacher who turns the gift into a demand, as in "We must believe in Christ." Being so loath to do anything that would deny God's graciousness in Christ, some of us are also loath to make any suggestion of a response. "Just tell the people the good news, and they'll react correctly. Don't promote works-righteousness."

Then why did Paul write, "Should we continue in sin in order that grace may abound?" That is, if God justifies the ungodly, why bother to be godly? Paul has no time for such twisted thinking: "By no means! How can we who died to sin go on living in it?" He goes on to spell out the response he wants. He doesn't leave it to our imagination: die to sin; rise to a new life in Christ (Rom 6:1-4).

6. Heinrich Ott, *Theology and Preaching* (Philadelphia: Westminster Press, 1965) 53, cited in Stuempfle, *Preaching Law and Gospel*, 15.

I find two other variations on the Problem-Solution pattern from two professors who used to teach at Concordia Theological Seminary in St. Louis, Missouri: Richard Caemmerer and George Hoyer. Caemmerer[7] proposed this format:

1. Goal
2. Malady
3. Means

Applying this pattern to Mark 7:1-8, we might state the goal as "To find a meaningful relationship with God." The malady would be something like, "Reducing our relationship with God to a set of rules may lead to nitpicking and hypocrisy, with no joy." The means would be something like, "Through Christ we get a new life."

Hoyer's format is expounded by one of his students, Paul Marshall.[8] It is similar to Caemmerer's "goal, malady, means"; it has the advantage of alliteration to help us remember it:

1. Point
2. Problem
3. Power

The challenge in all of these problem-solution structures is, how do we describe the solution? Whether the pattern calls it "God's agent, Christ," "our redemption in Christ," "means," or "power," how do we make this meaningful? Showing "our peril," "our sin and wretchedness," "malady," or "problem" is relatively easy; we have abundant experience of living under sin. Describing the way out is harder; many of us know less about living under grace.

Not only have I felt this challenge in my own preaching, I've encountered it in the homilies I've heard and read. The homilist may develop a picture of a child's being afraid of the dark: a storm comes, the power is off, and here comes mother with a candle for comfort. "Just so, Jesus is our light. Praise God. Amen." Well, yes; the preacher spoke of a malady and referred to a means to get rid of the problem. But did the homily proclaim the solution? *How* is Jesus the light of the world? *How* does he drive away the terror that immobilizes us? Or if we're preaching on John 8:32, *how* is Jesus the truth? *How* does he make us free? Or if we're preaching on John 10:10, *how* is Jesus our life? What does his giving us life abundantly look like?

7. Richard R. Caemmerer, *Preaching for the Church* (St. Louis: Concordia, 1959).

8. Paul V. Marshall, *Preaching for the Church Today* (New York: The Church Hymnal Corporation, 1990) 101–65.

Continuing my search for a format that would more likely show me and my students how to bring hope in Christ, I came upon "The Motivated Sequence," developed by Alan Monroe.[9] Monroe explained its name thus: "We shall call this pattern the motivated sequence: the sequence of ideas which, by following the normal processes of human thinking, motivates an audience to respond to the speaker's purpose."[10] Its potential for persuasion interested me, but the feature that attracted me was step 4:

1. Attention
2. Need
3. Satisfaction of the need
4. Benefits of living under the satisfaction of the need
5. Action

Step 4 was missing in the homily on "Christ Is Our Light. Praise God. Amen." The preacher hadn't shown us how Christ enlightens us and how his enlightenment delivers us from our fears. I've found many student homilies leaving out step 4. I've since discovered whole books of sermons skipping from step 3 to step 5, announcing that Christ has died for our sins and going on immediately to challenge us to live for him without first magnifying God's grace by showing us the blessings of living forgiven.

Is it unscriptural to show the benefits of living as a child of God?

> Happy are those who do not follow the advice of the wicked (Ps 1:1).
>
> The Lord is my shepherd. I shall not want (Ps 23:1).
>
> Blessed are the poor in spirit, for theirs is the kingdom of heaven (Matt 5:3).
>
> The fruit of the Spirit is love, joy, peace, patience, kindness, generosity, faithfulness, gentleness, and self-control (Gal 5:22).

It's all right to preach, "For those who want to save their life will lose it," but let's not omit the rest of Jesus' words: "Those who lose their life for my sake, and the sake of the gospel, will save it" (Mark 8:35).

Reflecting again on the daunting task of making homilies visual, I've found that the Motivated Sequence helps me focus on what begs to be made see-able, especially steps 2 and 4. As I've intimated before,

9. Alan H. Monroe and Douglas Ehninger, *Principles and Types of Speech* (Glenview, Ill.: Scott, Foresman, 1967) 264–89.
10. Ibid., 265.

it has always been easier for me to draw pictures of what sin does to us than to portray how grace blesses us. But keeping my eyes open, I discover more and more pictures of how the redeemed enjoy their status as children of God.

The Motivated Sequence may arrange itself in a homily something like this:

1. Introduction
   A. Attention; showing how the Scripture text appeals to our legitimate self-interest
   B. Announcement of theme

2. Body
   A. Need, as pictured or implied in the text
   B. Satisfaction, as pictured or implied in the text
   C. Blessings, as pictured or implied in the text

3. Conclusion
   A. Recap of the body of the homily
   B. Call to a response

I don't use this design exclusively, but I do now look at all my homilies to see whether step 4 is there. The hard work of describing how God's grace works has enriched my understanding of the good news and (I believe) the effectiveness of my preaching as well.

Summary

There are many who comment on the human condition, and some have much to teach us who occupy a pulpit. But that same pulpit sets us apart. We see a world "not as a hostile or evil place, but as a creation of a loving God who did not allow it to destroy itself, but sent his Son to rescue it."[11] What makes a homily Christian is that it brings hope in Christ. To insure that our homilies are Christian, we build hope in Christ into the structure. To insure its full proclamation, we visualize both the effects of sin and the effects of grace in our lives.

For Further Reading

Fulfilled in Your Hearing. Washington, D.C.: The Bishops' Committee on Priestly Life and Ministry, United States Catholic Conference, 1982, 17–28.

11. *Fulfilled in Your Hearing*, 18.

Skudlarek, William. *The Word in Worship: Preaching in a Liturgical Context*. Nashville: Abingdon, 1981, 65–77.

Stuempfle, Herman G., Jr. *Preaching Law and Gospel*. Philadelphia: Fortress, 1978, 11–74.

Exercises

EXERCISE 22

Examine homilies number 2 (page 209) and 11 (page 243) in the Appendix according to the five steps of the Motivated Sequence. Do they both have steps 4 and 5?

EXERCISE 23

A three-minute homily.

Your subject: a line of your choosing from the Apostles' Creed.

Your hearers: a men's group, whether at your church or in your community.

Your aim: to practice step 4, "blessings," and step 5, "action," in the Motivated Sequence.

Assume you've handled steps 1-3 already; introduce step 4 with a transition of one or two sentences in which you summarize your theme and steps 2 and 3, and then launch into step 4. (So you're also getting practice in making a transition.) During your time on camera, visualize the benefits of believing in whatever line you've chosen from the Creed. For example, if you took the line, "I believe in God," picture how we benefit from living in that faith.

In practicing step 5, show the outcome you hope for as something we want to do as the natural, grateful response to all God has done for us, especially to what he has done in Christ (not "We ought to," but "We get to").

Also, try to show both blessings and action in a series of scenes that could be pictured by a TV camera.

NINE

Releasing Our God-Given Creativity

The fine preacher, bishop, and homiletics professor, Gerald Kennedy, tells of a Methodist bishop who was asked about a preacher in his area. "Why," said the bishop, "he is dull. He is supernaturally dull." Then he said, "No one could be as dull as he is without divine aid." Kennedy further recalls an observation of Spurgeon about a preacher he said would make a good martyr: he was so dry he would burn well.[1]

As I've said before, dullness in the pulpit is a heresy: it teaches that the good news is unexciting, and that's false teaching.

How do we come up with ways to make the homily visual while still being true to the text? How do we arrive at the point of identification with the ways and self-interest of our people? How do we develop a cohesive and memorable structure? By the sweet agony of creativity. To those who lament, "I'm just not creative," I propose we reconsider Genesis 1:26: "Then God said, 'Let us make humankind in our image, according to our likeness.'" Being made in the likeness of the Creator means we are all creators in one degree or another. Just the fact that we have dreams while we sleep testifies to our capacity for creativity. Our challenge is to find ways to release our God-given imagination; I offer one possible strategy.

Those who have studied the process of creativity observe that it goes through these stages:

Discipline
Research
Incubation
Illumination
Verification

1. Gerald Kennedy, *God's Good News* (New York: Harper & Brothers, 1955) 13.

Discipline

Once while I was teaching at St. John's University, I asked my colleague Jon Hassler if he would lecture to my homiletics class on the use of language. (Jon Hassler is a much-published novelist, a writer-in-residence at St. John's who also teaches a course in creative writing.) He asked, "When does your class meet?" I answered, "At 8:00 A.M." "I can't come." "Why not?" "Because I write every day from 8:00 till noon." I said, "Great. That's what I've been telling my students: they've got to have discipline." A few days later, I asked him, "Could you speak on Monday at 4:00?" He said, "Yes." So we made it a campus-wide event, better in every way than the original plan.

But how can a pastor be as disciplined as Jon Hassler? I served congregations for thirty-three years. Don't I know how interruptions in our schedules are opportunities for ministry?

Of course. I also know about discipline-upsetters that may not be opportunities for being a pastor to hurting people, such as when tables needed to be set up in the fellowship hall and I was the only one around at the time.

Like many other pastors, I tried to make the best of it. Reflecting on it now, I believe these are the ways I aimed at keeping on target:

1. Set a definite schedule for study
   For me the best time to study is in the morning. My designated time for that was 8:00–11:00 A.M.

2. Focus
   I sorted out the phone messages and the mail that could be delayed till after my study time was over.
   In two parishes I had the luxury of having a study separate from my office. I was still available for anyone in need, but just the separate physical spaces made it easier to focus on preparing to preach.

3. Use broken pieces of time
   With a definite time scheduled for study and a focus on what I was about, I found I could get back on track even when derailed by legitimate interruptions. Fifteen, ten, or even five minutes can be valuable when you know what you're up to.

4. Block out enough time to allow for interruptions
   At the end of this discussion on discipline, I'll lay out my study schedule to show how I tried to compensate for the unavoidable discontinuities.

The hardest part of discipline is getting started. Creative writers have described their frustrations: how they chew their fingernails, sharpen every pencil, clean out the desk, turn on the computer—and sit there all morning while nothing shows up on the screen. Preachers have lost their focus while writing letters, planning meetings, seizing at anything at all to dodge the chore of getting started, and the longer the dodging goes on, the higher the anxiety piles up. How they envy those parishioners who have something physical to do, like making salads in a cafeteria or paper boxes in a factory or bundles of hay in a field.

I've found a way to get started on homily-making doing something physical. I copy the text, one verse to a sheet of paper. I write the verse only on the left side of the paper, leaving room for notes on the right. I put just one verse to a sheet so that if I need more space later for that verse, I can easily insert another sheet.

On the right-hand side, I go through a set routine (and that also helps me get down to work). I ask myself these questions and jot down my responses in this order:

1. What is the Holy Spirit saying to me through this verse?
2. What reactions does my panel of diversity have to it?
3. What questions do I have, to check out in my exegesis?
4. What has the Holy Spirit said to others through this verse? In exegetical works? In homilies in print?

I started developing this system in the 1940s after I heard a lecture by George Buttrick, from 1927 to 1954 the noted pastor of Madison Avenue Presbyterian Church in New York. (From 1954 to 1960 he was dean of Harvard's Memorial Church.) Buttrick showed us the system he was using at that time, which, as I remember it, included writing the Scripture verse on the left side and his comments and questions on the right side. After his death, as part of a tribute Joseph Sittler wrote:

> During a memorable week when I had duties at Harvard, I was the houseguest of George and Agnes Buttrick. It was at that time that George let me in on the disciplined way he had for years prepared for the weekly task of preaching. He had designed and printed up a form which was his worksheet for the coming sermon. In the left-hand column were the operational words from the Greek text; in the next column he entered the English equivalents and meanings of the terms as these were excised from lexicon and commentary. In the next (and each space from left to right was larger) were fundamental affirmations—theological, moral, spiritual, practical—which

the preacher felt properly derived from the text. The column at the extreme right contained allusions, illustrations, citations.

I do not recall that George suggested that such a meticulous method of sermon preparation was a prerequisite to a sound sermon, but I do know that the discipline of the particular method certainly had something to do with George Buttrick's long sustained career as a thoughtful, engaging, clear and edifying preacher of the Word of God.[2]

Your system for getting down to work may be different. I do recommend you try getting started by copying down each verse. I've discovered—particularly with the familiar texts—that writing down each word forces me to pay attention instead of gliding over. Sometimes I've been surprised at what I'd missed before. This came home to me during a stage when I thought I could save myself some time by asking a secretary to write down each verse for me. I soon went back to doing it myself, to give me something physical to do to get started and to force myself to see every word.

Two more things about disciplining ourselves by setting a schedule:

1. Know when to start working on the structure.

   To know when to stop doing exegesis requires discipline—because in the fascinating business of Bible study, there's always another rock to turn over.

2. Know when to start composing the homily.

   There's always the urge to make the outline better. I've discovered that when I've gotten a clear purpose in mind and a cohesive way to arrive at that goal, that's enough to get started composing the homily. Improvements in the structure will come while I'm writing or even when I'm rehearsing.

In my schedule I knew that my exegesis had to stop Wednesday at 11:00 A.M. I knew that I had to have a working outline by Thursday at 11:00 A.M. I took Fridays off. Since we had a service on Saturdays at 6:00 P.M., I knew I had to start writing on Saturdays at 7:00 A.M. My homilies were usually six pages long, double-spaced. Ordinarily I could compose one page per hour. By allowing ten hours, I could reduce the stress and make allowance for interruptions and still give me a little time for rehearsal. Counting additional rehearsal time (Sundays, 5:00 A.M. to 7:00 A.M.), my schedule had twenty-four hours of the week blocked out for homily preparation.

---

2. Joseph Sittler, "George Buttrick: A Tribute and a Reflection," *Christian Century* (16 April 1980) 429–30.

With the normal press of pastoral pauses, it often worked out to something like twelve hours, the minimum necessary for me.

Research (Exegesis, Prayer, and Contemplation)

Only God can create out of nothing. Novelists like James Michener will take a year or more to research Hawaii or the sugar beet farmers of Colorado before creating a novel. We heralds have no message at all except what the King has sent us to bring, so we want to know that message. Elizabeth Achtemeier, from her vantage point as professor of both Old Testament and homiletics, urges:

> First of all, we preachers—and we teachers of homiletics—have great necessity laid upon us to stay abreast of modern biblical study. There is no excuse for approaching some text . . . from the standpoint of the biblical research of 1930 or even of 1960. Our major task . . . is to be interpreters of the Word of God, and we fail our people if we do not utilize the best tools for interpreting the Word which modern biblical scholarship has to offer. That means keeping our libraries up to date and using library loan plans, usually available from every seminary. . . . It means taking advantage of continuing education courses on the Bible. . . . It means continual, daily, hard research and solid reading in the Biblical field.[3]

I join Elizabeth Achtemeier in pleading with her colleagues in biblical studies to think about how they teach the methods of exegesis according to how they can be used in preaching and the life of the Church.[4] I blocked out about nine hours for serious exegesis, but I never would have had time for thirteen or seventeen or twenty-three steps in exegesis that occasionally have been offered as the way to get ready to preach.

Prayer has been the process from the start with the question, "Holy Spirit, what are you saying to me in this verse?" Prayer is the attitude all the way through the research stage with the petition, "Holy Spirit, what have you said to other exegetes and other homilists?" Prayer is the posture as we commune in spirit with our panel of diversity with the request, "Holy Spirit, help me understand the people who'll hear me preach this message."

---

3. Elizabeth Achtemeier, *Interpretation* 35, no. 1, 18–31. Reprinted, *Pastoral Life* 36, nos. 5 and 6 (May, 31–38; June, 30–36); the quotation is in 36, no. 6, 35.
4. Ibid.

As for contemplation I make these adaptations from the *Spiritual Exercises* of Ignatius of Loyola:[5]

> 1. Imagine the place where what this Scripture talks about occurred. If your text is from the gospels, view in your mind the synagogues, towns, villages, and countryside through which our Lord went as he taught and preached. Put yourself into the skin of the people who saw him and heard him.
>
> If your text is from the Letters of Paul, imagine the place from which he wrote; put yourself into his skin; try to feel what he felt. Imagine the reactions of the first recipients of this letter.
>
> 2. Do the same with the people involved in texts from other parts of Scripture.
>
> 3. In addition to seeing and hearing what went on originally, try to use the other three senses as you contemplate the text. Smell and taste and touch what they must have smelled, tasted, and touched.

Incubation

The Word of God should simmer on the back burner, giving the subconscious mind a chance. This requires setting up our schedule for homily preparation with breaks in between—so the subconscious mind can go to work. This is why putting off homily preparation to the tail end of the week won't satisfy us—even if we should put in twelve hours in one sitting, there's no time for incubation.

Some insights on creativity have come from split-brain research. It has been thought that certain people afflicted with seizures could be helped by cutting the corpus callosum, a thick bundle of nerve fibers connecting the two halves of the brain. Researchers have studied these people because in them the left brain and right brain functions are clearly divided. The left brain is analytical; the right brain is intuitive. Formerly it was believed that either the right brain or left brain worked while the other rested; now that there has been extensive research on split-brain people, that idea is modified by the discovery that the two halves work best together. William Howell offers several references for those who wish to dig more deeply into this subject.[6]

5. *The Spiritual Exercises of St. Ignatius of Loyola,* ed. Robert Backhouse (London: Hodder and Stoughton, 1989) 25–31.

6. William S. Howell, *The Empathic Communicator* (Belmont, Calif.: Wadsworth Publishing Co., 1982) 110, note 5.

Howell quotes Carl Sagan about recent findings in brain research:

> The left hemisphere processes information sequentially; the right brain simultaneously, accessing several inputs at once. . . .
>
> There is no way to tell whether the patterns extracted by the right hemisphere are real or imagined without subjecting them to left-hemisphere scrutiny. On the other hand, mere critical thinking, without creative and intuitive insights, without the search for new patterns, is sterile and doomed. To solve complex patterns in changing circumstances requires the activity of both cerebral hemispheres: the path to the future lies through the corpus callosum. . . .
>
> I think the most significant creative acts of our or any other culture—legal and ethical systems, art and music, science and technology—were made possible only through the collaborative work of the left and right cerebral hemispheres. These creative acts, even if engaged in rarely or only by a few, have changed us and the world. We might say that human culture is the function of the corpus callosum.[7]

Dudley Lynch, a writer and trainer who helps people develop their creativity, has insights in problem solving in an organization, insights we can relate to creating homilies:

> If the problem requires "incubation"—to use a good hatchery word—then many of our company people are in trouble. Incubating a problem requires slowing the heartbeat and brainwaves. It requires giving up logical control of the mind. It is best augmented by walks in the woods, solitude, listening to Bach, meditation, daydreaming—by surrender. It is often a whole new world to the corporate mind.[8]

It may be a new world to some of us who occupy the pulpit, strategizing on how to incubate.

My plan was to have study sessions four mornings a week (therefore with a break between each session) followed by a day off (another break) before composing the homily. Such a schedule may not fit the circumstances of other homilists. I only suggest that anyone who is serious about being the best possible preacher he or she

---

7. Carl Sagan, *The Dragons of Eden* (New York: Random House, 1977) 169, 181, 185, cited by Howell, *The Empathic Communicator*, 94.

8. Dudley Lynch, "The Case for Disorderly Conduct: How to Get the Most out of Managerial Manpower," Management Review, February 1980 (New York: AMACON, a division of American Management Association, 1980) 17, cited by Howell, *The Empathic Communicator*, 93.

can be should consider arranging the homily-preparation time so as to allow for the mysterious and awesome process of incubation.

In later years I went a step further. I had four folders, labeled "Four weeks," "Three weeks," "Two weeks," "This week." On Monday morning I copied the text for my homily four weeks ahead, one verse to a sheet, and wrote brief answers to my first question, "What is the Holy Spirit saying to me through this verse?" That's all I did with that text that Monday morning, but I'm confident it was enough to start the juices bubbling in the subconscious mind. (I also discovered that being aware of the Scriptures coming up alerted me to material that might help me preach. Whenever I read something or observed something or thought of something that pertained to a text in one of the four weeks coming up, I'd jot it down and slip it into the folder to which it belonged.)

Illumination

All of a sudden—sometimes when you're doing something altogether different from homily-making—a new thought arises! Aha! Illumination coming from incubation.

One winter I had a contract to write a manual on organizing for evangelism. I was also making an ice-skating rink in the backyard. Sometimes I'd stop writing and put on my overshoes, my parka, and my mittens. Beulah would ask, "Do you have a blockage?" I'd nod my head and say, "Yes." I'd go outside and spray another layer of water on the rink. I'd come in, and she'd ask, "The blockage is gone?" I'd nod my head and say, "Yes."

I spoke earlier of the temptation to let setting up tables in the fellowship hall keep us from getting down to work on the homily. But it could be that setting up tables is just what we need to generate illumination, to put our homily preparation on the back burner, provided we've first disciplined ourselves to have something we can put on the back burner.

Verification

Not every flash of inspiration stands up under scrutiny. We need time to check out what has come to us (from who knows where). This is, again, an argument for spreading out our creative work over a span of time, certainly over one week or, still better, over more than one week.

Preaching More Than Once a Week?

The strategy laid out above aims at releasing our creativity for a one-homily-per-week schedule. The Roman Catholic priest preaches every time he celebrates the Mass, including the daily Mass and baptisms, weddings, and funerals. Pastors in some other denominations have evening services on Sundays and Wednesdays. Yet people compare us preachers (usually unfavorably) with other speakers who either (1) have only one speech they give to different audiences or (2) have a staff of writers. It's hard enough to preach well just once a week; how do we manage preaching more than once a week?

It takes extra work, and it works with overflow. We put in our major effort on the weekend celebration with about half the time or more spent on exegesis. We dig around in the riches we discover and find more than we can use. Not all of it will fit right away into one of the other preaching opportunities, but we tuck it away into the files and into the subconscious and it comes to the surface when we need to preach on occasions other than the weekend.

As a Lutheran pastor I've never had to preach at a daily Mass, but for fifteen years I did conduct Sunday evening services and for thirty-three years I did hold midweek services during Lent. I found it easier to meet these extra challenges if I developed a series that continued over a space of time, a study either of a Bible book or of Christian doctrine. The Roman Catholic daily lectionary offers continual opportunities for such series. For the thirty-three or thirty-four weeks of the year in Ordinary Time it arranges the gospel selections in continuity: Mark is read (weeks one to nine), then Matthew (weeks ten to twenty-one), then Luke (weeks twenty-two to thirty-four). The other readings are either from the Old Testament or from the Epistles, also in continuity so as to give a sense of what each book is about. The daily lectionary beckons the priest or deacon to nourish the people with Bible study, taking extra work but also working with the overflow.

Priest, deacon, and pastor may preach at baptisms, weddings, and funerals. It takes extra work to deal pastorally with the persons involved but out of the relationship developed comes the overflow out of which we preach.

Summary

I hold that we are all creative because we're all made in the image of our Creator. Our mirrors each capture different reflections of our Maker and different degrees of creativity. Nevertheless, we are all creative. We may learn how to release our creativity more productively when we follow five steps: discipline, research, incubation, illumination, and verification, with discipline at the top.

For Further Reading

Howell, William. *The Empathic Communicator*. Belmont, Calif.: Wadsworth Publishing Co., 1982, 88–97.
Skudlarek, William. *The Word in Worship*. Nashville: Abingdon, 1981, 52–60.

Exercises

Exercise 24

Begin working on John 20:19-31, the gospel reading for the Second Sunday of Easter in all three years. This exercise will give you practice on the first step: getting started.

> 1. Write each verse of the text, one verse to a sheet of paper. (Later, when some verses may require more space, you'll be able to add sheets where necessary and keep the material grouped for better access.)
>
> 2. Ask yourself these questions in this order and jot down your responses:
>
> What is the Holy Spirit saying to me through this verse?
>
> What reactions does my panel of diversity have to it?
>
> What questions do I have to check out in my exegesis?

TEN

Preaching on the Hard Topics

> The Son of God goes forth to war
> A kingly crown to gain.
> His blood-red banner streams afar;
> Who follows in his train?

Reginald Heber wrote this hymn for St. Stephen's Day (December 26), as we see in the second stanza:

> The martyr first, whose eagle eye
> Could pierce beyond the grave,
> Who saw his master in the sky
> And called on him to save.

We preachers may thrill especially to the third stanza, seeing ourselves as heirs apparent to this company:

> A glorious band, the chosen few,
> On whom the Spirit came,
> Twelve valiant saints; their hope they knew
> And mocked the cross and flame.

We admire the brave words of Jeremiah as he faces down his enemies: "Only know for certain that if you put me to death, you will be bringing innocent blood upon yourselves . . . for in truth the Lord sent me to you to speak all these words in your ears" (26:15).

We are gripped with the audacity of Amos: "Hear this word, you cows of Bashan, who are on Mount Samaria, who oppress the poor, who crush the needy, who say to their husbands, 'Bring something to drink!'" (4:1).

We are transfixed with the heroic vision of Martin Luther King, Jr.: "I have a dream my four little children will one day live in a nation where they will not be judged by the color of their skin but by the content of their character."[1]

Idolatry, oppression, and racism are still with us. If only we could follow in the train of Jesus, Jeremiah, Amos, Stephen, Peter, Paul, Martin Luther King, Jr. What glory to God if we could stir the unjust to repentance and win their hearts to virtue. Perhaps we have been to a churchwide assembly and heard a spine-tingling denouncement of housing discrimination and even voted for a statement against it. Then we come home. We visit with our fellow members. We find some of them fuming about the reports they have read in the daily paper about that church pronouncement. "See if I give them any more money!" Do we still yearn to follow in the train of John the Baptist?

The young deacon in the play and film *Mass Appeal,* outraged at how the parishioners loved their possessions, blasted the people in the pew and was rebuked by the priest who had survived in comfort by telling the folks only what they wanted to hear. "For the time is coming when people will not put up with sound doctrine, but having itching ears, they will accumulate for themselves teachers to suit their own desires" (2 Tim 4:3).

So how do we fulfill our vocation as prophets while still functioning as pastors?

A friend, Pastor Bob Konzelman, told me of an experience he'd had in high school. He was the drum major of the band. There was a parade in downtown Detroit where streets come to a hub like spokes on a wagon wheel. They were at the hub. He was strutting and prancing as all good drum majors should strut and prance when all of a sudden he felt he was strutting and prancing alone. Looking around, he saw that the parade had turned left on one of the spokes. He confessed to me that he ran to catch up with the band, to lead his followers in the direction they were going. Is that how we handle the tough questions?

When the gospel for the day has one of Jesus' hard sayings (e.g., "Whoever divorces his wife, except for unchastity, and marries another commits adultery" [Matt 19:9]), is that the Sunday we preach on the second reading?

The young deacon in *Mass Appeal* did not avoid controversy. We may know of real-life pastors like him who charge right into the hard sayings and, "[mocking] the cross and flame," suffer for it. Is

---

1. Diane Ravitch, ed., *The American Reader: Words That Moved a Nation* (New York: Harper Perennial, division of HarperCollins, 1991) 333.

non-redemptive suffering the way to go? That their suffering is non-redemptive can be read in one or more signs like these:

1. The people do not hear.

   No matter how loudly the preacher hollers "Thus says the Lord," what the Lord says is not coming through.

2. The people yawn.

   They see no connection between the oppression of women in Asia and their own praying, "Thy Kingdom come," and "Give us this day our daily bread."

3. The preacher is frustrated.

   With a vision of being faithful to the heritage of Jeremiah, Amos, and John the Baptist, this prophet is offended at the people's apathy and so the pot of holy rage only boils the more noisily.

How do we deal with controversial issues? How can we be prophets when we are also shepherds tending the flock, nurturing people we know by name, people who pray for us, who cry with us, who pay our salary?

In *Two Ways Of Caring*,[2] William E. Hulme says that both priest and prophet are essential: the priest to convey healing and reconciliation to the individual, and the prophet to speak for God to the spiritual and cultural conditions in society. How do we function as both priests and prophets? If we are going to suffer for our witness (and our Lord says it will be strange if that does not happen), how can we help make our suffering redemptive? How do we preach on the hard topics?

Before we can get to that, I want to emphasize the breadth of this subject.

To Preach Is to Risk

Let me clarify the term "hard topics." Certainly it includes bringing a change of mind on all matters of social justice and prejudice.

But the very words "change of mind" remind us of the Greek word *metanoia*, "repentance." And we know well that preaching repentance can evoke the wrath of King Herod's wife. Ever since Adam and Eve ran away to hide when God came looking for them, ever since Adam blamed God for giving him this woman who enticed him, human beings have been resisting a change of heart and

2. William E. Hulme, *Two Ways of Caring* (Minneapolis: Augsburg Publishing House, 1973) 35–37.

making alibis and getting angry at God for something they've done themselves and spilling over some of that anger on God's messengers.

Preaching *grace* is not necessarily received any better. When people understand the concept, they may well see it as endangering their self-respect. To have God's forgiveness coming free of charge—without any merit or worthiness in them—Paul explains that it is foolishness, a stumbling block. Read 2 Corinthians 11 for all the things Paul suffered because he preached grace instead of legalism.

That grace is still being resisted struck home when I was teaching homiletics and communication at St. John's. One of the Benedictine monks, Fr. Eric Hollas, a specialist in Reformation history, lectures from time to time in adult forums in Twin Cities Lutheran congregations. Returning from one of those guest lectureships, he said to me, "Why, Lutherans are Pelagians. They don't understand grace." I told him, "Eric, that's how we Lutheran pastors get our repeat business."

Mission is another ominous word. Who wants to hear about denying self, taking up the cross, turning the other cheek, being witnesses starting at our own Jerusalems, then going into all the world to preach the gospel to every creature, feeding the hungry, standing up for the oppressed, being peace-makers? And who wants to give money for that?

Notice that I have included *justice* under *mission*. James Empereur and Christopher Kiesling have shown us how prominent the issues of justice are in the three-year lectionary.[3]

So we have three major themes with the potential of riling our hearers: repentance, grace, mission. There is no getting around it. To preach is to risk stirring up resistance.

It took me a while to see this, but it should not have surprised me. Jesus in his parable of the sower shows that three of the four kinds of soil are hostile to the seed, the Word of God (Mark 4). He warns his disciples: "If the world hates you, know that it hated me before it hated you" (John 15:18). "Do you think I have come to bring peace on earth? No, I tell you, but rather division!" (Luke 12:51). George Sweazey observes: "Someone put it well: 'They did not crucify Jesus because he said, 'Consider the lilies of the field, how they grow,' but because he said, 'Consider the thieves in the temple, how they steal.'"[4]

3. James L. Empereur, S.C., and Christopher G. Kiesling, O.P., *The Liturgy That Does Justice* (Collegeville, Minn.: The Liturgical Press, 1990) 61–81.

4. George E. Sweazey, *Preaching the Good News* (Englewood Cliffs, N.J.: Prentice-Hall, 1976) 215–16.

Paul could understand hostility. He explains to the Corinthians, "Those who are unspiritual do not receive the gifts of God's Spirit" (1 Cor 2:14), and to the Romans, "The mind that is set on the flesh is hostile to God" (8:7). This refers not only to those outside the reign of God: Paul confesses that he too has problems: ". . . I am of the flesh, sold into slavery under sin" (7:14). The people in Corinth and Galatia who heard his letters read were also resisting God, and they were converts.

Repentance, grace, and mission—what else is there to preach about? And all of them can evoke hostility. It is plain that to preach is to risk. How then do we fulfill our calling both as prophets and priests?

We Need Not Be Alone

We do not want to do it by ourselves. For one thing, the emotional cost is too heavy. This daunting mission can make us feel as lonely as "a voice in the wilderness." We feel a kinship with the prophet Elijah, hiding in his cave, lamenting: "I have been very zealous for the Lord, the God of hosts; for the Israelites have forsaken your covenant, thrown down your altars, and killed your prophets with the sword. I alone am left, and they are seeking my life, to take it away" (1 Kgs 19:10). When this passage appears in Felix Mendelssohn's oratorio *Elijah*, the chorus that follows counsels:

> Lift thine eyes to the mountains,
> whence cometh help.
> Thy help cometh from the Lord,
> the maker of heaven and earth.
> He hath said, "Thy foot shall not be moved;
> thy keeper will never slumber" (Ps 121:1-3).

The prophet was despairing for no reason: the Lord was not only with him, he came to seek him out and to reveal himself, not in the wind, not in the earthquake, not in the fire, but in "a still small voice" (1 Kgs 19:11-12 RSV).

Nor was Elijah without human support: "Yet I will leave seven thousand in Israel, all the knees that have not bowed to Baal" (1 Kgs 19:18).

Nor do we need to be alone, if we keep looking to the hills and to the "seven thousand in Israel." Basic to our strategy for prophetic/priestly preaching is to discover all the support we can find. I can't say it enough: we must do this because the emotional cost of going it alone is too heavy.

So first we try to develop a cadre of backers, small or larger. I can illustrate how the priest/prophet benefits by an approach I used.

In 1960 I received a call to Lincoln, Nebraska, to a congregation whose building was located in what Lincoln could call its ghetto. The congregation had bought property a mile away on which to relocate. It was obvious that their building and site were inadequate, but I wondered if there were another reason they were wanting to move. So when I met with the church council prior to accepting the call, I asked whether the move to a different site was an attempt to escape from the ghetto. Unanimously they said, "No. Some of our members live here; we intend to keep serving them. And we've already been inviting our African-American neighbors, and we expect to keep doing that." On the strength of that commitment, I accepted that call.

I was eager for still more support. At our monthly meeting of Lincoln Lutheran pastors, I said, "I've talked to our synodical office in Detroit, asking for advice on how to go about integrating the two races. They told me their churches had agreed not to accept any transfer of membership for people who were trying to escape integration. Would you be willing to make the same commitment to us?" Unanimously they said, "We won't ask our congregations to vote on this because they aren't ready yet for that, but we promise you that if any of your people apply for membership here, we just won't submit their names to our church councils."

So as I began preaching on the hard topic of our mission to everyone, people would seek out a church council member and mutter, "Where did you find that pastor?" And that church council person would say, "I fully support him." When they would visit other Lutheran churches, they'd come back shaking their heads, "It's no use trying to run away."

The cadre of backers was growing. When one feisty old character kept protesting, a fellow member would chide him, saying something like, "Emil, the good Lord made the black people too." Emil would retort, "Yes, but he also made rats and mice." When I heard about that, I sought him out and told him, "Emil, that's not fair and you know it." We had numerous encounters, and I'm pleased to report that after a while, when he learned that I had a compost pile, he gave me a subscription to *Organic Gardening*. I treasured that gift. We all gained new respect for Emil; he'd turned 180 degrees from a widely known, loudly proclaimed position. When later we baptized an African-American baby and there were two rows of relatives and friends of the family sitting together, it was more than Emil could bear. As he got up and stomped out, we could overlook it with a smile. To his credit, Emil came back to church later.

Do They Trust Us?

When we feel we need to be prophets, and we're looking for human support, and the people don't trust us, can we blame them for not being willing to follow? George Sweazey has wise counsel:

> A minister should try to avoid controversial matters until he has been in a church long enough for the members to have confidence in him. He may not be able to pick his time if some crisis comes up in which he has to take a stand, but otherwise he should postpone the divisive subjects until people have had time to find out that he is devout, sane, and sincere. There is no reason to expect people to let their opinions be flouted by a stranger. A minister who has been in people's homes, helped them in their troubles, and been accepted as a friend can question their prejudices and get a thoughtful hearing. Controversy can be endured by those who know and respect each other.[5]

One way a priest/prophet fosters trust is by applying the principles laid out in chapter 4 on identifying with the people's ways and self-interest. If the homilist only delivers the generic message from the prepackaged homily service, and the people see no connection with their lives, giving them the (likely false) impression their preacher doesn't care about their struggles, how can trust be nourished? But if week by week the people hear homilies that identify with their ways and their legitimate self-interest, they can see that their priest/prophet understands their life. That cannot but cause their confidence in their homilist to grow.

What If the Issue Can't Be Postponed?

Sweazey recognizes that a crisis may arise before the priest has a chance to become known as a decent person. What to do then? I once came to a parish with an unresolved controversy. They had been debating whether to build a new gymnasium, and their voting was split fifty-fifty for and against. They decided to wait for me to help them work it out. I said, "It's obvious I'm the least informed person here. Are you willing to join me in a 12-week study of the mission of the church and the nature of this neighborhood?" I'm

5. Ibid., 213.

happy to say they responded well to this challenge. The controversy took care of itself. It happened that we didn't build a new gymnasium, but we did take several other courageous and expensive steps towards trying to fulfill our mission in that neighborhood.

So if a priest caught in a nettlesome matter isn't aware who or how many might be willing to give support, he would do well to offer a Bible study on the issue. Giving people a forum could be the medium of choice when dealing with controversial issues, because otherwise people may perceive the preacher as taking advantage of one-way communication, pulpit to pew. The shepherd/prophet must conduct the study ethically, following principles like those offered later in this chapter. Then if there's still a need to preach on the subject, the shepherd/prophet will probably not be alone anymore.

Does God Support Us?

Human support is desirable; divine support is crucial. Too many false prophets have claimed they've heard the voice of God. How can we be so sure we aren't also wrong? We can't expect spectacular manifestations (wind, earthquake, fire), only the still small voice that comes from praying through the relevant Scriptures. Steeping ourselves in the Word of God, praying to be fair to Scripture's intent, willing to listen to others who are also praying for the Holy Spirit's guidance, struggling to exegete the Scriptures to get the message accurately gives us the assurance to speak the truth as we understand it.

There is power in that.

The power of the still small voice is that we not only speak the truth but that we speak the truth in love (Eph 4:15). So in preparing to preach on controversial issues, the shepherd/prophet prays through the Scriptures while also praying for the people. The prophet feels the urge to throw a temper tantrum in the pulpit; the shepherd wants to gain the hearts of the people, to be as wise as serpents, harmless as doves (Matt 10:16).

In considering how to preach on the hard topics, we've seen so far that almost any homily can evoke resistance—for what else is there to preach about except repentance, grace, and mission? On the basis of Scripture and our own history, we've also considered the advisability of not going it alone. Above all, we want the assurance of the "still small voice," and so we search the Scriptures prayerfully. Before venturing out into the deep, we seek at least some human support. If none is readily apparent, we may offer a forum for jointly searching with others for the Holy Spirit's guidance in his word.

What do we do next?

What we are after here is how to let our theology inform our methodology. There are those who on that basis would say we need no methodology, that all we should do is just get up and give the people the Word of God. After all, isn't the effectiveness of preaching up to the Holy Spirit? Of course. But now we shall see how Spirit-led prophets and apostles took account of the hostility in those to whom they preached and adapted their messages to fit, not compromising the truth but opening ears so the truth could get in.

Biblical Models for a Methodology

Put yourself in the sandals of an Old Testament oracle whose king has committed a monstrous offense. As a prophet you're responsible for denouncing that sin. As a shepherd you aim not to score points but to gain a change of heart.

So you come to him with a story about a rich man with many flocks. His poor neighbor had only one lamb he kept as a pet. One day the rich man had company. Did he take from his many sheep to feast his guest? No. He stole the poor man's pet and butchered it for his table.

As you had expected, your king is enraged at this heinous miscarriage of justice and vows to punish the scoundrel. Without realizing it yet, your king has condemned himself. So you can raise your finger and say, "You are the man," and feel fairly sure he has heard you (2 Sam 11-12).

Put yourself in the shoes of a New Testament monotheist who finds himself in Athens and is challenged by skeptics to explain his new gospel. Upset as you are with all their idols, you do not fling the first commandment at them, but like Nathan you establish common ground: "Men of Athens! I see that in every way you are very religious. [Indeed!] For as I walked through your city and looked at the places where you worship, I found also an altar on which it is written, 'To An Unknown God.' That which you worship, then, even though you do not know it, is what I proclaim to you." Instead of quoting your Scriptures, you appeal to their writings: "As even some of your own poets have said, 'For we too are his offspring,'" arguing from that, "Since we are his children, we should not suppose that God's nature is anything like an image of gold or silver or stone."

It is true that Paul did not win many hearts in Athens, but he did not strike out altogether. Luke reports: "Some of them joined him and became believers" (Acts 17:16-34).

There are those who say that when Paul went next to Corinth, he repudiated his Mars Hill strategy: "When I came to you, brothers and sisters, I did not come proclaiming the mystery of God to you in lofty words or wisdom" (1 Cor 2:1).

But we notice that Paul wrote to the same Corinthians: "To the Jews I became as a Jew, in order to win Jews. . . . To those outside the law I became as one outside the law. . . so that I might win those outside the law. To the weak I became weak, so that I might win the weak. I have become all things to all people, that I might by all means save some" (1 Cor 9:20-22). I take this to mean that in Corinth Paul did not repudiate his Mars Hill policy: he affirmed it.

Common ground, apostolic mode of operation for bringing in the lost. Common ground, apostolic style also for shepherding the flock. In a day when even leading Christians held slaves and when the slaveholders' code required them to punish all runaways perhaps by killing them or at least breaking an arm, how would you deal with Philemon? Study that letter not only for what Paul says but for how he says it. Why does he keep referring to himself as "a prisoner of Christ Jesus"? Why does he compliment Philemon? Why does he remind Philemon that he and his runaway slave have the same spiritual father, namely, Paul? Why does he appeal to their jointly held belief in God's providence? Why does he leave his appeal open-ended?

Common ground for bringing in the lost. Common ground for being a pastor to one's friends. Common ground, a model also for disarming one's antagonists.

One day our Lord's archrivals dragged a woman in front of him, caught in the act of adultery. (Is adultery a solo act? Where was the man?) Since Jesus was known as the champion of grace, the teachers of the Law challenged him: "Moses commanded us to stone such. What do you say about her?" "Let anyone among you who is without sin be the first to throw a stone at her" (John 8:1-11).

Imitating the Biblical Models

We owe our appreciation of the usefulness of common ground to the Rev. Henry Ward Beecher, an American pulpiteer of the nineteenth century. In his *Yale Lectures On Preaching,* Beecher said he discovered this strategy through studying the sermons of the apostles:

> I studied the sermons [of the apostles] until I got this idea: that the apostles were accustomed to feel for a ground where they could

meet. Then they heaped up a larger number of particulars of knowledge that belonged to everybody; and when they got that knowledge, which everybody would admit, placed in a proper form before their minds, then they brought it to bear upon them with all their excited heart and feeling. That was the first definite idea of taking aim that I had in my mind.

"Now," said I, "I will make a sermon so." . . .

First I sketched out the things we all know. . . . And in that way I went on with my "You all knows" until I had about forty of them. When I got through with that, I turned round and brought it to bear upon them with all my might; and there were seventeen men awakened under that sermon. I never felt so triumphant in my life. I cried all the way home. I said to myself, "Now I know how to preach."[6]

During America's Civil War, Beecher went to Great Britain and made five speeches on behalf of the North. England's sympathy was with the South. For one thing, the aristocrats who controlled England feared the prosperity of democracy in America because that would spell the doom of feudalism. So English aristocrats were not unwilling to see their rival in commerce dismembered. For another thing, there was a synergy between English commerce and the South. The Confederacy was the great cotton producer of the world; England was the great cotton manufacturing community of the world. Indeed, the Civil War had so diminished England's supply of cotton that there was pressure building within Great Britain to send troops to join the South.

Adding to Beecher's difficulties in persuading England to stay out of the war was a British cultural assumption that a meeting did not belong to the ones who called it but to whoever chose to attend, and that it was fair play to prevent a speaker from being heard in order to take over the meeting. In Manchester, Liverpool, Glasgow, Edinburgh, and London, the clamor and the tumult were so impenetrable that it would be ninety minutes before Beecher could succeed in his effort to start speaking. He was still subject to continual heckling throughout his speeches,[7] but he even turned that to his advantage, establishing common ground through graciousness and humor: "It is a little inconvenient to talk against the wind; but, after all, if you will just keep good-natured—I am not going to lose my temper;

---

6. Henry Ward Beecher, *Yale Lectures on Preaching* 1 (New York: Fords, Howard & Hulbert, 1896) 11–12.

7. Lyman Abbott, *Henry Ward Beecher* (Cambridge: Riverside Press, 1904; Miami: Mnemosyne Pub. Co., 1969) 252–55.

will you watch yours? *[Applause]* Besides all that—it rests me, and gives me a chance, you know, to get my breath."[8] (Genial humor, especially when directed at oneself, is a peace-making weapon.)

Some of the common ground Beecher marked out:

> Slavery brings labor into contempt; freedom honors it.
>
> Slave labor promotes ignorance and vice; free labor promotes intelligence and virtue.
>
> A slave nation is a poor customer, buying the fewest and poorest goods. ("What carpets, what linens, what cottons can you sell to them? What machines, what looking-glasses, what combs, what leather, what books, what pictures, what engravings? . . . A little bagging and a little linsey-woolen, a few whips and manacles, are all you can sell for the slave.")[9] A free nation is a good customer, buying the largest and best goods. What Great Britain wants chiefly is not cotton but consumers.[10]

Was Beecher responsible for keeping Britain from supporting the South? It's hard to measure that; scholars disagree.[11] We do know that England did not intervene, and we can assume that Beecher's rhetorical strategy didn't hurt.

I found myself imitating the biblical models in an experience I had as a student in a state university course in persuasion. Earlier in the term, a classmate had quoted the Bible as part of his evidence in a speech. The professor had commented, "These days with an educated audience, no one quotes the Bible any more. It's been copied and translated so many times it just isn't trustworthy." I took this as my text for a speech.

---

8. John R. Howard, ed., *Patriotic Addresses by Henry Ward Beecher in America and England from 1850 to 1885 on Slavery, the Civil War, and the Development of Civil Liberty in the United States* (New York: Fords, Howard & Hulbert, 1891) 524.

9. Ibid., 526.

10. Ibid., 260–61.

11. David McCarthy, "Henry Ward Beecher," *Concise Encyclopedia of Preaching*, eds. William H. Willimon and Richard Lischer (Louisville: Westminster John Knox Press, 1995) 32.

One reason some historians may discount Beecher's influence in preventing Britain from supporting the South is that, while the Confederacy did seek help from Europe, European powers refrained from intervention for several reasons, chief being the inability of the South to win consecutive victories and thus be able to give the confidence that they could sustain their independence. Cf. James M. McPherson, *Ordeal by Fire: The Civil War and Reconstruction* (New York: Alfred A. Knopf, 1982) 215–18.

In establishing common ground, I first conceded what had to be conceded. I allowed that we in the Church have sometimes discredited the Bible by misusing it. The Church in Galileo's time tried to prove the world is flat by quoting Psalm 104:2: God has "stretched out the heavens like a tent." Well, you need flat ground to pitch a tent, don't you? As for the earth's revolving around the sun, the Church said, "No, the earth stands still because the Bible says, 'The earth is established; it shall never be moved'" (Ps 93:1; Ps 96:10).

I explained that the Church's position had come from Thomas Aquinas in the thirteenth century. Aquinas had gone back to Aristotle, a Greek philosopher four centuries before Christ. Aquinas had turned Aristotle's logic into a defense of the Christian faith—so successfully that when Copernicus and Brahe and Galileo questioned Aristotle's idea of the stars, it seemed to the Church they were attacking Christ himself. As for the statements in the psalms, I showed that what they actually communicate is the conviction that God and the earth are stable and that this is what makes life dependable. Because my primary audience was my professor (who did not know Scripture but was acquainted with Greek and Roman mythology) I observed that the Greeks and the Romans got no sense of security from their gods. In fact, they never knew what to expect if Zeus (or Jove) should wake up with a headache. So instead of investigating nature, the Greeks and Romans spent their time trying to outguess the scrapping and capricious gods. Modern science could only begin when people felt safe with a God who is steady, because it meant they could poke around in the earth and look at what was going on and count on it to work the same way tomorrow and the next day and the day after that.

As for the opinion, "The Bible has gone through so many hands, it's not reliable," I also conceded what had to be conceded: we have four thousand manuscripts of the New Testament but no originals, and these manuscripts have three hundred thousand discrepancies.

Having yielded this territory, I searched for more common ground. I found it in the professor's role as a scholar and in the scholar's desire to be fair. I had already demonstrated my willingness to be fair by making these concessions. I suggested it would be fair to look behind the statistics regarding the three hundred thousand variations. Doing so, we find that 95 percent of them make no difference, being mostly words misspelled or misplaced or left out and so on. Of the remaining 5 percent, none affect a Christian doctrine. I intimated that although the Bible has gone through so many hands, the evidence testifies not to its unreliability but to quite the opposite.

Proceeding with the common ground, the scholar's desire to be fair, I took the Book of Jonah as a reference point. A lot of sport has been made of Jonah's account of a great fish swallowing a man. But that is only the first chapter. When scholars analyze a piece of literature, they study not only the writing itself but the occasion, the audience, and the purpose. To be as fair to Jonah as we are to other works, I suggested that we read its remaining three chapters to see why the author wrote as he did.

Jonah had been ordered to preach repentance to Israel's worst enemy, Nineveh. He did not want to go since he was afraid of two things: that Nineveh would indeed repent, and that God in his grace would forgive the Ninevites—the last thing Jonah wanted to have happen. So he sailed in the opposite direction from Nineveh but found he could not escape God. Not being able to avoid his mission, Jonah did go to Nineveh; to his dismay, Nineveh did repent, and to his disgust, God did not destroy the city. Whether you read Jonah as history or as parable, the issue is still the same: not, "Can a fish swallow a man?" but, "Is the kingdom of God open only to our own kind?" The scholar's devotion to being fair requires us not to take the first chapter of Jonah out of context but to consider the author's intent.

I had taken a considerable risk in challenging the professor in front of the class. But he apologized to the group for having made an unfounded criticism and rewarded me with a high grade.

Structuring the Homily on Hard Topics

When dealing with a hard topic, the priest/prophet seeks to keep the people's ears open so that the Holy Spirit may have access to their hearts. We do not deny the Holy Spirit's power to work miracles of repentance in spite of the preacher's ineptness, just as we did not deny the Spirit's power to work miracles when the Word was preached in a holy tongue—Latin, King James English, or the blessed sounds of "the old country" (Germany, France, Italy, Poland, Scandinavia, etc.). But just as we finally saw the wisdom of translating the Spirit-energized Word into the *language* of the people, so now we are seeking to translate God's Word into a *form* that the people can receive. Great importance lies therefore with the way the priest/prophet will structure the message, so that the hearers do not shut off the dialogue before there is a chance to make the case.

The structure for preaching on the hard topics is the *unfolding format;* that is, we unfold only one part at a time and only when the people are ready to hear it.

That means that our introduction will open up a neutral inquiry and that our theme will not give away our proposal. Perhaps the theme will even be a question: "What Should Be Our Attitude towards . . . ?"

Using the unfolding format, we will not preview the supporting points. Instead we unfold them only as we come to them because the people might not be ready for point 3 until they have heard point 2, and they might not accept point 2 until they have heard point 1. So as we plan the structure of this sermon, we consider how the various persons in our panel of diversity might react as we decide which common ground includes the most people, making that point 1. That which would more naturally follow point 1 becomes point 2, and the remaining common ground becomes point 3.

The unfolding format means that the preacher will be fair. The preacher will concede whatever needs to be conceded; as in the case of my speech on the Bible's credibility, why defend what need not be defended? We may handle the concessions in one of two ways: making them all at once, in which case the concessions will likely become point 1; making them according to whatever point they may apply to, in which case they will likely come at the beginning of each point.

The unfolding format means we will not state our real proposal until the conclusion when the people can then see it as the natural outcome of all the common ground. So in sermons on hard topics, we have two working themes: the initial theme stated neutrally at the end of the introduction, opening up the discussion for fair-minded people, and the concluding theme stating the position we believe Scripture requires.

Suppose, however, that as we pray in our study and commune in spirit with the people in our panel of diversity, we perceive that after conceding what needs to be conceded and establishing all the other common ground, at least some of our people would still say no; what then? Leave it open-ended, as Paul did with Philemon. Leave it to the Holy Spirit working in our own heart and in the hearts of the people. Our concluding theme then will be something like, "Let's pray about this and talk some more." When Paul told Philemon, "Confident of your obedience, I am writing to you, knowing that you will do even more than I say," what specific thing had he asked for? Nothing at all, except "So if you consider me your partner, welcome him as you would welcome me." (He did mention the little matter of Onesimus's having stolen from Philemon: "If he has wronged you in any way, or owes you anything, charge that to my account." I get a kick from the next line, how he wipes out the debt he has just assumed: "I say nothing about your owing me even your own self.") But in this general statement, "knowing you will do more even more than I say," what was Paul hinting at? That Philemon should set Onesimus free? How much Philemon must have wrestled with this problem! How much we have had to struggle in facing up to the implications of our oneness in Christ—all because Paul did not ram it down our throats. The rhetorician William Norwood Brigance (who if he were writing in the 1990s instead of the 1960s would have used inclusive language) agreed with the policy we have noticed in Paul:

> Who ever heard of anyone changing his mind because of a speech? Well, people *do* change their minds in this changing world, and they are constantly making shifts of attitude. But they don't change them from hearing bull-headed argument. Thomas Jefferson was right when he said, "No one will ever change his mind on account of a mere argument," and he was justified in his intense dislike of personal arguments. With prophetic wisdom (for scientific investigation later proved he was right) he added that a man might "change his mind as a result of his own reflections and of what he has slowly digested."[12]

So when Paul fired no direct attack on slavery itself, he was giving Philemon the opportunity to digest the matter slowly, judging that it would have been too big a shift of opinion to expect abolition all at once. So too we as both prophets and shepherds will take the measure of the people and pray for wisdom to discern how far we can lead them, whether one homily will do the whole job or whether one homily will be just part of a campaign.

What effect did Paul's letter have on Philemon? What happened to Onesimus? If Philemon had followed the slave masters' code and either killed the runaway or at least broken his arm—as a warning to all other slaves in the neighborhood—I would expect that Philemon would have burned this letter. The fact that we have it in the New Testament suggests that he must have recognized Onesimus as his brother in Christ. Indeed, from the greetings at the end of the Letter to the Colossians, we infer that Onesimus had gained some stature in the Church (Col 4:9).

Here is an overview of the structure for a homily on hard topics:

    I. Introduction
       A. Opening up a neutral inquiry, showing its relevance to the people's legitimate self-interest

---

12. William Norwood Brigance, *Speech: Its Techniques and Disciplines in a Free Society,* 2d ed. (New York: Appleton-Century-Crofts, 1961) 174.

B. Statement of initial theme, expressed in a neutral spirit, perhaps as a question
(No preview of supporting points. Use the unfolding format, stating points only as you come to them.)

II. Body
A. Common ground most likely to be accepted by the most people in the liturgical assembly
B. Common ground flowing logically from point A
C. Common ground flowing logically from point B
(Conceding what must be conceded without violating our integrity, either making all concessions at once as point A, or conceding point-by-point.)

III. Conclusion
A. Recapitulation of initial theme and all points of common ground
B. Statement of concluding theme–the proposal, seen as the natural outcome of marking out all the common ground
(If the people would resist the proposal even when faced with all the common ground, we leave it open-ended as Paul did with Philemon. So we phrase our concluding theme something like: "Let's pray about this and talk some more.")

Here's a variation of the body of a structure for preaching to those who may oppose what we feel we must preach, an expansion of the problem-solution pattern:

II. Body
A. Definition of the problem
B. Exploration of the causes
C. Examination of possible solutions
D. Selection of best solution

Common ground is discovered in the process of defining the problem, exploring its causes, and examining all possible solutions, always being objective and always treating the opposing view with respect. If the subject is so volatile we can't expect it to be dealt with successfully in one homily, then we leave it open-ended, omitting "D. Selection of best solution."

The Ethics of Word-Choice and Evidence-Citing in the Homily on Hard Topics

We have seen how important it is to keep the people's ears open while preaching on the hard topics. Taking care in the way we arrange the order of our ideas is one way to do this; another is to take care in the way we choose our words and the way we present our evidence.

No Put-downs

We'll avoid any hint of a put-down, for two reasons. First, the ethical reason: Since all for whom Christ died are precious, ridicule betrays our high regard for those persons. ("The eye cannot say to the hand, 'I have no need of you,' nor again the head to the feet, 'I have no need of you'" [1 Cor 12:21].) Second, the pragmatic reason: Since we want to gain the hearts of those in the opposing camp, to make them look foolish will only harden their position.

No Loaded Language

We'll also avoid loaded language, again on the same two grounds of the ethical and the pragmatic.

Loaded language is unethical because the commandment against bearing false witness requires us to speak well of our neighbor and to put the most charitable construction on all the neighbor does. Preachers sometimes fall into this ethical snare because they're usually speaking in a homogeneous assembly where name-calling (in one congregation, "selfish business interests," in another, "radical labor leaders") doesn't roil the waters, and so there's no pain to signal the problem.

In addition to violating the law of love for our neighbor, loaded language is also unethical because it short-circuits logic, making it unfair. Loaded language ("red neck," "secular humanist," "long haired") evokes unreasonable emotion, causing people to jump to unfounded conclusions. The demagogue uses loaded language because it polarizes the audience, but do we Christian preachers want to be guilty of manipulating our people? Not according to David Buttrick: "Preachers are not manipulators. . . . Though some preachers may suppose that all is fair if we are determining salvation, and that devious rhetoric may be justified on the basis of 'It's for their own good,' such a pattern of thought is alien to the gospel."[13]

13. David Buttrick, *Homiletic: Moves and Structures* (Philadelphia: Fortress Press, 1987) 34.

We also avoid loaded language because it works against us, especially when preaching on the hard topics. If those who hold the opposing view perceive us as biased against them (and using loaded language will give them that notion), they won't hear us out. We're trying to reach into the innermost wellsprings of people's humanity. We won't compromise our own integrity, but in being faithful we'll be careful to avoid turning people off before we get to make our case. So we strive to be objective: we avoid hate-provoking words.

No Games

In keeping the people's ears open while preaching on hard topics, the ethics of evidence require that we play no games in the pulpit.

No "stacking the deck," bringing out only the evidence that suits our purpose, not being willing to acknowledge that God-loving people may have reason to have a different opinion.

No careless use of facts or unsupported assertions or glittering generalities. College- and seminary-educated clergy have learned to write papers in which all assertions are documented with footnotes. The same clergy will check all assertions for accuracy and reliability before declaiming them from the pulpit.

"Stacking the deck" and "glittering generalities" violate the commandment against bearing false witness, and so they're unethical. They're also not pragmatic, because sharp, fellow-believer/priests in the pew will discount the homilist's credibility when they hear unfounded assertions.

No Monologue

In trying to live up to our role as prophets of the living God, we may fall into the delusion that we always know the truth better than others. This distorts our eyesight when looking at how we present evidence: if we're right anyway, who cares about how we say it? Feeling superior also perverts our style of speaking—the words, the tone of voice convey the message, "Listen up, you peasants."

Writers on rhetoric recognize this ethical problem in other public speakers as well: "The truth or virtue of it we are to accept without proof. . . . The choice for the addressee boils down to whether he will say 'amen' or throw bricks."[14] "When employing a tough style,

---

14. Huntington Brown, *Prose Styles: Five Primary Types* (Minneapolis: University of Minnesota Press, 1966).

the speaker's tone is egocentric, brow-beating, no-nonsense, domi-neering, curt, covertly intimate, intense, and often omniscient."[15]

The Catholic bishops in the United States have recognized that homilists may also be tempted to feel superior:

> To preach in a way that sounds as if the preacher alone has access to the truth and knows what is best for everyone else, or that gives the impression that there are no unresolved problems or possibility for dialogue, is to preach in a way that may have been acceptable to those who viewed the church primarily in clerical terms. In a church that thinks and speaks of itself as a pilgrim people, gathered for worship, witness, and work, such preaching will be heard only with great difficulty, if at all.[16]

There is one who could have dropped out of heaven with all the answers, who would have robbed God of no glory had he done so, yet who made himself of no reputation, taking upon himself the form of a servant (Phil 2:5-8). He taught with authority and not as the scribes (Matt 7:29), yet he spoke dialogically. When the lawyer stood up to test him (not exactly a friendly posture), asking, "What must I do to inherit eternal life?" Jesus didn't hand down a pat answer but began a dialogue: "What is written in the Law? What do you read there?" (Luke 10:25-26).

Those rhetoricians who hold that monologue is unethical look for support to Martin Buber, Carl Rogers, Gabriel Marcel, Eric Fromm, and Paul Tournier. Building on the foundation of these thinkers, they claim dialogue is human and humane and that monologue breeds dogmatism and coercion. I'm not suggesting that there should be two persons speaking with each other in the chancel, but rather that the homilist should be in conversation with the people all the way from the text to the homily, from the study to the pulpit.

Some prophet/shepherds feel the pulpit is no place for contro-versy, the people having no chance to respond, that it looks like monologue, that the only place for hard topics is in a forum-type set-ting. I respect their opinion; I feel there may well be controversies where this is the medium of choice. But I believe it's also possible–and necessary–to be dialogical in the pulpit. Harry Emerson Fosdick

15. Richard L. Johannesen, "Attitude of Speaker Toward Audience," *Central States Speech Journal* (Summer 1974) 97; paraphrasing Walker Gibson, *Tough, Sweet & Stuffy* (Bloomington: Indiana University Press, 1966).

16. *Fulfilled in Your Hearing* (Washington, D.C.: The Bishops' Committee on Priestly Life and Ministry, United States Catholic Conference, 1982) 5.

wrote: "If however the people can be there too [with the priests in their study], so that the sermon is not a dogmatic monologue but a cooperative dialogue in which the congregation's objections, questions, doubts and confirmations are fairly stated and dealt with, something worthwhile is bound to happen."[17]

I refer you again to chapter 4 where I recommended choosing a panel of diversity to sit with you in spirit in your study, five or six people chosen to represent various parts of your congregation or parish (by age, gender, social condition, etc.), people with whom you commune—as though they were there—asking, "How do you feel about this verse, Mary? How do you feel about it, Tom?" It's hard to avoid being dialogical in the pulpit after having prayed through the text day-by-day in the presence of this panel.

Preachers: Authorities on the What, Not the How

Not too long ago, the preacher was known as "the parson" (or, "person"), the only one in the community who was educated. He could issue pronouncements on any subject. He could get by with glittering generalities and unsupported assertions. He could stack the deck and bring out only the evidence that suited him. Monologue with a vengeance. But now the farmer uses a computer to keep track of the gains in his livestock and is conversant with the markets in Russia and the crops in Brazil. Now the high school student may know more about chemistry and mathematics than the shepherd/prophet would ever understand. When our next-door neighbor Daniel was five years old, he invited my wife and me to his room to see his collection of stuffed dinosaur dolls. Beulah asked him, "Do you have names for each of these dinosaurs?" Five-year-old Daniel answered, "No, I just call them by their scientific names." Woe to the homilist who acts like a "parson."

The preacher's expertise is in knowledge of the Scriptures. Yet even here monologue can be not only unethical but foolish. David Preus, presiding bishop of the former American Lutheran Church (now part of the Evangelical Lutheran Church in America), observed that the preacher is an authority on the *what* but not necessarily on the *how*.[18] To illustrate, he referred to the Pentateuch: "When you reap the harvest of your land, you shall not reap to the

17. Harry Emerson Fosdick, *The Living of These Days: An Autobiography* (New York: Harper and Brothers, 1944) 215.

18. From an oral presentation to American Lutheran Church personnel. Permission to quote granted by David Preus.

very edges of your field, or gather the gleanings of your harvest; you shall leave them for the poor and for the alien: I am the LORD your God" (Lev 23:22; cf. Lev 19:9-10).

It's plain in this case that the *what* is that we shall be concerned about the down and out. But the *how* which worked well in the Holy Land in Bible times is irrelevant in our time where many of the poor live in an environment of pavement and whose only possibility for gleaning is to paw through dumpsters. So when dealing with matters of economics, the homilist can bring to bear the Bible's "preferential option for the poor" while deferring to others in the priesthood of believers who know something about how society works.

When Roman Catholic Bishops in the United States write their pastoral letters, they affirm their authority on the *what,* but they acknowledge the authority of others in the priesthood of believers on the *how* by holding hearings around the country to gain expert testimony before issuing their proclamations. Social action commissions of national Lutheran bodies have issued statements—not first *for* the Church but *to* the Church—for churchwide discussion before submitting the finished work to the churchwide assembly for a vote.

The prophet/shepherd, not having the resources of bishops or commissions, will still preach on the *what,* trusting the Holy Spirit to work in the hearts of fellow believer/priests to put it into practice, using their expertise to produce a workable *how* within their spheres of influence.

Summary

It's a glorious calling to be a prophet. If being a prophet should entail taking up one's cross, will that suffering be redemptive? We leave it to God to say, but Jesus did counsel us to be "wise as serpents and harmless as doves." So prophets are also shepherds. How do they fulfill both roles without compromising either?

The call to be both prophet and shepherd requires the preacher first of all to seek both divine and human support. Methodologically, the preacher follows biblical models in Nathan, Paul, and Jesus, marking out all possible areas of common ground, structuring the homily in such a way as to keep the people's ears open while making the case, "speaking the truth in love"—that is, being fair, objective, and ethical, recognizing that the preacher's expertise is in the *what* of the Scriptures, leaving the *how* to the wisdom of others in the priesthood of believers.

Although preaching any of the great themes of Scripture— repentance, grace, mission—is to risk evoking hostility, we are not paranoid, because we are not alone, and the King has given us models for handling his business.

For Further Reading

Burghardt, Walter J., S.J. "Preaching the Just Word." In *Liturgy and Social Justice*, Mark Searle, ed., 36–52. Collegeville, Minn.: The Liturgical Press, 1980.
Empereur, James L., S.J., and Christopher G. Kiesling, O.P. *The Liturgy That Does Justice*. Collegeville, Minn.: The Liturgical Press, 1990, 61–81, 82–108.
Sweazey, George E. *Preaching the Good News*. Englewood Cliffs, N.J.: Prentice Hall, 1976, 213–26.

Exercises

Exercise 25

Read homily number 13 in the Appendix (page 250), "Victims of the System."

1. Why were beards an issue in the early 1970s?

2. List the common ground established in the homily.

3. Is this deductive or inductive?

4. Any suggestions for improvement?

Exercise 26

Read Luke 14:25-33.
Identify any points to which your panel of diversity might be hostile.
Consider how much attention each point might deserve, lest one might be firing cannons at sparrows.
If there is a serious bone of potential contention, begin listing all the common ground you can find.

Exercise 27

A three-minute homily on a repentance, grace, justice, or mission topic of your choosing, addressed to a group of hearers of your choosing.

One area in preaching on the mission of the Church deals with improving our stewardship of time, talent, and treasure. Possible topics:

1. The satisfaction of making a will

2. The challenge of increasing your giving 1 percent per year: if it's 2 percent now, make it 3 percent for the coming year, 4 percent the following year, etc.

3. The joy of tithing

A pattern you might follow as you prepare:

1. List all the stumbling-blocks we all face in the topic you've chosen.

2. Develop all the concessions to the stumbling-blocks you can make without violating your integrity.

3. Mark out all the other common ground you can discover.

4. Find ways to draw word pictures of the common ground.

5. Develop an initial theme to be stated neutrally at the close of your introduction.

6. Develop a concluding theme stating your proposal. If your analysis suggests your hearers won't be ready to accept it even after your concessions and marking out other common ground, leave your concluding theme unstated. It will still be the purpose toward which your homily will move. When you find it prudent to leave your desired purpose unstated, then formulate a neutral concluding theme, something like, "Let's keep praying and thinking about this."

7. Develop a clear, cohesive outline that moves in a straight line from your initial theme to your concluding theme, with points stated from the people's point of view.

8. Memorize not the words of your homily but the flow of ideas. Think through your outline on your feet. Rehearse several times.

EXERCISE 28

Continuing with the text you began working on in exercise 23, John 20:19-31, ask yourself these questions in this order and jot down your responses on the sheet(s) having the verse the material pertains to:

1. If you can, ask: what does the Greek or Hebrew text say? (You may not only gain a clearer understanding but also benefit from getting some word pictures you can use to make your homily visual.)

2. What has the Holy Spirit said to other exegetes about this text?

3. What has the Holy Spirit said to other preachers (in published or recorded sermons) and homiletical commentators about this text?

ELEVEN

Making Homilies Textual

Andrew Blackwood tells of a backwoods exhorter who had the text: "Enoch walked with God: and he was not, for God took him" (Gen 5:24). Blackwood observes that the speaker might have explored the theme, "A Deepening Friendship with God," but instead, he followed a different trail:

A. Enoch was not an Episcopalian,
   for he walked; he did not dance.
B. Enoch was not a Baptist,
   for he walked; he did not swim.
C. Enoch was not a Presbyterian,
   for he walked with God.
D. Enoch was a Methodist,
   for God took him.[1]

This is an extreme example of using a text as a pretext. Yet it illustrates a practice not uncommon, where homilists do not do their best in exegeting the word of God, where they are not "rightly explaining the word of truth" (2 Tim 2:15). Not plumbing the depths of their text, not considering its context or its meaning as a whole, they grasp at some phrase or sentence and use it as a launching pad to take off into the wild blue yonder. Leander Keck observes that a phrase or a metaphor in the text "simply serves as a catalyst; the actual content of the sermon is derived elsewhere and frequently could have been suggested just as well by a fortune cookie."[2] No wonder some people say, "You can make the Bible mean almost anything."

1. Andrew Watterson Blackwood, *The Preparation of Sermons* (New York and Nashville: Abingdon, 1968) 61–62.
2. Leander E. Keck, *The Bible in the Pulpit* (Nashville: Abingdon, 1978) 101, cited in Sydney Greidanus, *The Modern Preacher and the Ancient Text* (Grand Rapids, Mich.: William B. Eerdmans Publishing Co., 1988) 123–24.

Other preachers, while not false to the Scriptures, may still not be true to the text they've read to the people. They're looking only for a subject like repentance or hope or perseverance. Then they make this topic a hook on which they hang a string of thoughts without developing the whole text.

We may learn something about the proper use of a Scripture *text* by looking at the etymology of the word. *Text* comes from the same Latin root as *textile*. The verb is *texere*, "to weave." So the text is the warp and woof out of which we weave the homily.

Why Use a Text Anyway?

For Roman Catholic priests and deacons, the very word *homily* implies a text: "the homily should flow quite naturally out of the readings."[3] Protestants usually call what they preach a *sermon*—always on a text, but not necessarily from the lectionary—but in Roman Catholic vocabulary, a *sermon* is a religious talk, perhaps on a doctrinal or ethical issue, without being confined to a text necessarily.

Even if the word *homily* presupposes textual preaching, we still may ask why this need be so. For Protestant preachers there's no commandment to use a text.

It is possible to be biblical and, most importantly, Christian, without being textual. But the Church has its reasons for the practice of preaching on a text. Here are the arguments I see for making homilies textual:

> 1. We have good historical models. When Jesus preached at Nazareth (Luke 4), he used a text from Isaiah. When Peter preached on Pentecost (Acts 2), he used a text from Joel. Justin Martyr says that the Church at worship in his day would read from the writings of the apostles, after which would follow an address admonishing the people to take to heart what had just been read.
>
> 2. We want to hear the Word of God. In spite of the fact that texts have been misused, having a text and expounding it is the simplest way to meet the desire to hear the Word of God.
>
> 3. We want to be able to test the preacher, to see whether he or she is bringing us the Word of God. A homilist may mis-

3. *Fulfilled in Your Hearing* (Washington, D.C.: The Bishops' Committee on Priestly Life and Ministry, United States Catholic Conference, 1982) 23.

use the text, but having a text at least makes it easier for the people to discern whether the preacher is true to Scripture or not.

There is plenty of scriptural testimony that testing the preacher is a responsibility of the people. Paul reminds the Corinthians that not even New Testament prophets are to be taken at their word but should first be weighed (1 Cor 14:29); to the Thessalonians he says, "Do not despise the words of the prophets, but test everything; hold fast to what is good" (1 Thess 5:20-21); to the Galatians he even holds himself accountable: "But even if we or an angel from heaven should proclaim a gospel contrary to what we proclaimed to you, let that one be accursed!" (Gal 1:8).

We shall expect our people to take the responsibility of testing us modern-day prophets seriously. Textual preaching probably makes this duty more manageable; topical preaching probably makes it more difficult. James Smart observes: "the topical form of sermon . . . usually permits the Biblical text to be touched only slightly. There is not room in it for any very careful exposition."[4]

4. The text limits the homily. The text gives the homily a starting place and an ending point.

5. The text allows the homilist to have something to say the next time. For me this may be the best reason of all. If every time I preach I cover Genesis to Revelation, I've soon preached myself out. Expounding a text and only that text saves the rest of our treasure to be shared later. The three-year lectionary that focuses on one Synoptic Gospel each year replenishes our storehouse even more because it pushes us to consider a particular evangelist's viewpoint. On the Thirtieth Sunday of the year of Matthew, on the Thirty-first Sunday of the year of Mark, and on the Fifteenth Sunday of the year of Luke, the gospel (Matt 22:34-40; Mark 12:28-34; Luke 10:25-37) has Jesus dealing with the question, "Which commandment of the law is the greatest?" But in Matthew and Luke the man who raises the issue is trying to trip Jesus up; in Mark the scribe is a genuine seeker. In Luke the lawyer posing a problem to Jesus tries to find a loophole, "Who is my neighbor?" and gets the parable of the Good

---

4. James D. Smart, *The Strange Silence of the Bible in the Church* (Philadelphia: Westminster, 1972) 22.

Samaritan in response. Being true to the text before us enables us to preach a fresh homily with something left over for next time.

6. Sticking to a text helps increase biblical literacy. We may lament the growing lack of knowledge of the Scriptures. But in spite of all the allurements that draw people away from worship, we still reach more people in the weekly celebration than by any other means. Although the religion section of the newspaper doesn't compare in size with the sports section, we're told there are still more people in all the churches on Sundays than in the athletic arenas. We may use this opportunity to increase biblical literacy by the way we preach, making sure each homily helps the people get better acquainted with a particular text.

Textual Preaching and Local Color

Helping the people get better acquainted with a particular text brings up a principle taught me by my homiletics professor Jacob A. Dell. He aimed to increase biblical literacy by having the sermon reflect the local color of the text. To him that meant the theme and its supporting points would also breathe the atmosphere of that Scripture. In a homily on Psalm 23, the theme and its main divisions will aim to sound like a discourse about the blessings that come from having the Lord as our shepherd and host.

If indeed the text is the warp and woof out of which we weave the homily, local color should be inevitable. Still there are homilies that evolve from prayerful study of a text yet show little relationship to that text. The homilists have brought us the end results of exegesis and meditation but haven't revealed to us the intermediate steps that got them there. Here is such an outline:

Matt 11:2-10

I. Introduction
    A. Question raised by text
    B. Jesus' answer to question

II. A person today
    A. A person's response today: "So what?"
    B. What do we respond to that person?
        1. Believe it
        2. Rhetoric
        3. Theological phrases

    C. That person's reply
    D. Now what do we do?

III. How we might respond
    A. Story, heaven and hell
    B. Say something about preaching
    C. Difference between heaven and hell
    D. Our possible response to the person

IV. Conclusion
    A. God's Word isn't confined
      1. The person's words
      2. Sunday
    B. If proclamation
      1. Nice words—no better than hell
      2. Only then it amounts to something

This outline has the obvious problem discussed in chapter 5, that it's preacher-centered, not people-centered. The preacher knows what it means; nobody else can see any immediate meaning behind "A person today," or "How we might respond." It also wanders off-course, and it's hard to see how the conclusion rises out of what has gone before.

Judging it in terms making homilies textual, this outline has no apparent connection with any text except that it mentions Matt 11:2-10 at the top. There's no weaving of the warp or woof of the agonizing of John the Baptist in his dungeon as to whether he'd thrown his life away in building up Jesus. There's no local color from the tender and sympathetic response of our Lord, "Go and tell John what you hear and see."

You may be able to improve on the following outline, but it does at least show its relationship to a particular text:

I. Introduction
    A. Many are searching for meaning.
    B. Is the gospel still relevant?
    C. John the Baptist's question is modern and vital: (theme) Are You He Who Is to Come, Or Shall We Look for Another?

II. Body
    A. Like John, we may have second thoughts about our commitment.
    B. Like John, we check the evidence directly.

III. Conclusion
    A. Recap
    B. We're blessed in the faith that Jesus is the one we're
       looking for.

Using the Whole Text

How much of the reading shall we use as grist for our preaching mill? My policy has usually been to accept the challenge of letting the entire passage speak to the people.

That doesn't mean I shut down my powers of discrimination, because, as far as I know, the makers of the lectionary were not divinely inspired. Sometimes it's hard to see why they included the final paragraph, and sometimes it's hard to see why they didn't include what comes next or what came before. In the Lutheran lectionary for the Third Sunday of Easter, Year C, they give us the powerful story of the risen Jesus directing the disciples to an unlikely haul of fish but they stop short of letting us hear the moving report of Peter's restoration to apostleship. This pivotal event appears nowhere in the entire Lutheran three-year cycle, at least the one in effect as this was written. The Roman Catholic lectionary does include Peter's restoration in the long form of the gospel but omits it in the short form. The mere fact that our lectionaries do offer longer and shorter versions of the readings suggests that we homilists are permitted some liberties in deciding how much of the assignment to take.

Yet I consider it my responsibility—as a rule—to search out the meaning of the whole passage, to deal with the questions the people may have from hearing the entire reading. Sometimes there's a verse standing out that begs for a homily to be woven from it, such as: "This is the victory that conquers the world, our faith" (1 John 5:4). There may well be occasions when we might take just that verse, to the glory of God and the edification of the people. But the chances are that in so doing we would overlook the context of that verse, how the apostle was dealing with the heresy of docetism, the contention that Jesus only seemed to be human. In chapter 2 I spoke of the docetists as trying to deal with the temptations of the world and spawning two opposing breeds: the "kill-joys" who said Jesus was too holy to be human (because being human is nasty, we should withdraw from the world and live as grouches); the "whoopee-makers" who also said Jesus was too holy to be human, but since they believed God only cares about what's spiritual, it made no difference what they did with their bodies—as long as they remembered their baptism, they could live it up.

This is what the apostle was confronting. To refute both errors, he taught that we conquer the world by our relationship with Jesus, who came "not with the water only [by baptism] but with the water and the blood," that is, as a physical creature. That's how John came to write: "This is the victory that overcomes the world, our faith."

This verse is part of the second reading for the Second Sunday of Easter, Year B, 1 John 5:1-6. If we should preach only on that verse, we'd stand a fair chance of depriving our people of the power they want, by not showing them how our relationship with the risen Christ strengthens us to live in the world. Not working with the entire reading, we might well overlook showing them the water-and-blood Jesus, so much in the world that they accused him of being a glutton and a drunkard, yet so much not of the world that the tax collectors and harlots he attracted never managed to make him to be like themselves. Not revealing why John wrote as he did, we might well shortchange our people of the riches of insight as to why our relationship to the risen Christ is essential to our daily walk.

It is possible to preach an expository homily by lifting out only a small part of the passage. It may be more practical as well. For example, Matthew begins his gospel with seventeen verses of the genealogy of Jesus. It's hard to read that aloud in church and keep people awake. Yet Matthew had a reason for starting that way. So I've preached on all of Matthew 1 by reading only one word, "Emmanuel." I had two parts:

1. God with us, rebels.
2. God with us, pilgrims.

Under "God with us, rebels," I dealt with the first seventeen verses, our Lord's family tree. I read only a verse or two at a time, giving a running commentary. Some notable branches, like Abraham, Ruth, and David, admirable for the most part but not perfect. Some characters we don't know much about, like Abijah, Jechoniah, and Zadok. And some rascals, like Jacob, Solomon, and Rahab. In all, some forty-two generations of the rebels of God. Such was the family into which our Redeemer was born. Such was the length to which our gracious God went to identify with us.

Under "God with us, pilgrims," I dealt with the rest of the chapter, how God was with Joseph in his quandary of what to do with his fiancee who had that strange story. "Oh, I see. Pregnant by the Holy Spirit. Sure." Then how God was with Mary in her agony, to be suspected by a good man and in danger of losing him as a husband, all because—as Gabriel had claimed—she was "highly favored." "God, thanks a lot." God with us, pilgrims—as we struggle when trying to do his will and getting into grief because of it.

Nevertheless, regardless of legitimate exceptions, I uphold the policy of usually using the whole text.

Using Only One Text

Shouldn't the homily deal with all three readings and the psalm that belong in the weekly celebration? As William Skudlarek observes: "But do not (repeat, do not) read the lessons from the lectionary and then ignore them completely in your preaching. To do so is a clear, indeed eloquent way of informing the congregation that the liturgy is something we do because we have to, but that it really doesn't have anything to do with life."[5]

During Advent, Christmas, Lent, and Easter, all the readings have some connection—if not with each other, then with the season. On the remaining Sundays, the second reading takes a letter from the apostles and reads it in series. The first reading—usually from the Hebrew Scriptures—is supposedly chosen to correlate with the gospel. (Occasionally the connection eludes me.) It has amazed me to see how some homily services—even books to help the preacher find his or her way through the lectionary—have discovered the "unity" in all three readings!

The plan I follow is similar to that offered by Skudlarek.[6] If I'm preaching on the gospel for the day, I preach only on that text and let it form the base on which I build a cohesive homily. But I keep my eyes open. The first reading likely has a connection and will probably provide me with some pictures I can draw. And it may well be that the passage from the epistles gives me insight into something in the gospel. The same with preaching on one of the other readings. I develop one text as best I can and strive to find the unity in that, keeping my eyes open to the other readings for insights. The cohesiveness comes from one text, not from trying to impose an artificial unity on all three.

Making a Textual Homily Outline

In chapter 8 I suggested getting down to work by writing each verse of the text on a separate sheet and proceeding step-by-step to

---

5. William Skudlarek, *The Word in Worship* (Nashville: Abingdon, 1981) 51.

6. Ibid., 31–44.

answer certain questions about that verse; now, what do we do with all this material? How do we distill it all into a cohesive, textual homily outline?

The plan I developed has these stages:

1. Summarize each idea on one line.

2. Summarize the people's reaction(s).

3. If the people's reactions include potential hostility, find common ground.

4. Develop a one-sentence statement of purpose for this homily.

5. Develop a theme expressing the unity of the text and having identification with the people.

    A. Look for connections between the ideas on your summary sheet.

    B. Summarize the connecting ideas, one sentence for each.

    C. Look for the unifying idea.

    D. Arrange the other ideas in logical order.

    E. Develop a working outline. You may want to use one of the various formats given in the chapter on "Making Homilies Christian." Try to make the theme and its supporting points cohesive and balanced, but for the sake of disciplining yourself to keep on schedule, don't spend much time now in polishing. A better form may well come as you compose the homily and even while you rehearse it.

Summary

Text comes from the same Latin root as *textile:* the text is the warp and woof out of which we weave the homily. Some homilists have abused texts, using them only as hooks on which to hang a string of allusions. Even so, using a text still bids fair to make the homily biblical and Christian. Having a text does help the people of God in their responsibility of judging whether their prophets are true to the Word of God. Having a text benefits the homilist, because by sticking only to the text he or she still has something to preach the next time. Bringing out the local color of the text helps increase biblical literacy.

The lectionary was constructed by competent scholars. Occasionally we may disagree with their judgment as to how much or how little of a reading we may use as a homily text. But for the most part, we serve our people best and we do ourselves a favor by challenging ourselves to find the meaning and the unity of the entire text.

The second reading during a large part of the year consists of reading in series Sunday-by-Sunday from letters by the apostles, with no designed connection with the other readings. It's fruitless to impose an artificial unity on all three readings when no such harmony was intended. Yet we don't ignore what the people have heard proclaimed. We preserve the cohesiveness of the homily by preaching on only one reading, keeping our eyes open for insights from the other readings.

We construct a cohesive, textual homily outline by systematically distilling the results of our prayerful meditation and exegesis of the text.

For Further Reading

Greidanus, Sidney. *The Modern Preacher and the Ancient Text.* Grand Rapids, Mich.: William B. Eerdmans Publishing Co., 1988, 1–23.
Marshall, Paul V. *Preaching for the Church Today.* New York: Church Hymnal Corp., 1990, 71–79.
Skudlarek, William. *The Word in Worship.* Nashville: Abingdon, 1981, 31–44.

Exercises

EXERCISE 29

Using the materials you've gathered in exercises 24 and 28, develop a textual homily outline with local color on John 20:19-31.

1. Follow the procedure recommended in the latter part of this chapter.

2. Make it not preacher-centered but people-centered, with complete thoughts either stated or implied, statements you want to focus on, statements summing up what you'd like the people to take home with them.

3. Have your homily outline cover the entire text.

4. Consider the other two readings that go with this gospel in Year A: Acts 2:42-47; 1 Pet 1:3-9.

5. As you formulate your purpose, theme, and supporting points, keep in mind what you've been practicing before:

A. identifying with the people's ways;

B. identifying with their self-interest;

C. making this a Christian homily by picturing both our sinful condition and how our hope in Christ redeems us from our plight. Consider the various formats suggested in chapter 8.

TWELVE

The Message Communicated in the Preacher's Character

When I was growing up in a Lutheran congregation, the conversation en route to church frequently included the following question, "Who is going to preach this morning?" Wily Lutherans that they were, the pastoral staff never announced that beforehand. The discussion on the trip home tended to focus again on who had spoken, countered by some half-hearted admonitions that it did not matter who preached—one of the earlier rhetorical lessons in assimilating conflicting messages.[1]

Again we're up against the theological question of content and form: doesn't all preaching depend on the Holy Spirit's working through the powerful Word of God? Isn't the personality of the herald irrelevant? Don't we follow the model of John the Baptist who said of Jesus: "He must increase, but I must decrease" (John 3:30)?

Again we affirm that it does all depend on the Holy Spirit's working through the powerful Word of God. But we cannot deny that the personality of the herald is significant: John the Baptist's decreasing of self and increasing of Christ is one of the features in his character that makes him persuasive.

Paul wrote of the persuasive power in one's character:

> Because our message of the gospel came to you not in word only, but also in power and in the Holy Spirit and with full conviction; just as you know what kind of persons we proved to be among you for your sake (1 Thess 1:5).

> As you know and as God is our witness, we never came with words of flattery or with a pretext for greed; nor did we seek praise from

1. Susan K. Hedahl, "The Model Preacher: Ethos and the Early American Pulpit," *Dialog* 29 (Summer 1990) 183.

mortals, whether from you or from others, though we might have made demands as apostles of Christ. But we were gentle among you, like a nurse tenderly caring for her own children. So deeply do we care for you that we are determined to share with you not only the gospel of God but also our own selves, because you have become very dear to us (1 Thess 2:5-8).

Aristotle lists three modes of persuasion furnished by the spoken word:

1. The personal character of the speaker
2. Putting the audience into a certain frame of mind
3. The proof or the apparent proof provided by the words of the speech itself

Not only does he rank the personal character of the speaker first, he also asserts: "Persuasion is achieved by the speaker's personal character when the speech is so spoken as to make us think him credible. . . . His character may almost be called the most effective means of persuasion he possesses."[2]

We want to distinguish between character and charisma. There are speakers, including preachers, who have so much charm, so much prestige, so much charisma, they're so attractive in body and face, they have such a commanding presence (perhaps three inches taller than anyone else, with a voice that sounds like God Almighty), with everything seeming to come so easily for them, they are tempted to shun the disciplines of study and prayer. To those blessed with charisma, we say keep on thanking God for that gift and use it humbly and joyfully in his service.

That the herald's charisma may seduce both people and preacher makes it a matter of ethics. So I choose to limit the discussion of the homilist's character to the issue of the moral principles of preaching, not the preaching of ethics but the ethics of preaching.

I was surprised at all the emphasis the discipline of rhetoric places on ethics. No doubt it springs from Aristotle's insight that the speaker's character is primary in the arsenal of persuasive weaponry. The reader will have noticed that the question of ethics has been raised already in this book:

1. The ethics of appealing to self-interest

2. The ethics of not appealing to self-interest

---

2. Aristotle, *Rhetoric* 1.2, 1356a, trans. W. Rhys Roberts (New York: Modern Library, 1954) 24–25.

3. In regard to children's sermonettes, the ethics of using the children to get laughs from the congregation

4. In preaching on hard topics, the ethics of word-choice and evidence-citing: no put-downs, no loaded language, no games, no monologue

The chapter on hard topics also brought up the issue of the preacher's temptation to feel superior and the ethical and pragmatic handicaps it presents to persuasion. There are at least a few other facets we may place under our microscope: A certain pastor boasts of graduating from college with a double major magna cum laude; another who's been to the Holy Land doesn't let the people forget it; still another who knows some important people just happens to find ways to drop a big name now and then; and still another has the habit of gesturing with the index finger up and shaking it at the people. All of these give the impression, at least to some, that they are saying, "I'm better than you are."

One would think we heralds of *agape* would be protected from a lack of humility, that just the heroic example of John the Baptist would keep us decreasing ourself and increasing Christ. But there are some things built into our vocation—good things—that create the temptation to do otherwise, and those good things are that we're called to be prophets, evangelists, and priests.

Our Attitude As Prophets

Responsibility weighs heavily on those who stand watch on the walls of Zion. But therein lies the snare, to assume that we are beyond contradiction. In the chapter on hard topics, I quoted Huntington Brown: "The truth or virtue of it we are to accept without proof. . . . The choice for the addressee boils down to whether he will say 'amen' or throw bricks."[3] Perhaps you're reacting as I first did: "This man is anticlerical. After all, we can't help we're called to proclaim, 'Thus says the Lord.'"

As I've wrestled with this, I've come to see that it's my attitude that's the issue. If I'm "dumping" on the people, if I consider myself superior, the one who has the authority to scold because I'm right, then the verdict of Huntington Brown is just. But if my attitude is one of fear and trembling, if I recognize that "Thus says the Lord" applies also to me, that gives it another tone.

3. Huntington Brown, *Prose Styles: Five Primary Types* (Minneapolis: University of Minnesota Press, 1966) 71.

Herbert Farmer allows the preacher to speak with authority but also observes: *"Deus cognitus, deus nullus.* A theology that knows every mortal thing is a sham."[4] The American Catholic bishops observe: "While preachers, like other people, cannot be expected to know everything, they are easily tempted to give the impression that they do. As one perceptive critic put it, preachers in their pulpits are people who speak ten feet above contradiction."[5]

Our Attitude As Evangelists

During the 1960s I became acquainted with some writings of Harry Golden, editor of *The Carolina Israelite.* In one of his pieces he said: "I consider Billy Graham a great Christian and an eminent gentleman. He is an evangelical minister of the Gospel who never tries to evangelize me."[6]

What? Did Billy Graham forget his mission? "Go therefore and make disciples of all nations" (Matt 28:19); "You will be my witnesses" (Acts 1:8); "I am a debtor both to Greeks and barbarians, both to the wise and the foolish—hence my eagerness to proclaim the gospel" (Rom 1:14-15); "For an obligation is laid upon me, woe to me if I do not proclaim the gospel!" (1 Cor 9:16); "So we are ambassadors for Christ, since God is making his appeal through us" (2 Cor 5:20).

How did Golden get the feeling that Graham never tried to evangelize him? It's clear he didn't perceive Graham as lording it over him. (There is a temptation for evangelists to feel superior: we have the truth.) What's more, Graham understands *agape.* We know about the brat who's well-behaved temporarily because Christmas is coming. We know about the salesperson who's friendly because he or she has a house to unload. We also know about the God whom Jesus described as making "his sun rise on the evil and on the good" and sending "rain on the righteous and on the unrighteous" (Matt 5:45). We recognize that in our fervor to share the gospel we shall not negate the gospel, that in our zeal to reach out to those without Christ, we dare not look upon them as scalps to be added to our belt. Billy Graham, even while yearning for the conversion of a person like Harry Golden, could still love him without making conversion a condition of that love.

4. Herbert Farmer, *The Servant of the Word* (Philadelphia: Fortress Press, 1964) 63.

5. *Fulfilled in Your Hearing* (Washington, D.C.: The Bishops' Committee on Priestly Life and Ministry, United States Catholic Conference, 1982) 5.

6. Harry Golden, *You're Entitle'* (New York: Fawcett, 1963) 125.

What I'm looking for is how to preach *agape* so that my attitude agrees with my doctrine. It may not be easy. I could rejoice in knowing the Holy Spirit has found me and brought me to faith in Christ, and that good fortune could give me a superiority complex. Here's how Gabriel Marcel describes our dilemma:

> The Christian in fact cannot in any way think of himself as possessing either a power or even an advantage which has been denied to the unbeliever. There we have one of the most paradoxical aspects of his situation, for in another sense he is obliged to recognise that grace has been bestowed upon him. This, however, only remains true on condition that the grace should inhabit him, not only as a radiance, but as humility. From the moment that he begins to be proud of it as a possession it changes its nature, and I should be tempted to say it becomes a malediction.[7]

Grace could indeed become a malediction. That's why Redd Foxx's sister-in-law in the TV series "Sanford & Son" was so obnoxious: a Bible-toting purveyor of the truth with nothing but disgust for the benighted pagan her sister, now departed, had married. Of course, this character is a caricature. We'd like to think no Christian homilist would exhibit such an attitude. I don't know any who do, certainly not consciously. But as I examine myself, I'm afraid there have been times when I may have erred in this direction. It could have happened as I sought to win people by showing them the attractiveness of the way of Christ and then, by contrast, the ugliness of the way of Satan—in so doing, making sweeping judgments that betrayed my sense of superiority over the rascals I was condemning. We shall surely not condone sin, and we are surely "obliged to recognize that grace has been bestowed upon [us]." But in picturing the distress of those without Christ—in order to gain hearts for the gospel—we pray that God's grace will inhabit us "not only as a radiance but as humility." "There but for the grace of God go I."

I emphasize, without diluting our passion for spreading the good news, we shall not violate the gospel as we proclaim it. Even the Lord of the nations portrayed in all his majesty in the Revelation to John doesn't invade the heart by force and take it by storm; rather he says: "Listen! I am standing at the door, knocking" (Rev 3:20). Artists, catching the spirit, have painted that door with no latch on the outside, signifying that the only way Christ chooses to enter is

7. Gabriel Marcel, *Homo Viator: Introduction to a Metaphysics of Hope* (London: Victor Gollanz, 1951) 159.

when we open the door from the inside. Richard Johannesen addresses public speakers in general but his caution applies to us as evangelists: "Although the speaker in dialogue may offer advice or express disagreement, he does not aim to psychologically coerce an audience into accepting his view. The speaker's aim is one of assisting the audience in making independent, self-determined decisions."[8]

Evangelism in the pulpit? Of course. One of the New Testament words for preaching is *euangelizo*. Not trying to coerce people but making the good news accessible to them, showing how it fits their need and brings them the blessings they want.

Our Attitude As Priests

There is a tale about a Puritan colonial preacher who was against a certain women's hair style known as the "top knot." He preached on the text, "Top Knot, Go Down." Challenged to produce chapter and verse, he pointed to Mark 13:15: "Let him who is on the housetop not go down." Is this a parable of the temptation that comes to us as priests? Does our role in representing the people before God and God before the people tempt us into believing we have a special place in the kingdom, that with our preferred position we may judge the cause as being so noble that anything goes? Do we think we know what's best for our people, even to deciding the color of paint in the church's kitchen? In one denomination where there was a dispute about historical criticism, a befuddled lay person was heard to exclaim, "I don't understand what this is all about; all I know is, I love the Word of God," suggesting that this person had heard speakers oversimplifying the issue. I have been on both sides of this question. I can testify from my own experience that love for the word of God is common ground between the opponents.

The Ethics of the Homilist's *Modus Operandi*

The way we homilists operate may have ethical implications. Some tend to avoid all unpleasantness, including unpleasant issues in the pulpit. The apostle urges: "Proclaim the message; be persistent whether the time is favorable or unfavorable" (2 Tim 4:2). This book

---

8. Richard L. Johannesen, "Attitude of Speaker toward Audience: A Significant Concept for Contemporary Rhetorical Theory and Criticism," *Central States Speech Journal* 25/2 (Summer 1974) 96.

offers a strategy for coping with hard topics, equipping us at least partially to "carry out [our] ministry fully" (2 Tim 4:5).

Sometimes homilists fear that homily feedback could be unpleasant, and so they avoid it—or if they get it anyway, they don't listen. This is related to the attitude of feeling superior, "ten feet above contradiction."

Some homilists avoid getting down to work in preparing to preach, letting everything else take precedence and trusting the Holy Spirit to make up the lack. My father's pastor-friends had a joke about a preacher who boasted of his reliance on the Holy Spirit: he could climb into the pulpit at any time, bow his head praying to be filled with the Holy Spirit's wisdom and eloquence, and then preach with no sweat, relying on what the Holy Spirit told him. The last time he tried this, the Holy Spirit told him, "Fritz, you've been lazy."

I suspect that some homilists procrastinate in their preparation because they don't get much joy from preaching. That may have something to do with their training (or lack of it). It may have had a discouraging form: "You struggle as best you can in finding something to say; you wrestle as best you can with how to say it; you stand up in class and preach as best you can—and we'll tell you what was wrong with it." I do hesitate to pass judgment on those who put off homily preparation because of this. If anyone reading this is afflicted with the disease of procrastination, I have two recommendations: If you're taking a course where this book is the textbook, and if you've been following the step-by-step learning process (or some other successful system), you probably have already experienced some success; you may need to review the part about discipline in chapter 8. If you're not taking a homiletics course, perhaps you can find a weeklong preaching workshop that will give you confidence, thus allowing you joy in your preaching, helping you to look forward to getting down to work.

The Apostle laid out our *modus operandi:* "Do your best to present yourself to God as one approved by him, a worker who has no need to be ashamed, rightly explaining the word of truth" (2 Tim 2:15).

A participant at one of my preaching workshops brought up the ethics of pastors who lead their congregations out of their denomination. It's possible they see themselves as modern-day "voices in the wilderness" standing firmly for the truth. It may also be they have fallen into the traps described in our discussion of the ethics of preaching on hard topics, especially stacking the deck, oversimplifying the issues.

What about Plagiarism in the Pulpit?

One of the issues in the way we homilists operate is how we use or misuse the homilies of others.

I remember reading somewhere about a person greeting the preacher at the door of the church by saying, "I have a book at home that has every word of your sermon in it, and I'll mail it to you this week." We can understand the preacher's relief when the book turned out to be a dictionary.

I have heard pastors whose sermons have been published tell of times when they've been invited to preach in another pulpit, and having sent their title and text in advance, the local pastor on the telephone has pleaded, "Don't preach that sermon here." When asked why not, the pastor hemmed and hawed and finally confessed, "Because I've already preached it here."

I know of a church that had guest preachers on successive Sundays, and on the second week there was an audible gasp when the homilist used exactly the same illustration the first homilist had used the week before. To make it worse, both pastors claimed the story as a personal experience.

A fellow pastor observed it would be a shrewd marketing strategy if publishers would bind their sermon collections so they looked like Bibles. That way, he said, we preachers could take the sermon books directly into the pulpit, sparing us the trouble of copying our messages.

I remember the bittersweet feeling I had when a pastor complimented me on a published sermon of mine. "It was great. It was easy to preach. My people liked it too." I said, "Thank you." I couldn't resist asking, "Did you give me credit?"

He could have quoted Kipling in his defense:

> When 'Omer smote 'is blooming lyre,
> He'd 'eard men sing by land and sea;
> An' what he thought he might require,
> 'E went and took—the same as we![9]

I can't pretend to have questions about plagiarism because I have such a noble character. It's rather by providential accident. When I was reading C. S. Lewis and Bonhoeffer for the first time, there came into our congregation a young Ph.D. in mathematics

9. Rudyard Kipling, "When 'Omer Smote 'is Bloomin' Lyre," *Parodies: An Anthology from Chaucer to Beerbohm and After,* ed. Dwight Macdonald (New York: Random House, 1960) 491.

who was also reading C. S. Lewis and Bonhoeffer. Before long he offered to teach a high school class. Wouldn't you know it, it turned out to be a course on C. S. Lewis and Bonhoeffer. With three high schoolers sitting around our Sunday dinner table, it would have been folly for me to have taken from these men and not have acknowledged them. So I quoted them directly, usually taking the book into the pulpit. I had the sensation it gave more credibility to my own material when I freely admitted these few lines were from someone else.

Having had my consciousness raised, I began to wonder how to handle material I wasn't quoting but using in paraphrase. In my papers in college, seminary, and graduate school, I acknowledged such help in footnotes. Shouldn't I show the same honesty in my preaching? I found it was possible and that it did not diminish my credibility but enhanced it. I can illustrate from a homily in print on the Beatitudes. It's for All Saints' Sunday and is entitled, "Is the Gospel for Women Only?" I'm quoting myself just after the introduction:

> I got some help for this sermon from an article, "Is the Religion of Jesus Effeminate?" It's in a book called *Jesus and Ourselves*, by Dr. Leslie Weatherhead, a prominent Methodist preacher, pastor of City Temple in London starting in 1936. He points out that Christianity is a woman's religion. That will be my first point: Christianity is a woman's religion. He's glad about it, and so am I.[10]

Should we acknowledge our sources? I think so. But this can be carried to a fault. There may be preachers who read a lot and cite every author, so that their messages are one quotation after another. I like their honesty, but I'd rather not preach that way. And which sources should we mention? Do we give an oral bibliography including Nestle's Greek text? There's a stylistic problem of clutter (and name-dropping, at least in appearance). Common good sense will tell us when we should cite our sources and when it would be pointless. We all know that reading other people's writings helps us be creative. Their words spark new thoughts in our heads. It's like hitchhiking in the brainstorming process; it started with something else but now it's our own invention. So why litter the landscape with a profusion of unnecessary oral footnotes?

Then there's the matter of borrowing from others when we're out of time. Preaching from weekend to weekend is hard enough, but then there are Christmas and Easter, Advent and Lent. I marvel at the incredible schedule of preaching that Roman Catholic priests

---

10. Alvin C. Rueter, *The Freedom to be Wrong* (Lima, Ohio: CSS Publishing, 1985) 46.

have with their daily Masses, not even counting the additional homilies each week for baptisms, weddings, and funerals. The people in the pews probably have small appreciation of the effort required. Doesn't the exigency excuse us from the ordinary rules of honesty as we serve the Lord so diligently?

When we're caught like this and the only way out is to use someone else's homily, why not just take the book into the pulpit, acknowledge whose work it is, and read it? I have done that. There would always be a good number of people who gave me positive feedback. Not that it didn't take time; I rehearsed the reading out loud several times.

Using Other People's Experiences without Permission?

"Let me tell you about a person who came to see me in my office last week." The homilist senses a rising tide of attention and notices that the coughing subsides.

Attentiveness grows when the homilist reaches into a treasury of real-life incidents and then pictures the blessings of living forgiven in stories that actually happened. Contrary to what some seem to think, pastors and deacons are not necessarily hothouse creatures. Not uncommonly do we see life at its worst and not infrequently do we get to witness gospel victories. So we feel impelled to let the world know. With all this in favor of revealing what goes on in our pastoral dealings with people, what's the problem?

Let's put ourselves into the skins of the people. Some are hurting. We say, "Why don't they come and see us for counseling?" They're saying, "Yes, and then become the subject matter of another juicy sermon illustration?" We could counter, "Of course I never reveal anything that goes on in my present parish." Or, "You must understand that I'm serving an area where no one knows anyone." The people are still objecting, "Whether now or twenty years from now, whether people know me or not, I still don't want my secret life blabbed about in public. So I don't trust you as a pastor."

Some Protestant preachers and Roman Catholic permanent deacons mine a lode of illustrations from their family life. Some Roman Catholic priests may tell stories about their nieces and nephews. The people are usually delighted to hear of the antics of the baby and the toddler. I find no fault with that. But the toddler soon becomes acquainted with the language and aware of the self. What then? We might explain, "Well, I only report the good things my child does." But don't "preacher's kids" have enough to contend with already? Why embarrass them by holding them up as exemplars of our life in Christ?

What to do? We want to publish the gospel. From personal observation we have evidence of its life-changing power. When we're scrambling for ways to picture step 4 in the Motivated Sequence—showing the blessings of living forgiven—shall we be denied this resource?

Not altogether. When the good Lord has brought solace or reconciliation or freedom, the person or couple or family may be willing to celebrate that victory in the communion of saints. Why not ask permission to share it? If given, we explain to the congregation that we relate the story only with the consent of the people involved. It should be made clear that even if it would pertain to a previous parish, we still won't tell the experience without leave. And if a story of a family member begs to be told, it too must contain an acknowledgment of permission. If the owners to the testimony to God's grace are agreeable, the likelihood is strong that it will be a memorable celebration.

There's another kind of privacy I think should be respected. I'm thinking here of the little things that go on in daily life: not in the realm of the confessional but just ordinary things that—if related in a homily—would make the participants uneasy.

I recall one summer afternoon when I came to a house and saw the father in the backyard with his son repairing a bicycle. They were facing the other way and didn't notice me at first. It was obvious the son was all thumbs. It was a pleasure to observe how patient the father was with the lad. I saw this as a gospel victory. He could have berated the boy for being so clumsy, but instead the same justification by grace through faith that was covering all the father's mistakes was empowering him to tolerate his son's awkwardness.

It was a perfect homily illustration of the benefits of living forgiven. But I couldn't use it as it was. Not then anyway. If I were the father's pastor when he dies, I'd be free to tell it at his funeral as a testimony to the grace of God in his life. (Even then I'd probably want to ask the son's permission.) But until then, to report it in public even without mentioning names would embarrass both father and son: the father for being singled out for saintliness and the son for being shown up for ineptness.

But what if I used this scene for the plot of another story? I could transfer the action to the kitchen. I could say, "Let's imagine a thirteen-year-old boy moving the dishes from the dishwasher to the cupboard. Let's say he accidentally breaks a dish from a set, one that can't be replaced." Then I could invent a parent who'd react, perhaps first with anger and then with forgiveness. It would be true to our life in Christ but not associated with any particular household. It came from the private lives of two people and yet wouldn't violate their privacy.

Perhaps you don't agree with all of this. If the good Lord would only give us a twentieth-century Moses and visit him or her on some convenient mountain, we could have a sure set of guidelines. I welcome your reactions.

Summary

Thinking about the message in the preacher's character raises again the theological issue of content and form, whether the art of homiletics tends to deny the effectiveness of the Holy Spirit's working through the Word of God: isn't the *who* of the herald irrelevant? Don't we follow the model of John the Baptist: "He [Jesus] must increase but I must decrease?" (John 3:30).

In contrast to those preachers who are seduced by their charisma to rely on charm instead of substance, John the Baptist's decreasing of self is one of the persuasive features of his personality. The way we use charisma, a gift from God, is a question of ethics.

The apostle Paul backed up his claims by appealing to the people's perception of his credibility.

Aristotle—three hundred years before Christ—observed that a speaker's character is the "most effective means of persuasion he possesses."

This book has already discussed some factors of the homilist's ethics in previous chapters: the ethics of appealing to self-interest and the ethics of not appealing to it; the ethics in children's sermonettes in Protestant churches of using children for laughs, manipulating them to spout preposterous answers for the amusement of their elders; and in preaching on hard topics, the ethics of word choice and citing of evidence.

In this chapter we have reflected on other aspects of the ethics of preaching, how our good roles as prophets, evangelists, and priests may lure us away from humility. Even though we speak in the name of the Father, Son, and Holy Spirit, we make sure to speak that word first to ourselves, giving our homilies a different tone than that of sergeants barking at recruits. We keep praying God to preserve us from an attitude of feeling superior, from an attitude that regards our people as objects instead of persons, from an attitude that says our cause is so noble, anything goes.

Our aim is that our character will proclaim a message consistent with the gospel. Our aim is to grow in the likeness of Christ, not violating people but aching for them: "Jerusalem, Jerusalem, the city that kills the prophets and stones those who are sent to it! How often have I desired to gather your children together as a hen gathers her brood under her wings, and you were not willing!" (Luke 13:34).

For Further Reading

Halvorson, Arndt L. *Authentic Preaching*. Minneapolis: Augsburg Publishing House, 1982, 11–30.
McLaughlin, Raymond W. *The Ethics of Persuasive Preaching*. Grand Rapids, Mich.: Baker House, 1979.
Skudlarek, William F. "The Ethics of Preaching," in *Ethical Issues in the Practice of Ministry*, ed. Jane A. Boyajian, 38–43. Minneapolis: United Theological Seminary of the Twin Cities, 1984.

Exercises

EXERCISE 30

Using the outline you developed in exercise 28, write a full-length homily on John 20:19-31. Try this procedure:

1. Convert the high-level abstractions in your homily outline into scenes that could be shot with a TV camera, using your skills gained from chapter 6.

2. Write for the ear, using your skills gained from chapter 7.

3. Pray about your attitude: are you talking top-down, or are you dialogical—a forgiven sinner bringing hope to fellow-forgiven sinners?

THIRTEEN

Nonverbal Preaching

When my wife-to-be was in college, she sometimes went to visit her sister on weekends. One time the Sunday was Sexagesima (according to the historic Church calendar, part of a three-Sunday shifting of mood from Epiphany to Lent). The pastor of her sister's church had a problem with the *s* sound. He whistled it. Since he was hard of hearing, he whistled it louder than other whistlers whistle. When he announced the readings for Sexagesima Sunday, Beulah giggled so much she had to leave.

I hesitate to write on this. (Because of what my wife would have thought of the opening paragraph? No; I mentioned this in a column in 1988, and she gave me permission for that.)[1] But because of what I discussed in chapter 2, that it may tend to confirm an opinion some have that homiletics deals only with the trimmings of theology, not the essentials, that homileticians may be all right, but remedial English teachers could do the job just as well. I am including this chapter on nonverbal preaching because it follows naturally after a discussion on the message communicated by the homilist's character. If what we are is so relevant to what we say, then our nonverbal preaching also wants to be consistent with our character and our content.

I still remember the impact of an experience I had with my first class of homiletics students at St. John's University, after they had all preached their first homily in a parish. We had worked together as a class on the gospel for the day. They had also turned in a paper exegeting the text. We struggled together in class on how to structure their homilies. The week before they preached they gave oral

1. Alvin C. Rueter, "People-Centered Preaching," *Emphasis* (August 1988) 5–6.

progress reports. They rehearsed their homilies with a partner from the class who gave me a written critique. They supplied me with a final outline. So I had an idea of the content of their homilies and the sense that the content was good—in some cases even excellent. What was the feedback from the parishioners and pastors? Commendatory. What did these good folks usually remark on in their critiques? The content, as I'd hoped? No. They noted the student's "presence"; the voice; the eye contact; the freedom of the gestures. I'm glad they did well in delivery, but for heaven's sake, that wasn't the main thing I was teaching them! Yet the people's reaction only confirms how impressive nonverbal preaching is, and how it can work against us if it's badly done.

It's frustrating, after all the years we've put into theology and all the hours we've poured into praying and exegeting the text, that the two-edged sword of the Word of God may be blunted by seemingly irrelevant matters. My sister-in-law's pastor couldn't help he was hard of hearing, and he didn't realize he had a whistling problem. His people understood that. But if we have the capacity to overcome the trifles that threaten to undo our message, then by all means we want to try. Nonverbal preaching may not rank with Christology, ecclesiology, and eschatology, but it would be too bad if these grand themes were drowned out by the static caused by our ineptness. We take Paul's outlook as our own: "We are putting no obstacle in anyone's way, so that no fault may be found with our ministry" (2 Cor 6:3).

Eye Contact

"We have several pastors and rarely do they in worship ever look at the congregation. They are always reading to us—even announcements. . . . [They] hardly ever look up at us and when they do look out at us it is only briefly." This is an excerpt from the letter I mentioned in chapter 7, "Making Homilies Oral." It's by a layperson who had read a notice about my preaching workshops. He loves his pastors and appreciates the content of their homilies: "What they say is great and correct—*it's the method!*" I gather he feels strongly about this; his handwritten letter is nine pages long. He was hoping to influence me to press his case with my students, my peers in the ministry, and my colleagues in seminaries. He permitted me to quote him, although he didn't give his name and address. He has a B.A. and a four-year graduate degree, but he's so hungry for a word that seems more like it's coming from his pastors' hearts that "even if they made an error in the use of English, I'd love it!"

My anonymous correspondent is distressed because his pastors rarely look him in the eye, and when they do, it's only briefly. What's his problem? Doesn't he talk on the telephone and listen to the radio? Without eye contact? And he mentions his pastors (plural), which seems to imply his church building must not be small. So let him sit in the back. When preachers are that far away, you can't tell if they're looking at you or not, can you?

Yet why do TV news anchors close by saying, "We'll see you tomorrow?" I say under my breath, "No, you won't; you can't see us at all." The stock in trade for news anchors is credibility, just as with us preachers and all others who address the public. Quoting again from Aristotle: "It is not true, as some writers assume in their treatises on rhetoric, that the personal goodness revealed by the speaker contributes nothing to his power of persuasion; on the contrary, his character may almost be called the most effective means of persuasion he possesses."[2] And our eyes are a large factor in how people perceive our character. We may not trust people who don't look at us. If we suspect a child is embroidering on the truth, we may say, "Look me in the eye and say that." So when news anchors tell us, "We'll see you tomorrow," it's no trivial thing; they need to have us believe them.

Well then, what about the forms of communication that don't permit us to look into the soul through the windows of the eyes? In those cases we go with what we have. On the telephone, it's the voice: "You sound stronger today than yesterday; you must be getting better." On the printed page, it's the tone: "I can identify with this writer; she understands how I feel."

But if the author is right there in the room with us, we want the whole person and we crave the eyes. They are always looking above us. What's up there? Am I missing something? They always have the head down. Are they preoccupied, aloof? They do look up quite often but only at two spots. I'm sitting somewhere else; don't I count? Or if I'm one of the targets, why all the attention to me? What have I done wrong? They keep panning the entire nave, back and forth, a steady rhythm. Are they afraid to look at anyone in depth?

What's going on here is empathy. When the preacher has trouble with eye contact, we feel uncomfortable because it seems that he or she isn't comfortable with us. So it doesn't make any difference how large the sanctuary is; the people in the back pew of the

---

2. Aristotle, *Rhetoric* 1.2, 1356a, trans. W. Rhys Roberts (New York: Modern Library, 1954) 24–25.

rear balcony can still feel whether the pastor is at ease with them or not.

I wish I had the name and address of my correspondent so I could tell him I push my students to preach without notes (which ought to facilitate eye contact but doesn't necessarily; more about this in chapter 15.) I bring this up because of the experience of one of my students (and I tell this only with his permission). He went blank every time in the three-minute exercises without notes. At the end of the term, he–like the rest of the class–was required to produce a complete homily in manuscript. His was a delight: evangelical, textual, visual, oral, cohesive. My written comment: "Wow!" He was doing it all: identifying his proposal with our legitimate self-interest; using oral language with no complicated, zig-zag sentences; showing the benefits of living forgiven; building it all in a way he could see it and ordering it all in a way we could remember it. I asked him privately to get ready to read it in class the first day of the second semester. It was exciting. He was in every word, and so were we. Our tables in that classroom were in a horseshoe pattern, but he kept everyone in his line of sight, including those of us at right angles to him. (One author claims that even with a manuscript, we should have eye contact at least 85 percent of the time;[3] my student was doing that.) I asked his classmates if they'd had any difficulty attending to him. Not a bit. A manuscript homily, yet it was an oral event. It was oral when I'd read it silently in my office. The preacher had been communing with his people all during his preparation and was still doing so as he brought it to us face-to-face. The eye contact had begun in his study.

That's why eye contact is vital. It testifies to our empathy with the people who are right there under the same roof. There's a reciprocal empathy in them. Their antennae can sense whether we're tuned in with them or not. A large part of their sensing antennae is in their eyes–and they look for our corresponding awareness of them in our eyes. That's how I interpret my correspondent's hunger for a word that comes from his pastors' hearts, so much so that "even if they made a mistake in the use of English, I'd love it."

Body Language

If you get to visit other churches, you may see a preacher here and there gripping the pulpit with both hands and never moving.

3. Jo Sprague and Douglas Stuart, *The Speaker's Handbook*, 2d ed. (San Diego: Harcourt Brace Jovanovich, 1988) 266.

The pulpit rail is a convenient place to park the hands; what could be more natural than that? Perhaps that's true; but hanging on for dear life? You may see another pastor again and again shoving the glasses back into place. Why not? If the glasses slide down, shouldn't they go up again? Another homilist may be adjusting the glasses even if they're not sliding down.

Why should anyone quibble about such little things? Isn't the Liturgy of Word and Eucharist paramount? Yet trifles though they be, they're not insignificant. Like others, I work at listening, but I can't help being distracted by these nonverbal messages. Why is the preacher immobile and rigid? Or the opposite: why is the homilist in perpetual motion—swinging the arms, hunching the shoulders, swaying back and forth, shifting the body weight from one leg to the other? Why doesn't the preacher go to the optician and get those spectacles adjusted? Or if the glasses aren't sliding, what does the gesture of adjusting them mean? Or why is there so much smacking of lips? Bothersome body language, a molehill when compared to our privilege of sharing the gospel, can become a mountain in the eyes of some people, shutting off the vistas God's Word could show them.

Since having one's message done in by seeming insignificant factors is just as annoying to other public speakers, rhetoricians have been examining *kinesics:* the study of body motion and its role in communication. Translating what they've discovered into the language of homiletics, we can say a number of things about how movement affects the congregation's reaction to preaching.

> 1. Whether we homilists look at the lector who is proclaiming the Word or instead take the opportunity to smile at someone in the pew, we're sending a message.

> 2. How we walk to the pulpit communicates an attitude: are we hesitant? Or cocky? Shouldn't our walk rather signify that we're both alert and relaxed, that we have a Word from the Lord we're eager to bring?

> 3. Although a moving stimulus (like a children's choir getting ready to sing) draws attention away from a nonmoving stimulus (like a reader at the lectern), this doesn't sanction random motion. Using the same gesture repeatedly—scratching an ear, drumming the fingers, fingering the cross around our neck, playing with the notes—undoes the impact of all our hard work of preparation.

Why do we let this happen? I'm guessing it's because we may be losing our concentration. As I also remarked on page 10, the good golfer preparing to putt doesn't let the chirping of a squirrel get in the way of the challenge at hand.

Continuing with what kinesics can tell us about preaching:

> 4. Purposeful movement brings physical relief both to us and the good folks before us. It helps because our muscles can't stay in one position too long without tiring. We knew this before we heard it from the kinesics scholars. But I didn't know about recent studies that seem to show that purposeful movement by the speaker relaxes our hearers. We don't need specialists to tell us that when people are bunched in the benches, they get tired from being restricted. But it was news to me that through empathy—feeling what they're observing—people penned in the pews can have a change of muscle tension; that is, when we homilists have purposeful movement, the people subconsciously sense the tensing and relaxing of our muscles, and they participate in that with us.
>
> It also takes no scholarly research to know that random activity distracts and sends the message that the homilist is uneasy. But the kinesics scholars show us another reason why perpetual motion is stultifying: through empathy the preacher's continual swinging and swaying never gives the people's muscles a chance to relax.
>
> 5. Purposeful movement also helps us focus on the main ideas. If we were speaking on a platform, we could pause at the conclusion of one point and then move to another position on the dais before beginning the next point. The pulpit and perhaps also the microphone circumscribe that sort of activity somewhat. We can still pause at a transition, turn our attention to another part of the congregation, and begin the next part.

In my college classes in public speaking, I asked my students to lecture on certain chapters of the textbook, to acquaint them further with communications theory, to give them more practice lowering the levels of abstraction, and to provide another occasion to speak before a group. One student had some experience as a mime. It happened that the pages assigned to her group included body language. It was exciting to see how many moods she could convey without saying a word. The British poet Ben Jonson wrote, "Drink to me only with thine eyes, and I will pledge with mine." That's again about eye contact, but when he read that first to his love, I suspect every muscle in his body was aquiver.

The Tone of Voice

Somewhere I remember reading about the efforts of Mark Twain's wife to clean up her husband's language. One day she began using all his curse words, apparently to echo back to him how unpleasant and disgusting he was making himself sound. After listening to her a while, Twain observed, "You know the words, but you don't know the music."

If people have a subliminal sense of who we are and how we feel about them from our eyes and body language, they also read our tone of voice. If we have the words right but the music wrong, they hear it.

Suppose it's Ash Wednesday, and the homilist is taking the role of Joel and working with the first reading: "Yet even now, says the Lord, return to me with all your heart, with fasting, with weeping, and with mourning; rend your hearts and not your clothing" (Joel 2:12-13a). Just for fun, try reading that aloud in the manner of Sergeant Snorkel barking at Beetle Bailey. See how the tone of voice contradicts the prophet?

Suppose the ushers have returned to the altar, and the minister is saying:

```
                        receive
            as we                   the Sunday
     And now                              offering
                        bow
         all                       our heads
      let us                            in prayer.
                  in heaven,
         who art                  Hallowed be
  Our Father,                          thy name.
```

The words are right; the melody is wrong. What conclusion might the receiver draw from the nonverbal message? "You're stuffy"; "You're not thinking about what you're saying."

Some newscasters, even on national networks, may do something similar:

> And now for the evening *news.*
> We turn first to our nation's *capital.*
> Congress gave another blow to the *president.*

What reaction might there be to the nonverbal messages riding on the notes of this speech melody? "You're sincere, but you're trying too hard"; "You irritate me."

Suppose the homilist has no melody at all. All on the same note. All at the same rate. All with the same volume. How are the people likely to respond? "When do you ever catch your breath?"; "Please don't wake me till it's over."

I concede there's a benefit to a speech pattern; it has to do with the oral tradition out of which much of our Scriptures have come. How useful it was when we were memorizing poetry as school children to do it in singsong:

> Listen my children, and you shall *hear*
> Of the midnight ride of Paul Re*vere*

Just so, it must have been useful in the Hebrew oral culture for Jesus to shape his words into a rhythm that could charm its way into the minds of the people and help it stick:

> *Blessed* are the *poor* in *spirit,*
> for *theirs* is the *kingdom* of *heaven.*
> *Blessed* are *those* who *mourn,*
> for *they* shall be *comforted.*
> *Blessed* are the *meek,*
> for *they* shall *inherit* the *earth.*

We recognize the value of such a pattern in facilitating oral tradition, but we'd probably do our people a disservice if we read the Sermon on the Mount in a singsong fashion. So how do we improve our tone of voice? How do we make emotional color and speech melody attractive without being noticeable?

We feel ourselves into it. When reading something like the Beatitudes, we study the text, meditate on it, pray about it, and then note which ideas are key. We stress those words even if they're not on the beat, and especially if they're not on the beat. The following may not be how you'd do it, but it's one possibility:

> Blessed are the *poor* in spirit,
> for theirs is the kingdom of *heaven.*
> Blessed are those who *mourn,*
> for they shall be *comforted.*
> *Blessed* are the meek,
> for they *shall* inherit the earth.

In the first two, I've tried to show contrasts: *poor-heaven; mourn-comforted*. With the third, I'm taking the view that we often doubt the meek will accomplish anything, so I'll stress that they *are* blessed and that they *shall* inherit the earth.

When we're leading the congregation in prayer, the same policy applies. As Benedict advises his monks in praying the psalms, we take care that the mind is in harmony with the voice.[4]

It's the same when we're preaching: we feel ourselves into it. We're not caught in the trap of trying to be perfect, every word exact and correct, because then there's a chance we'll be communing with the paper (even when the paper isn't there). We're in rapport with the people, we're speaking in oral style, and we sound like normal human beings.

Summary

The subject of this chapter is what some rhetoricians call paralinguistics, the message that goes along with the message—indeed sometimes drowning out the message. Through empathy people read our eyes, posture, gestures, and voice to judge how we feel about them and how we feel about ourselves. It's exasperating, after all the years we've spent in studying theology and after all the work we've put into exegeting the text and then shaping our message into proper form, that our people get diverted by some mannerism, not even hearing the good things we've been saying. I've come to believe that nonverbal preaching is not immaterial: it makes a difference in our ability to communicate effectively, and it has theological significance as we seek to *be* the gospel even as we say the gospel.

Paul said the following in a different context; can we apply it also to our mission as homilists? "We are putting no obstacle in anyone's way, so that no fault may be found with our ministry" (2 Cor 6:3).

For Further Reading

Bradley, Bert E. *Fundamentals of Speech Communication: The Credibility of Ideas*. 6th ed. Dubuque, Iowa: Wm. C. Brown Publishers, 1991, 223–45.

Dahnke, Gordon L., and Glenn W. Clatterbuck. *Human Communication: Theory and Research*. Belmont, Calif.: Wadsworth Publishing Co., 1990, 50–69.

4. *Rule for Monasteries,* 19, cited in William Skudlarek, *The Word in Worship* (Nashville: Abingdon, 1981) 101.

FOURTEEN

Preaching at Funerals and Weddings

When I was in college, I had a professor of English who expanded the horizons of each course to include whatever he wanted to talk about. One day it came to him that even though only two of us in the room were preseminary, he should comment on the practice of preaching at weddings. "Don't do it," he said. "The couple is so smitten they won't hear you anyway; it's a waste of breath."

It made sense to me then. So for several years in the ministry, I never gave a homily at weddings. I saw that the rite in our previous *Service Book and Hymnal* was not forceful in promoting the idea; after mentioning the possibility of singing a hymn and chanting a psalm came the statement, "If there be an Address, it may then follow." The present *Lutheran Book of Worship* also is permissive: "An address may follow."

I had the honor of assisting at my grandson's wedding. His bride's church is of another Protestant denomination. The wedding was reverent and memorable, but there was no homily.

As for preaching at funerals, I've heard substantially the same argument: "The family isn't able to hear preaching; better to read Scripture and poetry and offer prayers and be done with it." Our former service book was noncommittal: "Then may follow a sermon." The present *Lutheran Book of Worship* offers no choice: "The sermon follows the reading of the Gospel."

What do you do when the funeral director calls to ask, "I have a family here without a pastor. Will you please help us?" Isn't it fair to say, "I don't know them; how can I preach to them? Shouldn't they be satisfied if I limit myself to readings and prayers?"

In times past Roman Catholic priests could offer the Mass without preaching. Now they give homilies at every Eucharistic celebration–

which means they always preach at weddings and funerals. Roman Catholic deacons also often preach at weddings and wakes.

So there are two minds about preaching at weddings and funerals, and I've had both of them. I've slowly come to the conviction that we should preach every time, in spite of the fact that some of those present may not be in prime condition for hearing the Word.

Why did I change my mind? For one thing, years ago people sometimes asked for typescripts of the service so they could go over it again. In recent years people have requested audio or video recordings. If they weren't receptive at the time, they might well be so later.

Again, at funerals and weddings I've usually seen people in the pews who rarely go to church at any other occasion. God willing, even if the principals were unable to hear, surely his Word might find root in the hearts of at least some of those strangers.

Then I began to understand that it wasn't true in every case that the ones immediately involved weren't receptive. In the marriage preparation work, we'd either begun or strengthened our relationship. In planning together, the couple may have sensed some feeling of ownership as they considered the question, "What do you want your wedding to say to the people who come?" That may well have helped them to listen. In the case of a bereavement, there had usually been numerous pastoral calls during the illness that led to that death, and so the family and I rarely had any trouble being in rapport at the funeral.

But what about funerals for people we don't know? If the pastoral relationship is crucial, shouldn't we omit the homily for them? Can it possibly do any good?

I want to arrive at my answer in a roundabout way. When I was young in the ministry, a mortician undertook to educate me on how pastors should conduct themselves at funerals. Among other things he was "death" on obituaries. He had logic to back him up: "The obituary has been in the papers. The people in front of you know the dead person better than you do. The obituary is a relic of the past and a waste of time." For a while I heeded his counsel. But something was amiss. These funerals were impersonal.

I would always try to get acquainted with the mourners beforehand, but too many times it was awkward. Perhaps other pastors don't have my problem, but I've found that some who have dropped out of church are embarrassed talking with clergy. As I tried to figure out how to help these mourners be more at ease with this "holy" stranger, I began asking, "Would you please answer a few questions to help me write the obituary?" It gave me a structure for a pastoral conversation. I'd start by asking the date and place of birth. Then the church of the dear one's baptism and confirmation. Then about schooling, marriage, children, other mourners. Was he or she sick for a long time? Each of these questions gave the mourners an opportunity to open up, giving me insight into the lives of both the deceased and the bereaved. In the language of communication theory, I was doing audience analysis. Even though the circumstances dictated only minimal time together before the service, I was still able to build a measure of relationship that made it easier to establish rapport in the funeral. Reading the obituary in itself helped make it more personal, and the interview process also aided me in finding connections with the mourners in the readings and the homily.

What Do We Say in Funeral Homilies?

I remember a funeral for a man who found me hard to appreciate. First we had a service in our church. Then we had another one forty miles away, where he had grown up and where he would be buried. This allowed acquaintances in each neighborhood to attend, but since the family and some of the friends would be at both places, I felt I should prepare two funerals. It didn't help that it was a hot and dusty day. I'm afraid my exasperation showed. A few days later, the man's daughter came to see me. She was bitter: "No feelings. So impersonal." She was right. I'll never forget that encounter.

BE CHARITABLE

Why couldn't I have followed the model of Paul? In his First Letter to the Corinthians, he addressed people who were splitting the Church, who were practicing immorality, who were making a shambles of the Eucharist, who were attacking his authority as an apostle. Here's how he greeted them: "I give thanks to my God always for you because of the grace of God that has been given you in Christ Jesus . . . so that you are not lacking in any spiritual gift" (1 Cor 1:4, 7). If Paul could thank God for the grace given to these rascals, then I could have done the same for this man who'd given me some grief. That has led me to the first principle I've developed in what to say at funerals: be charitable.

BE TRUE TO YOUR THEOLOGY

If the funeral is not the time to shake the finger, it's also not the time to forget your theology. How do nonuniversalists handle the funeral homily for a person whose life bore no visible fruits of faith in

Christ? You may be a universalist; then this issue is irrelevant to you. You and other respectable theologians argue from the standpoint of grace that God's unmerited love encompasses all. My problem is that I see a God so gracious he won't force himself on anyone; he stands at the door and knocks, waiting for the person to open from the inside. I see a God so gracious that if someone doesn't want him now, he won't compel that person to live with him forever. I see Christ the King separating the sheep from the goats and saying to those who had not recognized him in "the least of these," "Depart from me . . . ."

So in trying to be both charitable and true to my theology, I turn my attention to the mourners, putting their dear one in the best possible light, speaking to their loss, commending them to the Comforter.

BE BIBLICAL

Related to being faithful to our understanding of Christian doctrine is that in our funeral preaching we want to be biblical. That is, we don't say things the Scriptures don't say, such as: "This accident was the will of God." It's true the Creator has ordained that two things can't be in the same place at the same time. But we can't infer that it was his will that this car and this bicycle should have collided and killed this youngster. It is biblical however to promise that God will make good come out of this evil. We can't predict what that good thing will be, but we can assure ourselves that "all things work together for good for those who love God" (Rom 8:28).

Neither can we say, "This illness was the will of God." Why did Jesus go around healing people? Why do we hope for the ultimate healing of our bodies in the resurrection?

Nor shall we say, "You shouldn't cry; you should rejoice." A well-meaning student giving a funeral sermon in class admonished us not to sorrow. I told him I felt like punching him in the mouth, that I was still grieving for my seven-year-old daughter. The Bible counsels, "Weep with those who weep."

Richard Rutherford has an insightful comment:

> It is unfortunate when presiders at funeral liturgies confuse paschal joy with joviality, whereby the secular mood of denying faith influences liturgical expression of a faith that takes death seriously. Christians rejoice in faith because a dead person enters a new form of union with God, a subtle part of the mystery of death. Christian joy, which accepts death in faith, cannot deny grief. Like other people, Christians grieve not because of what they believe has hap-

pened to the deceased but because they have lost a loved one. Injustice is done to the bereaved when the *Ordo,* which offers so much by way of Christian support and hope, is misused as an attempt, however unconsciously, to cover up grief and the reality of death with saccharine eulogies, canned music, and sentimental rhetoric. . . . By deepening their own paschal faith and accepting their own mortality, presiders at funeral liturgy must realize the duty to attend to the spiritual needs of the faithful while respecting the reality of loss and bereavement.[1]

SHOW EMPATHY

Morticians may deal with several mourning families every week; they can't afford to spend the emotional energy to get involved with all that grief, so they must be professional. Clergy want to be professional also, but I've come to believe we could go too far with it. Since Paul does allow us to "weep with those who weep," and since Jesus wept at the tomb of Lazarus, I don't see why we can't let our feelings show. A good many of those we bury were dear to us. We loved them, and they loved us. There have been times when I've had to stop and do a little crying before I could go on. I've never apologized for that.

SHOW THE BLESSINGS OF LIVING FORGIVEN

What about eulogies? It's not in my tradition to give them because even in a funeral chapel, my heritage sees our function as leading in worship, focusing on the grace of God. Out-and-out eulogies seem to be out of place. But to highlight how God's grace manifested itself in the life of the departed is different. In chapter 8, "Making Homilies Christian," I advocate the policy of showing the benefits of living forgiven: that is, after declaring that the gospel meets our need and before issuing the challenge to follow Christ more faithfully, reflecting on the blessings of our life in Christ. The funeral homily offers a special opportunity for picturing those benefits. At a memorial service for someone in whom God's grace has borne visible fruit, what could be more natural than to describe that fruit? The Revelation to John almost invites that kind of funeral homily: "And I heard a voice from heaven saying, 'Write this: Blessed are the dead who from now on die in the Lord.' 'Yes,' says the Spirit, 'they will rest from their labors, for their deeds follow them!'" (Rev 14:13). On the basis of the first half of the verse we remind ourselves how the grace

1. Richard Rutherford, *The Death of a Christian: The Order of Christian Funerals,* rev. ed. (Collegeville, Minn.: The Liturgical Press, 1990) 130–31.

of God makes it possible to die in the Lord and be blessed. In the second half of the verse, we thank God for the deeds of our dear one that will continue to memorialize him or her in our hearts. Even when we don't know the deceased, practicing the policy of being charitable, still being true to our theology, and making use of the information gained in visiting the bereaved, can't we thank God for the specific ways in which the dear one's life was a blessing to those left behind? The difference is in the focus: the eulogy glorifies the person; the homily magnifies the Lord.

What Do We Say in Wedding Homilies?

William Skudlarek counsels:

> The purpose of preaching at a wedding is not to relate personal anecdotes about the couple's courtship, to offer them helpful hints for a happy married life, to present a theology of marriage and the family, or (God forbid, but it does happen) to condemn the evils of divorce, birth control, and/or abortion. Rather the gospel is preached to enable husband and wife to give themselves fully to each other in love and to call them and the witnessing congregation to celebrate that love as a sign of God's continuing presence in the church.[2]

The wedding homily (like all other homilies) grows out of the Scriptures. The wedding homily (like all other homilies) identifies with the legitimate self-interest of the people. The wedding homily (like all other homilies) reminds the people of our hope in Christ.

To bring all this off effectively, we do something else we also do always: we analyze the audience. We've learned something about the couple in our marriage preparation work. But the bride and groom won't be the only people present; there are the attendants, the families, the friends, the neighbors. How do we analyze them?

One way is to look at their connection with the Church. Many will be our parishioners. Some will be solid members of other Christian denominations. Some may be dropouts from the kingdom.

Another way is to look at their marital status. There may be children present who are being formed by this experience. There will be singles: younger and older, never married, divorced, and bereaved. Among those married will be those who are happy about it and those who feel differently. There may also be those living together without benefit of marriage.

2. William Skudlarek, *The Word in Worship*, (Nashville, Abingdon, 1981) 105.

All we have to do is speak the living Word to this couple so that all who overhear can–through the Spirit's power and guidance–make connections for themselves. (And people sometimes kid us on how soft a job we have. The irony is, the better we preach, the easier it seems.)

To manage this huge task of identifying with the legitimate self-interest of this heterogeneous assembly, there's something else we do in wedding homilies (as in all other homilies): we're visual. The Robert Frosts, the Arthur Millers, the Ernest Hemingways, the Garrison Keillors describe particulars. People make connections with particulars. We'd think it would be better to preach universal truths so that people could provide their own particulars; but that way leads to sleep. Rather, we show them particulars and so help them induce their own universals. Out of our acquaintance with the couple in the marriage preparation, we learn how to speak visually to them. In doing that, we open up a lot of channels for the Holy Spirit to work with in the conglomeration of persons in the pews.

Summary

Protestant clergy have been of two minds as to whether we should preach at weddings and funerals. Roman Catholic priests may have omitted preaching in the past, but since Vatican Council II, they preach at every Eucharist. Roman Catholic deacons often preach at weddings and wakes. The debate has sometimes been whether those most affected are able emotionally to receive the Word. But we notice these factors persuading us to seize the opportunity:

1. People have requested typescripts or audio or video recordings of the service, signifying that if they weren't able to receive the Good News at the time, they may be able to do so later.

2. Among those besides the principals attending are people who rarely go to church otherwise, who may overhear our words on the blessings of living forgiven.

3. In spite of the emotional atmosphere at funerals and weddings, the chief mourners or the bridal couple often are still receptive, especially when the priest, pastor, or deacon has developed a good relationship with them beforehand.

4. When having a funeral for people whom the homilist doesn't know, the priest, pastor, or deacon may begin establishing rapport before the funeral by asking questions related to writing an obituary.

Policies we may follow in preparing to preach at funerals: be charitable; be true to your theology; be biblical; show empathy; show the blessings of living forgiven.

The policies we follow in preaching at weddings are the same as for any other homily: be scriptural; identify with the people's ways and self-interest, focus on our hope in Christ. Analyzing the wide diversity of those usually attending weddings may daunt us until we remember that people connect with particulars. So we preach visually and specifically to the couple—whom we've come to know through our marriage preparation work—and the others present, children, singles, married, will overhear and induce their own connections.

For Further Reading

Richard Rutherford. *The Death of a Christian: The Order of Christian Funerals*. Rev. ed. Collegeville, Minn.: The Liturgical Press, 1990, 127–37, 147–49; 234–45.

William Skudlarek. *The Word in Worship: Preaching in a Liturgical Context*. Nashville: Abingdon, 1981, 103–11.

Exercises

Exercise 31

Prepare a funeral homily outline on Psalm 23. Make it people-centered and textual. Use the whole psalm. (Notice that in verse 5, the imagery changes from shepherd to host.) Not as part of the outline but in a paragraph or two, describe the deceased so we may see how you connect with the mourners.

Exercise 32

Prepare a wedding homily outline on 1 Corinthians 13:4-7. Make it people-centered and textual. Use the whole text. Not as part of the outline but in a paragraph or two, describe the couple so we may see how the homily connects with them.

There are two special challenges in this text:

> 1. An abundance of ideas. How will you group them into a theme and two or three supporting points, to make them easier to underline for the ear?
>
> 2. The absence in these verses of any mention of how we get the power to love like this. How will you make this homily a Christian message?

FIFTEEN

Remembering Your Homily

For two years I worked in a public relations firm in downtown Minneapolis coaching business executives in public speaking and meeting the press. One day a salesman showed up. He'd been an associate pastor in a church where the senior pastor was known for his preaching; it seemed to me that this associate must have had some extra pressure to excel in the pulpit. Whatever was motivating him, during his time in this parish he'd come up with a system for speaking without notes and he'd wanted to help my clients by sharing this system with them. It seemed as though he'd come to the right place because I favor speaking without notes. How did his system work?

He'd speak his sermon into a cassette recorder. When he went into the pulpit, he'd have the cassette machine in his back pocket. He'd have an ear plug connected to the machine. He'd hear the words and then repeat them to the people.

"Just a minute. Isn't there a time lag? How can you speak the words while you're hearing them without getting confused?"

"The price includes three lessons on how to do it."

I thanked him for thinking of my clients and showed him to the door.

I give the man credit for trying to cope with a vexing problem: how do you remember all those golden words etched onto the paper with your sweat? The panic-potential of this worry was recognized long ago. The Greek goddess of memory was Mnemosyne (from whose name we get that mouthful of a word, *mnemonics,* which means a technique for improving the memory). The Greeks thought so much of memory they imagined that Mnemosyne was the mother of all the Muses by Zeus. The first century B.C. Roman rhetorician Cicero and the first century A.D. Roman rhetorician Quintilian observed that memory was one of five parts of oratory: invention, arrangement, style, memory, and delivery.[1] In fact, a system of memory was developed by Simonides of Ceos (556–468 B.C.) He'd been at a banquet where the roof fell upon the guests. He had left the hall a moment before. He was able to identify the crushed bodies because he could remember where the living banqueters had been seated.[2] From this he developed the theory that memory depends upon order and that those who want to recall events or words should arrange places and symbols on which to fasten the ideas. Modern adaptations of Simonides are: tying a string on your finger to remind you to do something; associating a person's name with a thing or a place.

Textbooks of that day developed the theory further: "It is necessary, if we wish to remember many things, to provide ourselves with many places. . . . We think it is better to arrange the places in order . . . and it is a good idea to arrange them in fives. . . . It is better to locate the places in a deserted region rather than a populous neighborhood, because the throng and the walking about of the people disturb and weaken the marks of the images."[3] Ouch. Not only do I have to remember the homily, I must remember all the places and images and what they stand for. It's not a help; it's a double burden. My salesman/associate pastor was addressing a serious difficulty, even though I couldn't accept his solution.

For centuries after Quintilian, rhetoricians kept advocating memory as one of the five indispensable canons of oratory. But by the middle of the eighteenth century, the textbooks on rhetoric dropped the subject. Why? Is it because it's so difficult that we'll solve it by ignoring it? Or perhaps a journal article has it right: "Long ago Plato foresaw this when he remarked that the invention of writing by the Egyptian God, Theuth, caused learners to trust external written characters rather than themselves.[4] That he was right may be judged from the number of speakers who read their addresses."[5]

Yet reading homilies in the pulpit isn't always the answer. In chapter 7, "Making Homilies Oral," I reported the plea of parishioners, "Don't read your sermons."

1. Cicero, *Oratorical Partitions* 1.3; Quintilian, *Institutes of Oratory* 3.3.1.

2. Cicero, *Oratorical Partitions* 2.86; Quintilian, *Institutes of Oratory* 11.2.11.

3. Cornificius, 3.23, cited in Bromley Smith, "Hippias and a Lost Canon of Rhetoric," *Quarterly Journal of Speech* 12, no. 3 (June 1926) 141.

4. Plato, *Phaedrus* 275.

5. Smith, "Hippias and a Lost Canon of Rhetoric," 144.

In the opinion of Gerald Kennedy:

> This whole concept of the Christian message as good news demands a delivery free from manuscript and notes. That statement will start an argument in any preachers' meeting, but I have yet to meet a lay[person] who disagrees with it. [Those] who sit in the pews are agreed that, other things being equal, they will choose the [one] who can speak without notes every time. They have a true feeling that real preaching is direct, simple, and without written barriers. In fact, they go further than homiletical professors think proper. But they are right, and we will do well to trust their judgment. When John Wesley preached his famous sermon "On the Death of the Rev. Mr. George Whitefield" on November 18, 1770, he remarked that "it was on the 29th [of December] that he first preached without notes." Wesley rightly assumed that such an occasion should never be forgotten.[6]

In my early preaching workshop brochures, I was afraid to list this topic as "Preaching without Notes," thinking it would scare potential registrants away. So I put down the subject, "Putting Ourselves in the Pew." My reasoning went, "If we can't remember what we're going to say, how can we expect our people to remember it?" But that was about the time I was beginning to develop my ethics of preaching. I soon rejected this title for its questionable morality, appearing to offer one subject while actually delivering another, a "bait and switch" tactic. I then began listing this presentation as "Preaching without Notes" and found that it not only satisfied my taste for honesty, it also didn't seem to turn registrants away. But after more study and observation, I came to see that preaching without notes—a method I still prefer—is not the only way. Whether it's reading a manuscript, speaking from an outline, speaking from an outline almost as detailed as a manuscript, memorizing a script, not memorizing but still speaking without notes—whatever system you choose, you can find great preachers who've employed your method. So I now call this topic, "Remembering Your Homily," with the caution that this chapter still has a bias towards no notes. In my preaching workshop brochures there was a subtitle showing that partiality: "The Dangers and Delights of Preaching without Notes: How to Do It without Rambling and without Getting Stuck."

Truth to tell, I use all the systems myself, including reading a script. But whenever I have time enough to prepare, I prefer to

---

6. Gerald Kennedy, *God's Good News* (New York: Harper & Brothers, 1955) 35.

preach not by memorizing but without notes. I find no other way that gives the same sense of rapport—at times almost a sense of rapture. The people are with you. You're thinking on your feet and they know it. One preacher went home from one of my workshops and tried preaching without notes and reported with satisfaction, "It was like a moment of eternity." That recalled for me a cartoon series I used to enjoy in my boyhood called "The Willetts." It would show scenes from time to time of some delicious experience such as being at the "Ol' Swimming Hole" and the caption would read, "When you'd love to live forever."

No wonder John Wesley couldn't forget the first time he preached without notes. It was like a moment of eternity.

If you feel preaching without notes is out of the question, then consider the difficulties of whatever other systems there are.

The Difficulties of Memorizing

It's possible to memorize your homilies and make them come off alive. But it takes a lot of time and skill. Actors memorize. The good ones make us feel as though they're speaking from their hearts to ours. In the past the giants of the United States Senate memorized their addresses, spending weeks in rehearsal. Their worthy opponents would rise to compliment them but countered by saying, "The speech by the honorable senator smelled of the lamp." (Meaning, the senator had spent hours way into the night working on his speech by the light of a kerosene lantern.) And the honorable senator would rise to protest, "Oh no, I spoke from the heart." But we preachers don't have weeks to rehearse each homily. Lacking that time, our efforts at memorizing may become the struggling to recall what comes next, communing with the manuscript, not with the people. What one critic had to say of a secular speaker may also apply to some preachers who memorize: "I know a very distinguished man who memorized every word of each address and did it with amazing skill. But I always felt that his slight preoccupation with the effort of memory drew an unfortunate veil between him and his audience."[7] One rhetorician observes: "In real public speaking you participate in *communion* with your audience. Memorizers don't participate in communion. They recite."[8]

---

7. William Norwood Brigance, *Speech: Its Techniques and Disciplines in a Free Society* (New York: Appleton-Century-Crofts, 1951, 1961) 74.

8. Ibid., 75.

The Difficulties of Reading

It's possible to read the homily and do it well. I've discussed the difficulties of reading in chapter 7, about the lack of eye contact, cohesiveness, visualness, and orality. All these bad things don't have to happen: the problem is not in the reading but in the writing. Reading a manuscript also tempts otherwise faithful pastors to glide over the hard work it takes to get a homily to hang together on its own. As I noted in chapter 5, the only thing holding some homilies together is the paper they're written on. No wonder the only recourse is reading. In my preaching workshops, I've also discovered there are some manuscript preachers who don't rehearse. It's all on the paper, so why worry? The homily was alive on Friday as they finished it, and then they don't look at it until they face their congregations. Admittedly, if Saturday is the day off it should be the day off. But is it really permissible not to see the manuscript again until you ascend the pulpit?

What if someone gave money so your church could buy a TelePrompter? That would overcome the objection that reading reduces eye contact, wouldn't it? Yes, but the TelePrompter by itself wouldn't improve what's written; it could still be incohesive (because you don't have to worry about remembering what comes next), and it could still be in essay style with its complicated sentence structure so that even the homilist may not know where the thought is going next.

Suppose you conquer all the handicaps of reading and craft a homily that's cohesive, visual, and oral; suppose also that you rehearse enough so you can deliver it well. I still think you can do it better without notes. Your aim has been to get it into such a shape that your people can remember it. Then why can't you? (especially since you've worked on it for days).

The Difficulties of Preaching from an Outline

Say what we will about memorizing or reading, the homilists who use those methods have submitted to the discipline of writing. Even though they bring an essay instead of an oral discourse, they're still likely to be exact, with their words chosen carefully. That's not always the case with those who speak from an outline. If they follow the outline closely and if the outline is cohesive, they may not ramble, but they may bore or offend the people with cliches, over-used words, or grammar that's less than correct.

It is also true that some homily outlines aren't worth following. In chapter 5 I spoke against what I call preacher-centered outlines intended to jog only the preacher's memory, of no use to the people. If we could just get over that and produce people-centered outlines! Yet even when we overcome this handicap the same problem exists as with memorizing or reading, that we could wander into the trap of interacting with the paper instead of with the people.

The Difficulties of Preaching without Notes

If rambling, over-using certain words, and making grammatical errors are problems for those who speak from an outline, the possibilities for such abuses could be as much or greater for those who speak extempore. As for interacting with the paper instead of with the people, extemporaneous speakers can have the same problem as those who take an outline into the pulpit; the paper may not be in front of them, but they may still be so wrapped up with themselves or their content that they are concentrating only on what to say next, still trying to read what's in the manuscript. I know about this first-hand: being in the pulpit striving desperately to recall what's on the top of page five.

"The More Excellent Way"

Yet for all the difficulties, when I can get enough time to prepare, I still am happiest when I preach without notes. There is nothing like the rapport I get this way. In one of my papers at the University of Minnesota, I wrote about the elation I experience in preaching extemporaneously, saying it must be something like the "high" a drug addict feels. My professor wrote in the margin, "You don't really want to use this image, do you?" Perhaps he's right; I do confess to an addiction, praying that in the next homily I'll have such freedom from the paper that the Holy Spirit will have no hindrance in working in the hearts of the people and that we may all feel the electricity of that interaction as we're lifted out of ourselves into the presence of God himself.

If you're apprehensive, I don't blame you. I have the same terror every time. During most of my preaching career, the order of service inserted a hymn between the reading of the gospel and the homily. As the congregation sang, I was praying. It wasn't about lofty things; it was arguing with the Lord: "Why wouldn't it be all right to take the notes into the pulpit this time?" Usually I left my manuscript on the bench, and as I preached, I was glad I did.

How Do You Do It?

When the subject of memory came up in my introductory speech course in college, I'd ask the class clown to stand before us and tell the story of Goldilocks and the Three Bears. (One clown—when he arrived at Mama Bear's bed—stopped to ponder, "Why weren't they sleeping together?") In my seminary course, I'd ask someone to stand and tell the parable of the Good Samaritan. In neither situation was there ever a problem. In both cases there was action we could see, told in an oral style, to an orderly flow of ideas. There you have it. We can preach without notes when our homilies are visual, oral, and cohesive.

When done well, it looks simple. Don't be fooled.

Some pastors, upon hearing I advocate preaching extempore, have told me, "I prefer a sermon that's prepared." They're reacting to the difficulties mentioned above, rambling and less than perfect word choice. I tell them, "I'm not talking about impromptu preaching. What I'm recommending takes not less preparation but more." It means not copying sentences from a commentary (or even from a book of sermons or a homily service) but working them over into oral style and lowering the level of abstraction. It means not just putting down any idea that comes into mind but struggling to find unity. And it means rehearsing on your feet. This is the acid test. If I keep getting stuck at a certain place, that's a signal something's out of place—or shouldn't be included at all. Without the paper to prompt me, my mind just can't make the connection. That's a clue the listeners won't be able to make it either. So even though the hour of preaching might be dreadfully near, I still have to sit down and analyze what's illogical in my structure and fix that up, even taking something out. It takes not less preparation but more.

To show by contrast what I mean, here are a couple of sentences from a homily in print:

> To keep from blaming God, to learn from those things we suffer and to grow even closer to God through our hardships has got to be about the most difficult thing for any of us. To see him not as Cause but as Comforter, not as Scapegoat but as Strengthener, not as the reason for suffering but as the Rescuer, has got to be the most important stance from which any of us view him.

How does this measure up to our standards?

Is it cohesive? Yes. It's orderly and logical. The two sentences hang together. They balance each other and set up a rhythm that helps us anticipate what's coming.

Is it visual? Well, it's not as abstract as some preaching I've heard or read. But I still don't see the flesh and blood. It took the author of Job forty-two chapters to illustrate lines like, "to keep from blaming God, to learn from those things we suffer and to grow even closer to God." The homily couldn't recite all the dialogue between Job and his friends and between Job and God, but it could give the gist of it, and that would be flesh-and-blood action I could see—and remember.

Is it oral? The words are simple but the sentences are not. The reader can manage it and appreciate the artistry, but the listener has to keep in mind all those things in the front half of each sentence before getting to the predicate. Do you see why a homily like this must be read? The same thing that makes it hard for the listener to remember is what makes it hard for the homilist to recall.

Other preachers express their hesitancy like this: "I like to preach from a manuscript because otherwise I overuse some words and rely on cliches and maybe, when I'm fumbling, I'll use filler-words." I recognize the danger. If I could be a benevolent despot for fifteen minutes, I'd make it a felony ever to say "you know" and "basically" and "if you will."

I try to avoid this hazard by writing out every word of the homily, taking care that it's in oral style, making continual revisions even while I'm rehearsing. When I speak the homily out loud, if I hear myself repeating words and phrases that could evoke monotony, then I'll look for new words. By going over the homily several times on my feet, the key phrases come out pretty much as I have them in the manuscript. Writing out every word helps eliminate cliches and boring repetition, and diligent rehearsing will help recapture much of the phrasing, but if I can't recover every precious syllable, I'm still not lost, because I don't memorize the words, I memorize the structure. If I were to try to recall the order of words, then if I couldn't retrieve the next word I'd be stumped. I don't rehearse the order of the words but the flow of the scenes. Then I can put myself into the pictures and simply report what I see.

Other homilists give voice to different qualms: "What if I'm in the pulpit and I get stuck? You say, if we preachers can't remember our homilies, how can the people? But after all, the people in the pews aren't under the same pressure as we are." Amen. I know the strain, and I've gotten stuck often. What I do then is restate my people-centered theme and the people-centered major parts covered to that point, saying something like, "Friends, what we've talked about so far is this. . . ." Usually this gets me into the train of thought again. But there were three or four times when even that didn't do it. After floundering for what seemed to be eons, I finally said, "Friends, I'm lost. I just can't remember what comes next." Didn't the people laugh! After the merriment died down, I got back on track. We enjoyed it so much there have been times I've been tempted to fake a memory loss.

That shows what the situation really is: you're among friends. Some—perhaps many—are even praying for you. Most want you to succeed and would admire you all the more for bringing them the homily in the same wonderful style you use when dealing with them one-on-one.

Sometimes when a student has labored through preaching from a manuscript, I'll ask him or her to give us the flow of ideas. Almost without fail the student does so without looking at the paper. I point out that the student did know the message and could have given it without notes—because he or she has just done so—and to the same audience, the same friends.

I read my quotations, even the Scripture verses I know by heart. This sets them off from my own material and (I suspect) may even enhance it.

I know the objections. I raise them to myself often. That must be why I panic every time I go into the pulpit. More than once I've thought of myself as being like Peter venturing out of the boat to walk on the water. When he considered the danger, he began to sink. He'd forgotten that up till then, he'd been looking to Jesus and so he was making it. Or if I don't think of that, I remind myself of a principle of the kingdom Jesus announced at least twice: "For those who want to save their life will lose it, and those who lose their life for my sake will save it" (Luke 9:24; 17:33).

Summary

The rhetorical canon of memory, remembering what you want to say, challenges every public speaker, including preachers. There are problems with every system: memorizing, reading, speaking from an outline, preaching extempore (carefully prepared but without notes in the pulpit). Electronic marvels like the TelePrompter don't eliminate the problems; if the discourse is badly written and the preacher reads poorly, the gadget doesn't take away the listeners' pain. When some people hear that I advocate preaching without notes, they may say, "I prefer a homily that's prepared." I tell them: "So do I. It takes work to craft a homily that doesn't need the paper to hold it together but hangs together so that even the people can follow it. It takes work to create pictures for every idea in the

Scripture text. It takes work to write and rewrite every sentence in oral style. I'm talking about more preparation, not less."

Although there may be emergencies when we can't avoid going into the pulpit without preparation, this is not the normal mode of operation; speaking without notes is not the same as preaching impromptu.

Whatever system of memory you prefer, you can find excellent preachers who do it your way. If your homily is cohesive, visual, and oral, it will work whether you read, memorize, speak from an outline, or preach without notes.

I use all the systems, but when I have enough time to prepare and rehearse, I prefer to preach without notes because the rapport can be electrifying.

I write out every word in oral style. But I don't try to recapture the sequence of words; rather, I memorize the structure and the flow of pictures. I rehearse out loud on my feet and put myself into the pictures and report what I see. With diligent rehearsal I'm able to recover most of the phrasing that's on the paper—but if while I'm preaching, I can't recall the next word, I'm not stumped—because I've memorized the structure and the flow of pictures. If I do get lost, because my structure is people-centered, I can simply say, "Friends, you remember that the homily today is [and here I restate the theme] and that so far, we've discussed [here I restate the people-centered points covered up till now]. That usually gets me back on track.

The objective is to forget about myself and to concentrate on Christ and his good news for the people.

For Further Reading

Brigance, William Norwood. *Speech: Its Techniques and Disciplines in a Free Society.* 2d ed. New York: Appleton-Century-Crofts, 1952, 1961, 67-89.

Exercises

Exercise 33

According to your instructor's choice, give a three-minute, five-minute, or full-length homily, without notes and without memorizing the words.

Purpose:

1. To imitate the African-American preacher in telling stories from the Bible.

2. To experience what can happen when the homily is visual, oral, and cohesive.

(If the class schedule permits one of the longer options, that will allow each homilist more time to develop the characters and the context.)

Your hearers: those present in the room with you.

Review the section in chapter 6 subtitled "Learn from the African-American Preacher," pp. 67–71.

Study these excerpts from Henry H. Mitchell, *Black Preaching* (Nashville: Abingdon Press, 1990): 64–67, 73–75, 93–94.

Study homily number 14 in the Appendix (page 256), "Everlasting Treasures," by a black preacher, James Thomas. Notice especially how he develops the idea that Jesus who was rich then became poor so that we through his poverty might become rich.

Study homily number 15 in the Appendix (page 261), "The Dog," by a white preacher, Rick Witucki. Notice how he expands on Jesus' words, "Even the dogs would come and lick his sores."

If possible, attend an African-American church and/or listen to a recording of African-American preaching.

In all examples, notice how the African-American preacher uses imagination based on study of the Bible text. As Henry Mitchell puts it, it's "the imaginative use of the helpful insights of the scholars."

Take one of these Scriptures as your text: Mark 10:35-45; Gal 6:1; Luke 12:13-21; Gal 6:7-8; Luke 14:7-11; Eph 5:1-2; Luke 16:19-31.

When you begin rehearsing, first think of your purpose. That's the destination towards which your homily is pointing. Then think of how you'll begin. Then recall the way that you travel from your starting point to your destination, fixing in mind your outline and the flow of scenes.

As you rehearse, some lines will come out as they appear in the manuscript, but do not try to memorize which words come next. Memorize which scene comes next, and then simply report what you see as it's happening.

SIXTEEN

A Checklist for Developing Your Homily

Making the Homily Textual

A. Write each verse of the text on a separate sheet.

B. On each sheet also write:

1. What is the Holy Spirit saying to me through this verse?

2. What are the reactions of my panel of diversity (five or six people, each representing a segment of the congregation)?

3. What has the Holy Spirit said to others through this verse? (notes from exegetical and homiletical works).

Making the Homily Cohesive

A. When the exegesis has to stop, summarize your findings on another sheet of paper, one idea to a line.

B. Summarize the likely reaction(s) of your panel of diversity.

C. If the people's likely reactions include potential hostility, list the areas of common ground, one line to each idea.

D. Develop a specific purpose of this homily stated in one uncomplicated sentence that you can remember.

E. Using all the summaries, look for connections between the ideas.

F. Look for the unifying idea; develop that into your theme, being careful to have it show identification with the people.

G. Arrange the other ideas as supporting points.

H. Make the theme and its parts logical and cohesive, but don't spend too much time now in polishing them. Better forms will come when composing and rehearsing the homily.

I. Test the outline for its cohesiveness:
   1. Do the parts add up to the theme?
   2. Do the ideas cluster?
   3. Do theme and parts express identification?
   4. Does your outline have diagnosis and hope in Christ built into it?
   5. Does your outline show the benefits of living under your proposal?
   6. Does your outline have an introduction? (Do you start where the people are and show them how your proposal concerns them?)
   7. Does your outline have a conclusion? (Does it recapitulate the theme and its major parts? Does it have a call to action that reflects the purpose you charted for this homily?)
   8. Is your outline people-centered, easy to underline for the ear?
   9. Is your outline clear enough and simple enough so you can remember it? (If you can't remember it, how can the people?)

Making the Homily Oral

A. Is your structure in oral style?
   1. Will the people be able to tell when your introduction ends?
   2. Will they know what your theme is from listening to your introduction?
   3. Will they know when the first part starts and what it is and when it ends and how it relates to the theme?
   4. The same for the succeeding parts?
   5. Will the people know when you get to the conclusion? Do you summarize the homily in order to give the greatest force to your call to action?

B. Is your language in oral style?
   1. Are the verbs mostly active?
   2. Are the sentences mostly without dependent clauses?
   3. Are the sentences mostly short?
   4. Do they avoid too many modifiers? (Modifiers that define are good; modifiers that comment are suspect.)

5. How do the words sound out loud? Are some words or some sounds over used?

6. How much can you cross out without destroying the meaning or the mood?

7. Are there some ideas you should repeat or re-state (to help the people grab hold)?

8. Whether or not you preach without notes, is the language simple enough—and the sentence structure simple enough—so that you could deliver it that way?

9. Can you put yourself in the pew and examine each sentence as to whether you could understand it, having only your ears to go by?

Rehearsing and Delivering This Homily

A. Are you physically fit? (There will be exceptions you can't help, when you draw on your adrenalin and rely even more on the Holy Spirit's power.)

1. Did you get enough exercise the week before? enough sleep the week before?

2. Is your body relaxed (not holding on to the pulpit for dear life)?

3. Are you breathing from the diaphragm (able to project your voice without being whiny or raspy)?

4. Is your diction clear (your tongue and jaws loose, speaking every part of every word)?

B. Are you excited about your message?

C. Are you concentrating on the people instead of yourself?

D. Do you have eye-contact with the whole assembly?

E. Do any parts of your homily need to be revised? (Do you always get "stuck" at a certain point? Is this a clue that the ideas don't cluster at that place? Do you need to move something to another part of the homily—or perhaps throw it out? Do you discover some better ways of phrasing? Are there some more lines you can cross out? Are there some parts that need to be clarified or expanded?)

An Acronym (CONVERTS) As a Checklist

C = Christian, Cohesive
O = Oral
N = No notes
V = Visual
E = Ethical
R = Rehearsed
T = Textual
S = Self-interest

APPENDIX ONE

Do We Need God?

Luke 7:1-10

The new fact in our time, so we are told, is the disappearance of God from the human scene. Tennessee Williams, in *Sweet Bird of Youth*, has one of his characters say, "I believe in the silence of God, the absolute speechlessness of Him, is a long, long, and awful thing—and the whole world is lost because of it."

For the past decade, theological writings have been full of God's demise. And some secular people have gloated over the idea.

More disturbing than this, however, may be our own experience of God's absence. Men seem to be living all around us as if there were no God—or worse yet, as if they didn't need him if he is still alive. Our question, then, is do we need God? Much of our life is going to hang on the answer.

There are two types of people I might well miss in answering this question. There are the unbelievers. The rigid, immovable unbelievers. Those who quickly reply, "Do I need God? No, I don't. My life is full without him."

On the other hand, there are the great believers who say that it's a silly question. "I'm not looking for him because I've already found him. He's my God, and he's with me here."

However, most people fall in between these two extremes. They believe there is a God, but they are not too sure just as to how, or where, they can find him. If you stop any group of people on the street in Madison and ask them if they believe in God, a surprising 90% will say "Yes."

In spite of this, the need of God is certainly not as desperate as the need expressed by the writer of the 42nd Psalm: ". . . as a hart longs for flowing streams, so longs my soul for thee, O God." As David Read has observed, "If there is any kind of longing going on here, it's after power, money, or sex, certainly not after God." For we make our plans and regulate our behavior, most of us, without any specific awareness of God's direction.

A Gospel for the Secular Man

My guess is that God is peripheral rather than central in our lives. You may be somewhat like the fine father in this congregation who admitted to me this past summer that he had begun to take long ski weekends last winter, and then he said, "We began to wonder whether we needed the church. Skiing seemed to take care of the basic needs of our family." Some others have told me of their surprise in finding that they, too, had stopped bothering about God, giving up worship and prayer. "And you know, pastor, life went on as usual."

That is why I believe the text in the Gospel of Luke has such significance. Here we have a man, in many ways a highly secularized, sophisticated man of the first century, who found a strong affirmative need for God in his life. He was a Roman soldier, an officer of the hated army of occupation. He was also a man who differed markedly from the usual centurion who commanded Rome's military garrisons in occupied countries—an arrogant, coarse, and often a brutal type of person. The man from Capernaum comes through as a fine, sensitive, real human being.

Here was a man who had what some people want so desperately. He had power! "I say to one, 'Go,' and he goes; and to another, 'Come,' and he comes; and to my slave, 'Do this,' and he does it." Like a secularist in any age, he could have patterned his life without any reference to God. He could have been a self-satisfied officer living in the lap of Greek culture in an occupied country. Or he could have been "on the make"—as many fortune-hunting soldiers of any army, content with a life of sexual adventures or fortune-hunting. But this kind of life didn't satisfy him.

Listen to his words: "Lord, I am not worthy to have you come under my roof . . . but say the word, and let my servant be healed." Such humility, faith, and awareness of God! And it resulted in a genuine and heartfelt response on the part of Jesus.

Is there any way that the gospel can break through to the secular man in our day in the way it did to this man? Does the man in the scientific, enlightened twentieth century still need God? Permit me to respond to these questions from three different points on the compass.

What Is Relevant

I think we should acknowledge first of all that the questions are not new. The so-called "man come of age" is actually as old as the Garden of Eden. From the dawn of history men and women have been listening to that whisper from the garden: "Eat, and you shall be as gods. You don't need God."

As a pastor over these years, I have yet to hear any basically new questions or objections raised against God's goodness or his existence that I didn't hear in the first five years of my ministry! Thus, to suggest that we adjust our message of the Church to the mood of the moment in the name of "tolerance" is the "playing of an old record" for me.

We might well ask, "Relevant to what?" For at times a fire siren on the highway may be more relevant than the sound of a Beethoven symphony, but does that make it more important in the long run? And the morning newspaper may be more relevant (if you want to see how the Wisconsin Badgers did) than a play by William Shakespeare. Does that make the morning newspaper more relevant than Shakespeare's insights?

I would not argue with those who want to make the gospel relevant to their lives, to put it into words and actions that ordinary people can understand and live with.

But I am convinced that it cannot be done merely by attempting to adjust the message to the secularists—to make it relevant to their point of view, to chisel it down until they'll accept it. Rather, something has to happen to *them*. They have to suddenly become aware of their dependence on something other than things, or power, or sexuality.

Remember there's a "givenness" to the gospel that nothing is going to change. You can't sandpaper it down.

Scripture reveals simply that all men need God, but he remains God. And we do not tailor the presentation of the Gospel to those who don't think they need him. We let God be God.

God in Our Blood

This line of thought often leads to the next point—that you are often closer to God when you think you are farthest away. And you're often farthest away from God when you think you are closest.

There is no doubt that mankind has a deep natural memory of God, half buried and half forgotten. In a real sense we've got "God in our blood." Alan Richardson, the English theologian, said, "The life of every man is full of pieces of unrecognized knowledge of God, intonations of his divine heredity which he has never learned to call by their proper name."

I like that old story of the Russian girl—brought up as an atheist— who after taking a governmental examination was worried about the answer she had given to the question, "What is the inscription on the Sarmian wall?" She had written the answer of Karl Marx, "Religion is the opiate of the people," but she wasn't quite sure. After the exam, she walked seven miles to check. Sure enough, there it was. Quickly forgetting her Marxist ideology, she crossed herself and said, "Thank God, I had it right."

There are many sophisticated people who still have this spiritual reflex in them. It is even among those who offer the most brilliant arguments against God's existence or goodness. Radicals, rebel writers, poets, dramatists, are often preoccupied with God-thoughts. They are God-saturated people—sometimes in reverse.

As a man who struggled for faith, Martin Luther understood this ambivalence. He wrote: "Nobody in this life is nearer to God than those who deny him. He has no children more dear to him than those of Job and Jacob who wrestle with him and cannot let him go."

God's Search for Man

Actually, the role of man and God according to Scripture is reversed. And this fact ought to make some of us uneasy, or hopeful, as the case may be. Seventy-five years ago, a poem was published in England by an unknown drug addict. His name is now world famous— Francis Thompson. His poem, called "The Hound of Heaven," was described by *The New York Times* as ". . . one of the first English lyrics that makes the popular appeal to all nationalities and faiths. Basically it is a poem about the seeking God—His pursuit and final capture of a human soul."

In the final analysis that's what the Bible is all about—from Genesis to Jesus. One of the first questions in the Bible is, "Adam, where are you?"—Man, where are you hiding?

The glorious scriptural hunt begins at this point. The account is of God's search for man, not man's search for God. Someone else has spoken out of the cosmic silence—left his footprint on the desolate sand of human culture. God breaks through in our human awareness in the flesh and blood of human life.

Nearly 2,000 years ago it happened, and because it all happened, we're here today.

Perhaps one of the best modern parables of this is found in the story of that famous Japanese Christian, Kagawa. As a young man in Milwaukee, I heard him speak, and I'll never forget the impression this small, foreign-speaking individual made on me. He spent many years of his life in the slums of Kobe. He was a little man without any physical strength—one lung had been decimated by tuberculosis. Practically blind by the time I saw him, he had been told by doctors in America many years before that he couldn't live much longer. But when he went back to Japan, he said, "If my life is to be short, it will at least be full." It was!

One day, we're told by his biographers, Kagawa went out to preach in the streets of Kobe about the love of God—dismal streets with rain falling and rough men laughing. They chided him: "You little man with your funny talk about God. What do you know about him? Does anybody know whether God loves or even exists?"

It seemed they had the strong side of the argument. For even as he tried to answer, he coughed up blood. And they laughed again, though now partly out of pity. "If God loves," said one, "why doesn't he do something for you? A small wind could blow you over."

But the persistent little man lifted his arms, wiped the blood from his mouth on his sleeve, and went on with the story about the love of God. And gradually in that cruel street the mocking voices became stilled, and the realization began to sink in that right before their eyes was the proof of what he was saying. A little man was standing there, sick and cold. And yet he was telling them that God loved him.

Is this not the fantastic appeal of Calvary's cross? He loved us enough to let this happen to his Son. Who can resist that kind of love? Do you need God? Maybe the question ought to be, do you need love?

Not a Matter of Choice

There are only two valid responses to Calvary. Everything is there that makes men *disbelieve* in God, and everything is there that makes men *believe* in God. There can be none other. The one thing you cannot do with Calvary is to retreat into some sort of neutrality.

Life gets made up one way or the other. Pascal, the French writer, put it beautifully: "This, however, is certain, either that God is or that God is not . . . this is not a matter of choice; you are committed, and not to wager that God is, is to wager that God is not. Which side then do you take?"

I'll leave the matter to you and to the Holy Spirit. One thing you cannot do, is say, "I'll think about it later." Life will make up your mind.

Reprinted from *Augsburg Sermons, Gospels, Series C*, 1973, 168–73. Used by permission of Augsburg Fortress.

Much More!

John 16:12-15

As Christians we believe in the God of the "much more." When Jesus made clear to his followers that he would be returning to his Father and that they, in turn, would be persecuted, they were plunged into grief. So he went on to say more about the Holy Spirit whom he would send as their Counselor and Advocate. Jesus said: "I have *much more* to tell you, but now it would be too much for you to hear. But when the Spirit of truth comes, he will lead you into all the truth" (John 16:12-13 from *Good News for Modern Man*).

Jesus' early followers weren't ready at that moment for all that he could have said to them or shown them. Neither are we at any given point in our development. Jesus teaches and guides us only to the degree that we are ready and able to receive. His greatness, however, is limitless and unsearchable. Always he has much more for his disciples than they can stand or understand. So Jesus today, on this Trinity Sunday, acquaints us with God the Holy Spirit. He puts us under his tutelage. He sends him to be in us and with us.

The Holy Spirit is God active today. He is God our contemporary. He is God in and with us now to continue the teaching, illuminating work of the Son. He is the God of horizons—horizons that "move forever and ever as we move." He is the God of Christian growth. The Father's unexpended resources, untouched possibilities and unrecognized glory become ours through him.

Most Christians, happy for all that God the Father means to them, nevertheless look for more. Their experience with God the Son teaches them that they have only begun to know the love and strength, the understanding and challenge, that he wants to give. God the Spirit stirs this awareness in us. He draws us beyond the present point in our Christian development. To the degree that we rely upon and cooperate with him we become mature Christians. To that degree we forge ahead into the "much more" of Jesus Christ, we discover over and over again the God of glad surprising. Serendipity flourishes where he is present and welcomed.

The "much more" with which Christians can be blessed by the Holy Spirit has several dimensions, three of which Jesus mentioned in John 16:12-14. There we see untouched possibilities regarding the truth, the future and the glory of Christ. The Holy Spirit leads and speaks. As he does so, there result 1) much more insight into the truth, 2) much more vision for the future and 3) much more appreciation of the Savior.

Made Insiders

Jesus promised that the Holy Spirit would lead his followers into all the truth. He makes Christians insiders when it comes to the truth. He works to make us more and more at home with what life is all about, as God has put it together. As a good guide leads canoeists into wilderness country or as a good teacher guides students towards full awareness of a subject or as a good host and hostess lead their guests into the warmest atmosphere of the home, so the Holy Spirit leads Christians into all that counts and all that lasts.

Truth has many dimensions. There is truth in medicine, in geology and in history. There is the truth in music, in poetry and in art. Awareness of any of these dimensions is a discovery made possible by God. The truth into which the Holy Spirit leads us illuminates dark places and dark lives. It exposes what is false and fractured and fatal. It fosters what is right and whole and vital. It exposes what is evil and hateful. It nourishes what is good and loving. The Holy Spirit puts us at ease with the mystery of life. He helps us live fruitfully with its unexplained anguish and ecstasy, its unexplored height and depth. Jesus is the truth. God is truth. Responsiveness to the Holy Spirit increases our understanding of God. He leads us into God as the very atmosphere, or force field, or home within which we live and move and have our being. God makes life possible; God puts life together; God holds life together; God makes life worthwhile. God is life. God is where it's at. When we follow the Holy Spirit, the God-dimension becomes more and more a familiar country. The Holy Spirit is Insight Divine. With him leading us we expect to understand more of how he sees our trials and pleasures, our plans and problems, our identity and our relationships. We come to see that nothing can separate us from the love of God. We learn more of how to interpret and harvest our experiences as Christ would interpret and harvest them.

Through the Holy Spirit God is real to us, he is "nearer than breathing, closer than hands and feet." Because of the Holy Spirit we follow not simply a set of commands, we follow God.

Filled with Expectation

Jesus also said, the Holy Spirit "will not speak on his own, but he will speak of what he hears and tell you of things to come." "Things to come" are possibilities for the future. They are expectations yet to be fulfilled; they are hopes yet to be realized. "Things to come" include what is coming to the world and who is coming to the world. They include what the world is coming to and what you and I can become. From the Holy Spirit comes much more awareness of the future promised by God, opened up by God and shaped by God. From him comes a vision of both possibility and destiny.

On the one hand, the phrase "things to come" refers to things such as the end of the world, the final return of Jesus Christ, and the arrival of the new heavens and earth. They include the resurrection, the judgment and eternal life. They point to the victory of Christ and the Lamb upon his throne. They inspire the vision of multitudes without number singing, "Worthy is the Lamb that was slain to receive power, and riches, and wisdom, and strength, and honor, and glory and blessing."

On the other hand, "things to come" refers to all the possibilities open to us and to mankind *because of God.* The "much more" of God spells itself out in a vision of what we ought to be and can be through Jesus Christ. It quickens us with hope for the future by sketching the changes for the better that can come through faith and through grace. No matter what our circumstances the Holy Spirit enlivens us with the certainty there is more to come—more fulfillment of the promises of God and more growth in the grace of Jesus Christ. His beckoning words point us toward heaven. They also teach us how to live in it here and now.

God active today is also the God of all our tomorrows. He is inspiration for the future because he is future-oriented. He is Hope Divine. Right out of the councils of heaven the Holy Spirit inspires a vision of the kingdom of God. Sometimes we say about a good teacher or a creative person that he "opens things up" for us. That is what the Holy Counselor does for Christians and for the church. He opens the door to the God-intended future. He sets before us a door that no man can shut and he accompanies us through it. He is the God of hope and of horizons.

When, at times, life seems meaningless or empty, let us look to the Holy Spirit. When the future seems closed, let us ask him to show the way. When the future seems closed or when the possibilities seem endless, let us listen for his word about "things to come." Through him we can live forward in "marvel and surprise."

Captured by the Glory

Third, Jesus told his followers, the Holy Spirit "will give me glory, because he will take what I have to say and tell it to you." Much more appreciation of the Savior springs to life when we pay attention to the Holy Spirit. Much more adoration of Jesus breaks into words and deeds when through Scripture and Sacrament we are taught by the Spirit. He is God with us showing and telling and giving from Christ. He is Glory Divine.

Not until the Spirit is allowed to glorify Christ for us and to us will the Christian adventure grip us. Not until that glory captures us will the happiness reach the heights. Not until then will it reassert itself against the assaults of the world, the devil and our own flesh.

Spiritual things are spiritually discerned. Thus when the Christian life begins to drag, let us look to the Spirit. Let us ask him to glorify Christ for us. When we turn to the Bible, or come to worship, or talk with God in prayer, or try to do his work, let us look for the "much more" of the Spirit. As Luther said, he is "sacred Ardor, Comfort sweet." He "gives life" (2 Cor 3:6). He can raise dry bones and dull souls. He can loose the tongue and speed the feet. Where Christians surrender to him there is more of joy, there is more of praise, there is more of life that glorifies God. In the thick of any experience the sublime is always at hand through him.

Received in the Fellowship

All of this "much more" Jesus promised to the company of his followers. What we have been talking about belongs to his people. That is, it happens to us individually, but it is best experienced together. The insight into truth is for the Christian fellowship and for its members. The vision of things to come is given to the body of Christ and in it to its individual members. The richest realization of the glory of God flourishes in the family of believers. No one Christian grasps it all, whether we refer to the truth, or to the things to come or to the glory of the Lord. We need God's revelation to one another, just as we need not only Matthew but also Mark, Luke, John, Paul, Peter and James. The Spirit's leading of *all,* his illumination of *all,* and his inspiring of *all,* together compose the "much more" of our Lord.

For the ever-growing enrichment of life in Christ we need to come together and to be together. In worship and study, in fellowship and ministry, we need the company of believers. In this fellowship we can know and be changed. With it we shall hear what the Spirit says to the churches (Rev 2:7).

We Press On

A traveler sat one morning having breakfast in a lodge high on the mountains. Through the window he could see great snow-covered peaks, green forested slopes and a brilliant blue sky. He exclaimed to the waiter that he had never expected to see such beauty anywhere. Whereupon the waiter replied, "Yes, but wait till you see the other side!" That is Jesus' word to his people. Much more is available! More insight into the truth. More vision for the future. More appreciation of the glory of God!

Reprinted from *Augsburg Sermons, Gospels, Series C* 1973, 164–68. Used by permission of Augsburg Fortress.

Third Word from the Cross Is Concern

John 19:25-27

Alvin C. Rueter

Central Lutheran Church, Minneapolis, Minnesota

Three Hour Service, Liturgy of the Word
13 April 1990

Purpose: To meditate on Christ's concern for the individual; to support us in our desire to show concern for Christ in our midst.

   I. Introduction

      A. How crucifixions were done

      B. In the midst of a global mission, Jesus shows concern for an individual

  II. Theme: The Third Word from the Cross Is Concern

III. Body

      A. Concern for the individual
        1. In our world of computers, we need this reminder
        2. The Heavenly Father knows when sparrows drop dead

      B. Concern for the helpless individual
        1. Mary, helpless in her grief
        2. Mary, helpless in her economic condition

      C. Concern shown through other individuals

 * 1. The women at the cross responding to Christ's concern
       for them, showing concern for him.
       a. Where were the men?
       b. It was dangerous to be there
       c. Oh, that we could have been at the cross
    2. John's sweet reward: to care for the mother of Jesus
       a. Why not the family of Jesus?
       b. We have no clue as to why not
       c. Oh, that we could have taken care of the mother of
          Jesus

IV. Conclusion
    A. The third word from the cross is concern
       1. Concern for the individual
       2. Concern for the helpless individual
       3. Concern shown through other individuals, as hands and
          feet of the body of Christ

    B. As we meditate on the third word from the cross, we're
       strengthened in our desire to show our Lord's concern to
       his mother and brothers and sisters in our midst

* I had to omit part III.C.1 because the homily was getting too long for the time
allotted.

The Third Word from the Cross Is Concern
John 19:25-27

Alvin C. Rueter

Central Lutheran Church, Minneapolis, Minnesota
Three Hour Service, Liturgy of the Word
13 April 1990

(The subheads are underlined to show how we manage type and
white space to make the main ideas stand out for the eye; these
lines were not said while preaching this homily. The lines in italics
show how we underline the main ideas for the ear.)

Introduction

In olden times they considered crucifixion the most cruel and
shameful of all penalties. It was usually only for slaves, or the

underclass, or people without Roman citizenship. The officials liked to place the crosses next to a highway and if possible on high ground—so that the greatest number of people could gawk and jeer—and tremble at the power of the Roman government.

None of the evangelists tells very much about how they crucified Jesus. We know they nailed his hands because Thomas traced the nail prints with his fingers. We know that Jesus was high enough off the ground that to give him a drink, they had to put it on a reed to reach his mouth. That's about all we can say for sure. It's possible there was what they called "a seat," a block or a pin on which the body could rest. There could also have been a step on which the feet could stand. But whether or not Jesus had a seat and a step, we know he'd already been whipped with a cat-o-nine tails—leather strips with bits of metal or bone on the tips to make them bite deeper into the flesh—and we can faintly imagine the excruciating pain of hanging from spikes even if he would have had a seat and a step, and we can empathize with the relatively minor discomfort of not being able to swat the insects feasting on his blood—and we can marvel that in the midst of all this—acting out how much "God so loved the world"—in the midst of all this, when he sees his mother and the disciple whom he loved standing near, he said to his mother, "Woman, here is your son!" And to the disciple, "Here is your mother!"

That leads me to suggest as my theme, The Third Word of Jesus from the Cross Is Concern.

A. Concern for the Individual

In showing regard for his mother even while hanging from spikes, we *notice first that he shows Concern for the Individual.* We need this reminder. In our world of computers where we all go by numbers, where people can't remember our names, or if they do, they probably can't spell them anyway, where our letters to the government are put in stacks and weighed instead of read—we get the notion that God must be like that too. We can't blame government officials for sending us form letters signed by a machine—how could they deal with us personally? And God has all the people in Ethiopia and South Africa and Lithuania and Outer Mongolia and Brazil and Peru and Guatemala and Nicaragua to look after—wouldn't he be still further removed from us? Wouldn't a single individual mean still less to him?

Comes then the Son of God both to declare and to demonstrate that our Heavenly Father is so much on top of everything that he notices when a sparrow drops dead. He knows so much about you that he could tell how many hairs you have on your head if the need for that information ever comes up. *The Third Word from the Cross is altogether in character with our Lord's Concern for the Individual.*

B. Concern for the Helpless Individual

More than that, we also notice that he shows Concern for the Helpless Individual. Mary, helpless in her grief. The old man Simeon—when Joseph and Mary had brought the baby Jesus to the Temple—Simeon had prophesied: "And a sword will pierce through your own soul too" (Luke 2:35). Artists have empathized with Mary at the cross in their paintings, and so have musicians who've composed music expressing her grief in pieces that are called "Stabat Mater."

Helpless in her grief. And also helpless in her economic condition. We can only guess at Mary's age by remembering Jesus was 30 when he began his ministry, putting her in her late 40's or early 50's. But that wouldn't make her helpless, would it? She'd have her pension from Joseph's carpenter business. She'd have her Social Security check from the Roman government on the third of every month. I'm afraid not. She did have the advantage of living in a Jewish society. Other nations didn't have the Torah—the Hebrew Bible—with its frequent urgings to take care of widows. But these frequent mentions of the widows' plight only underscored the problem of their helplessness. The New Testament report of the widow who put two mites into the Temple treasury—that this was all she had—this was no exaggeration.

Concern for the Helpless Individual—showing itself in the Third Word From the Cross.

C. Concern Shown through other Individuals

And how does the Lord show Concern for the Helpless Individual? Through the Concern of Other Individuals: "Then he said to the disciple, 'Here is your mother.' And from that hour the disciple took her into his own home."

That's the way our Lord does it: his concern shown through the concern of other individuals. And what a sweet reward for "the disciple whom Jesus loved." Our Lord gave him the privilege of taking care of his mother!

Now why didn't Jesus give this privilege to his family? Was it because as we read in the Gospel of John that "even his brothers did not believe in him?" It's hard to say, because that unbelief wasn't permanent. We learn that between the Ascension and Pentecost, Mary the mother of Jesus and the brothers of Jesus were with the disciples in prayer (Acts 1:14). So if the kinsfolk of Jesus were unbelievers before Good Friday, they didn't stay that way. We just haven't got a clue as to why Mary's family didn't come to her rescue.

We could protest, "Well, if I'd been a relative of Jesus, I'd have taken care of her. I'd have been embarrassed to have someone outside the family do it for me."

Trying to put myself into the situation like this led me to remember a part of Roland Bainton's performances of Martin Luther's Christmas sermon:

> "But there was no room in the inn." Of course there was. There was all the room in the inn. But nobody would give up a room. Shame on you, wretched Bethlehem. You ought to have been burned with brimstone.
>
> And don't let you people of this congregation think you'd have done any better if you were there. I can just hear you say, "Oh, we'd have loved to take care of the baby Jesus. We would have washed his diapers."
>
> Yes, you would! If you'd have been there, you wouldn't have done a bit better, and if you think you would, why don't you do it for your neighbor in your midst, who is Christ among you?
>
> [transcribed from "Christmas Is," Augsburg Publishing House, Box 1209, Minneapolis, MN 55440 LP album, Code 23-1462, recording of Roland Bainton made at Yale Divinity School, 12-18-68]

We notice that after Easter, the Lord kept showing Concern for the Helpless Individual Through Other Individuals. In one of the New Testament letters, we read: "Religion that is pure and undefiled before God, the Father, is this: to care for orphans and widows in their distress" (James 1:27). Written by James, likely the James whom Paul calls the brother of our Lord (Gal 1:19), the James reputed to be head of the church in Jerusalem. (I'd guess that by now he was also helping take care of his mother.) We know that believers in Jerusalem sold some of their property to share with the needy. Early writers tell us that before long, Christians began picking up abandoned babies and giving them Tender Loving Care. Christians were among the first to establish hospitals. *The whole concept of charity and social welfare had its start in Christ's Concern for the helpless individual, a concern that exhibits itself in his Third Word From the Cross, a concern shown by the disciple whom Jesus loved, and still being shown through other individuals, members of the Body of Christ, his hands and feet in the world.*

Conclusion

As we draw this homily on the Third Word from the Cross to a close, we can allow that "Woman, here is your son; . . . [Son], Here is your mother" is not the whole Gospel. Someone besides Christ could have said this too. But these two sentences are thoroughly in character with all that we know about our Lord, the *concern he has for the individual, especially for the helpless individual, and his mode of operation, showing that concern through other individuals—the hands and the feet of the body of Christ.*

As we keep on meditating on the Third Word from the Cross, we gain new delight in the privilege of taking care of the Lord's mothers and brothers and sisters in our midst.

Do I Give up Praying Too Soon?

Luke 18:1-8

(An example of a one-point homily: the theme is illustrated by one example after another.)

I've heard marvelous stories of people who've prayed and found their prayers answered. I've heard testimonies like that from some of you. I've heard reports from hospital chaplains. One that sticks in my mind is of a young man hopelessly sick. The physicians didn't think surgery would help but they didn't know what else to do. So they tried it. The young man was up and around and out of the hospital in a week. The surgeon had seen this happen before and so he asked, "Did he belong to a group and did this group pray for him?" They checked it out and learned this was exactly the case.

When I hear of experiences like that, I sometimes wonder, "Why don't my prayers get answered?" The doubts increase when I hear Jesus making a wide-sweeping promise such as he did in the Upper Room as recorded in John 16: "Truly, truly, I say to you, if you ask anything of the Father, he will give it to you in my name." Is that really so? If Jesus said it, it must be true. Then why don't my prayers get answered?

There may be a number of reasons, as we see from other Scriptures. But today's Gospel focuses on just one thing: persistence, sticking-to-it. Going by just this story—and others like it—if I want to know why my prayers don't get answered, I have to ask, "Do I give up praying too soon?"

The parable of the widow and the judge speaks for itself. But let me fill you in on some of the background.

There was this judge. Jesus called him "unrighteous" and said he neither feared God nor regarded man. William Barclay in his *Daily Study Bible* observes this was clearly not a Jewish judge, since all ordinary Jewish disputes were taken before the elders and not into the public courts. Larger disputes went before a three-judge panel, one of whom was chosen by the plaintiff, one by the defendant, and one by a neutral body. Since there was only one judge here, Barclay concludes it must have been a Roman magistrate, one of those who was probably looking for a bribe or who would bend under pressure from someone with influence. The Jewish people called the likes of him "robber judges."

Then there was this widow. The Law of Moses dealt more kindly with widows than the law of other nations of that time. But still there was no legal provision for her care, except that it was up to the family—especially the eldest son. That's why he got an extra share of the inheritance. If he didn't do his duty or if he just didn't have anything, the widow had nowhere else to go. There was no Social Security check on the third of the month. She was just up against it. We may see her as the symbol of all who are poor and defenseless. No one to stand up with her before the judge, and the judge was looking for a bribe.

Defenseless—except for one weapon, persistence. For a while the judge refused her pleading, but she kept coming and she finally wore him out. He said to himself: "Though I neither fear God nor regard man, yet because this widow bothers me, I will vindicate her, or she will wear me out by her continual coming."

Since Luke says that Jesus told this parable "to the effect that they ought always to pray and not lose heart," when I wonder, "Why don't my prayers get answered?" I need to ask, "Do I give up praying too soon?"

Luke reports another parable of our Lord with the same encouragement to persistence. It comes in chapter eleven where we read that Jesus told of a friend who came to this man's house at midnight, wanting to borrow three loaves of bread—because a friend had just arrived on a journey and there was nothing in the house to set before him. The neighbor tried to put him off by saying, "Don't bother me; the door is now shut and the children are with me in bed." He had good reason to protest. Let me describe his problem.

He was not in a three bedroom rambler. He had just one room. One end had the floor a bit higher. You could call it a split level hut. The lower end was the winter shelter for the ox, the donkey, the goats, and the dog. The higher level was where the family cooked and ate and slept. At nightfall the people would unroll their mats on the higher level and lie down in their clothes. Often the household would consist of three or four generations including widowed sisters and aunts. I can understand that the man inside had plenty of reason to say, "Don't bother me. The floor is covered with bodies and I don't want to step on anyone. I can't get up to give you a thing."

But the man outside wouldn't quit. And so as Jesus observed: "I tell you, though he will not get up and give him anything because he is his friend, yet because of his importunity he will rise and give him whatever he needs" (Luke 11:8).

Importunity means being persistent to the point of nagging. Another translation uses the word *shamelessness*.

In both parables Jesus argued from the lesser to the greater. He doesn't *liken* God to less than perfect people; he *contrasts* him with them. If the neighbor who was aroused at midnight and the judge who cared neither for God nor man—if these people would eventually give in to a persistent petitioner, won't the Heavenly Father be all the more likely to do the same? Especially since he doesn't regard our pleadings as a nuisance?

After the parable of the neighbor pounding on the door at midnight, Jesus goes on to say: "Ask, and it will be given you; seek, and you will find; knock, and it will be opened to you." In the language Luke used to report Jesus' words, it actually reads: "Keep on asking, and it will be given you; keep on seeking, and you will find; keep on knocking, and it will be opened to you."

In Matthew and Mark there's a vignette, a sketch of how to do it: how to hang on, how to keep on asking, how to keep on seeking, how to keep on knocking.

It's about a woman. That in itself was against her. How could a woman in that culture approach a man in public? She was from the district of Tyre and Sidon, now a part of Lebanon. An outsider. On top of that, a Canaanite, of the race that occupied the Promised Land when Joshua crossed the Jordan to take it away from them, a mortal enemy of the Children of Israel. And like the widow in Jesus' parable, nothing going for her except persistence, in spite of the obstacles.

She was pleading for her daughter who was possessed by a demon. I think she must have felt our Lord was ignoring her. I can identify with that. There are times when I must have given up praying too soon because it seemed God was ignoring me. But this woman kept on asking, kept on seeking, kept on knocking. The disciples grew sick of her: "Get rid of this pest." Then Jesus said something that really should have demolished her: "I was sent only to the lost sheep of the house of Israel." That doesn't sound like our Lord.

But she still kept on asking. She came up and knelt before him and begged, "Lord, help me." We get an inkling of what Jesus the master teacher was up to; he must have been drawing her out because the next thing he came up with was: "It is not fair to take the children's bread and throw it to the dogs." We notice he did not say "mutt" or "cur" or "hound dog" or "mongrel"–which were the customary words for Gentiles–but that he said "pet dog," a member of the family. She noticed it too and right away she said, "Yes, Lord, yet even the pet dogs eat the crumbs that fall from the masters' table. The apostrophe comes after the *s* on *masters' table.* So *masters* is plural. A pet dog has many masters–every person in the house. It's not hard to imagine that some of the younger masters might even have been sneaking a few crumbs to their pet dog on the sly. It was a master stroke; she caught our Lord in his own words. A dog, was she? Well, she was hanging on like a pet bulldog.

Her persistence paid off. Jesus exclaimed, "O woman, great is your faith! Be it done for you as you desire." The gospel writers report that her daughter was healed instantly.

Do I give up praying too soon?

There are some striking pictures in the Hebrew Scriptures about hanging on in prayer. There's Jacob, having run away from home because he'd cheated his brother Esau out of his birthright, now coming home after many years, bothered by his conscience. The Scriptures say he wrestled with God all night, hanging on and saying, "I won't let you go unless you bless me."

There's Moses who one time was holding up his rod; I suppose you could say it was a way to pray. The rod had been God's instrument in so many acts of deliverance. Here they were now in the wilderness, attacked by the Amalekites. So Moses went on top of a hill and held up his rod, and as long as he held it up, the army of Israel was winning. But whenever his arms grew tired and he lowered his rod, the army of Israel was losing. So they gave him a stone to sit on while Aaron and Hur held up his arms, Aaron on the one side, Hur on the other side. "And so his hands were steady until the going down of the sun." Joshua's army prevailed.

There've been times when you and I might also have grown weary. We thought we'd been holding up our arms in prayer for a good long time. We thought we'd been hanging on like pet bulldogs and not letting go. But we had so many reasons to give up. "That job I want; surely others are praying for it too. How can God give it to all of us?" "The money I need: think of all the people in the Third World who live on $100 a year. Why should God listen to me, when compared to them, I'm so well off?" So we get tired and discouraged and we give up. No wonder Jesus remarked, "When the Son of man comes, will he find faith in the earth?"

That's why we also need our Aarons and Hurs to stand by us and help us keep holding up our arms in prayer, like the group surrounding the young man undergoing surgery, who bounced out of bed in a flash. That's why we need the company of believers to encourage us and sometimes to correct us and always to take us to the top of the hill so that like Moses, we can take in the larger view. We also need the company of believers to remind us of God's promises and his larger plans. In the assembly of worship and in our other contacts with the communion of saints, we're reminded of instances like that of Christ in the Garden of Gethsemane. He prayed, "Let me get out of this; yet thy will be done." Did he get out of it? No. Was God's will done? Yes. Did God's kingdom come? Would we have wanted it any other way?

Do I give up praying too soon?

This isn't the only issue involved in our prayer life. Lack of persistence isn't the only reason our prayers aren't answered. But it's the theme of the Gospel for today, the reason the parable was told, that we ought always to pray and not lose heart. To keep our hearts growing in faith, he gave us the Eucharist so that we too may hang on like this widow. "And will not God vindicate his elect, who cry to him day and night? Will he delay long over them? I tell you, he will vindicate them speedily."

Alvin Rueter, *The Freedom to Be Wrong* (Lima, Ohio: CSS Publishing Co., Inc., 1985), 21–26. Reprinted by permission of CSS Publishing.

APPENDIX FIVE

The Freedom to Be Wrong

Luke 18:9-14

Alvin C. Rueter

I want to begin with a situation that might happen to a young person. I hope those of us who are older will think back to our youth and put ourselves into the same story.

Let's say you're still living at home and going to school. On a Saturday night you take the family car. Let's admit you're an excellent driver and that you have the right to think of yourself as careful and prudent at the wheel. This is the image your parents have of you and you're pleased with that. Good for you. You are with the gang at your favorite gathering place and you are taking some of them home. Everyone is laughing and you are backing up—and all of a sudden, crunch. Never happened to you before. Quite a blow to the rear fender and to your self-image. When dad sees the dent in the morning. . . . If you're like many of us, driven by the need to be right, you'll be tossing in bed all night, testing out one alibi after another.

Here's a husband fighting with his wife. It's plain he's in the wrong, and he may even realize that. But he's the macho type and John Wayne would never surrender, would he? So he just hollers louder.

Here's a set of parents concerned about keeping their children's respect. They may believe they should never admit a mistake.

Hung up on the need to be right.

How much this cripples us we can observe in a scene Jesus once drew, about a man who prayed: "God, I thank thee that I am not like other men, extortioners, unjust, adulterers, or even like this tax collector" (Luke 18:11).

This was a Pharisee, Jesus said. We may snicker at his boasting and we may dismiss him as a hypocrite but when we check his record, we find that if he were like other Pharisees, he was really trying. For example, he mentions adulterers. The Pharisees seemed to know that the essence of adultery is lust. That's why some of them—when they went around in public—always kept their eyes closed (so they wouldn't see any women). The folks called them "Bleeding Pharisees," because they kept bumping into trees. Hung up on the need to be right.

Paul had been a Pharisee. He used some crude language to describe how useless his former way of life had been—when he's tried so hard to be blameless. One place he tells about this is in 1 Corinthians 15. Our versions show how he makes the translators blush. When he said he's also seen the risen Christ, the translators have him say, "Last of all, as to one untimely born, he appeared also to me" (1 Cor 15:8). Since he wrote this to be read in a public assembly of worship, I assume he had no qualms about having his real language heard by church people. So I feel I have the right to tell you what he actually wrote: "Last of all, as to a dead fetus, he appeared also to me." That's how sad it is, to be under the compulsion of justifying yourself. That's something of the difficulty of living with the need to be right.

Now I'd like to tell you of the advantages of living forgiven.

Suppose somebody attacks you or me: "Sir," or "Madam," "what you just did was silly." Now if we're trying to make it as an abortion, then we'd answer, "Is that so? Well, I've seen you do a lot worse." You know where that would lead. But when we live forgiven, we rather respond, "Is that so? Tell me more." If it develops that what we'd done was foolish—then since we know that Christ has already atoned for that mistake, we make no alibis. We just admit it, apologize for it, and try to do better. What's so hard about that? But when we need to be right, it's impossible.

When parents live forgiven, they're free to be wrong. Since Christ died for their sins, they may say to their offspring, "We're sorry; we made a mistake." Does that diminish respect?

There are some tortuous problems that parents and young people may need to work out. They have their own points of view. The parents who live forgiven are free to say, "We don't have all the answers. We're not even sure we're right. But because we love you and because of what we do know and because we're afraid of what may happen, here's what we wish you'd do." Does this destroy authority?

As for that dent in the rear fender, there are so many situations like that in my past and I handled them badly. But Christ's atonement covers those mistakes too, and so I'm learning not to dwell on them. The gospel is continually giving me a fresh start. Now that I'm a bit more aware of what it means to live completely forgiven for Christ's sake, if I could live those situations again, I'd do them something like this:

> Dad, I guess I'm not as careful as I thought I was. Last night I was taking some of the gang home and we were laughing and I wasn't paying attention and as I was backing up in the parking lot, I went too far and I ran into a telephone pole and I'm sorry . . .

How would Dad have reacted? Frankly, I think he'd have been confused. I've noticed that's what happens to others. They expect you to make alibis. That they can handle. Then they can fight back, and if they have the need to be right, the argument will have given them a chance to strut their stuff. But when you admit you're wrong, you knock out all their wind, simply because the gospel has given you the freedom to be wrong and the freedom to admit it.

When we humble ourselves like the tax collector, when we refuse to try to justify ourselves by making alibis, then Jesus says we're exalted. I suppose that can mean several things, but for me the best thing I've discovered so far is this relief I get when I don't have to be right.

How refreshing it would be if this gospel could be let loose in the world, so that we and all our neighbors could live forgiven! What a revolution for the good if peoples and parties and nations could just admit, "We goofed. Please forgive us. We'll try to do better."

How pathetic when anyone has to croak, "Nobody's going to shove me around." It's tragic when people get hung up on the need to be right.

The Good News today is this: that the good Lord has justified us for Christ's sake, and that this empowers us to live with the reality that we're less than perfect. God love you!

Revised and reprinted from Alvin Rueter, *The Freedom to Be Wrong* (Lima, Ohio: CSS Publishing Co., Inc., 1985), 27–31. Reprinted by permission of CSS Publishing.

Grateful for the Giver

Luke 17:11-19

Alvin C. Rueter

Imagine a man who will conduct forty to fifty funerals a day, burying nearly 4500 people in all. Among those dying would be his wife. Towards the end the deaths would be so frequent that the bodies would just be placed in trenches without burial rites.

Imagine also that this person would be so thankful for these experiences he'd write a hymn that would be sung by Christians 300 years later on another continent.

A fantasy?

Not if you're describing Martin Rinkart, a Lutheran pastor of Germany during the Thirty Years' War. He lived in a walled city, the walls being the reason it was a place of hiding for thousands of refugees. The over-crowding brought on epidemic and famine. All other officials and pastors fled, leaving Rinkart alone to care for the dying. The hymn he composed: "Now Thank We All Our God." For you see, gratitude does not depend upon the circumstances.

Imagine another man, one who would be wiped out financially. Let's make him a farmer, and let's say there was just too much rain—everything covered with water. Let's also specify that when the land reappears and dries a bit, he'll offer one-seventh of his remaining assets as a thanksgiving to God.

Incredible?

Not if you're describing Noah. For you see, gratitude does not depend upon the circumstances.

Invent an army general whose lines of supply would fall apart. Let's say his men will be starving, their uniforms ragged, their shoes bottomless. When the ordeal is over, he'll issue a proclamation of thanksgiving.

A fairy-tale?

Not if you're describing Washington, "the father of our country." For gratitude does not depend upon the circumstances.

Create a character who'll have no family and no home. He'll be afflicted with a loathsome disease, perhaps one that causes matter to ooze from the eyes, making people hate to look his way. Decorate his body with scars all over from rods and whips and stones. Let's say that in nearly every letter he writes—even when he's in jail unjustly— he thanks God for the privilege of suffering for him.

Unreal?

Not if you're speaking of the Apostle Paul. For gratitude does not depend upon the circumstances.

Here's a man making $500 a week, his wife earning $300 a week, and together they offer $2 every Lord's day for the Gospel. Here's a widow with a pension of $400 a month of which $160 is for rent and $20 is for her pills. And she also offers $2 a week for the Gospel.

Untrue to life?

Every congregation's books can tell this story. For gratitude does not depend upon the circumstances.

We see this vividly in Jesus' healing of the ten lepers, for the circumstances were the same for all but the gratitude was not.

They all had leprosy; that is, they were all dying by inches. Leprosy is a curse of the skin. There are sores that may end up as holes, exposing the joints. The ears can swell up and hang down. The nose might disappear and the tongue become thick and cracked. Whether all ten were equally deteriorated made little difference. It was only a matter of time; what one was, the others would become.

They all had the same living conditions; that is, they were all outcasts. They were required to cover their faces and leave their hair uncombed. They had to warn others to keep their distance by crying out, "Unclean! Unclean!" Anything they touched and any house they entered was pronounced unfit for others until it was cleansed by a special ritual. If they *did* come to a synagogue, they had to sit in a special place. You and I might have felt sorry for them—but their families probably not. Their rabbis taught that leprosy was God's punishment for some gross sin. The marks of their sickness etched into their bodies were big signs reading, "Here walks the scum of the earth!" So their misery did not excite pity but scorn.

Yes, they all had the same living conditions.

They even shared a trust in Jesus. They all went to him. They all came as close as they dared. They all appealed for help. Their prayer we borrow every Sunday: "Lord, have mercy upon us!"

More than that, they all obeyed Jesus. He ordered them to show themselves to the priests (the Department of Health of their country). And they all went before they had any sign of a cure, for as Luke reports, "As they went they were cleansed."

They were furthermore all alike in being healed. Leprosy deadens the sense of feeling, but now there was feeling in their fingers. Leprosy gives an unholy tint to the skin, but now there was pinkness in their flesh.

As they heard the priest declare them fit to be with, they were probably all alike in their excitement:

"I haven't seen the old farm in years."

"I wonder how my shop's been doing."

"My little boy was just crawling when I had to leave home. I'll bet he can pick me up now."

We can see them, each looking at each other in open wonder, all in the same circumstances. But nine scattered to the winds, and only one turned back to offer thanks.

It's painfully clear then that gratitude does not depend upon the circumstances. What can account for the difference between the nine and the one?

II

It could well be this, that the nine wanted the gift but not the Giver. They were out to exploit God, to get what they could from him. Like others today, they only needed him when they were in a spot. Something like some soldiers in World War II who gave us the proverb, "No atheists in foxholes." When the bullets and the bombs were screaming, oh how they prayed. (Couldn't do any harm.) But when the crisis was over, so was the praying. It was in this sense the nine former lepers were still sick. The public health department pronounced them whole, but Jesus did not.

Any relationship that's exploitive is sick. Where a man uses a woman or a woman uses a man—even though they might be married—the relationship is sick. People using their neighbors—that's sick. In a re-run of "The Mary Tyler Moore Show" we saw Mary staggering home under two overflowing bags of groceries. In comes neighbor Phyllis who thanks her for "picking up a few things" since she was going to the store anyway. Then we saw Mary take out just one quart of milk for herself while Phyllis grabbed all the rest and carried it all away. Funny but sick.

The Bible sometimes shows us leprosy as a picture of sin. This disease of the nine that deadens the sense of feeling and eats away muscle and organ and bone is a symbol of how selfishness numbs our conscience and consumes our integrity.

Our Lord by his selfless living and dying and rising has cleansed us of the gnawing guilt that erodes our personality and befouls our human relationships. Our faith in him makes us well. Nurtured by Word and Sacrament, we grow in the assurance of being loved by God. Nurtured by Word and Sacrament, we are becoming whole. Nurtured by this grace that comes to us without our deserving it, we are becoming more like God, more able to love others without their deserving it, more able to love them without our trying to use them, more able to be clean in our relationships.

That this happens (or can happen) to you and me helps us understand what Jesus said to the Samaritan. Didn't the nine also become clean? Didn't Jesus admit that when he mused, "Were not ten cleansed?" Why did he tell the one thankful one, "Your faith has made you well," when the nine were also cured? Yes, they'd lost their leprosy, but they hadn't found the Samaritan's humility. They enjoyed the gift, but they didn't want the Giver.

The nine had experienced the grace of God that lets his rain and sunshine bless the evil as well as the good. The nine—by the grace of God—could gather with their nine families for a dinner of reunion. The nine—by the grace of God—could also enjoy the chatter and chuckles of cousins and the aromas and tastes of roasts and desserts. For the grace of God comes without strings; it delivers daily bread even to the wicked without their prayers. It often delivers even cake.

But the children of God (whose faith has made them well—that is, whose humble trust has taken hold of his offer of forgiveness through Christ), these have learned to know the Giver, so that their delight in his gifts is multiplied. Like the grateful leper, they can't think of the blessings without thinking of God, and they can't think of him without offering him thanks.

We could sum it all up then by saying our gratitude and our giving and our service to our neighbor don't depend upon our circumstances but in being made whole, or right with our Lord. We're grateful for the Giver.

Preached at American Lutheran Church, Lincoln, Nebraska, and published in Alvin Rueter, *The Freedom to Be Wrong* (Lima, Ohio: CSS Publishing Co., 1985), 17–20. Reprinted by permission of CSS Publishing.

The Uglier She Gets

Ephesians 5:25-27

Alvin C. Rueter

You're at a wedding. You barely made it, because you took pains to be scrubbed and shined and combed.

As you sit in the pew, you enjoy the lovely work of the organist, and you admire the poised and thoughtful ushers. The parents of the groom walk down the aisle, straight, proud, and well-dressed. Then of course, the mother of the bride. She has an orchid, and she is beaming. Her hair has obviously been set by topnotch talent.

Next, the soloist shares the result of years of discipline, and he thrills you with his voice. The bridesmaids glide in on cue, in varied pastels, erect and graceful, every eyelash in place. A flower girl trips down to the front, shy and glistening.

Oh yes, the groom. He and his brigade have slipped in also. Shoes polished like mirrors, trousers sharp as knives.

And now, here comes the bride. Her hair is stringy. Her face is grimy. Her fingernails are jagged. And her dress? She took it out of the trunk this morning. It reeks of mothballs. It's creased, and it's stained with gravy and beer.

Far-fetched?

Take another look:

> Husbands, love your wives, just as Christ loved the church and gave himself up for her, in order to make her holy by cleansing her with the washing of water by the word, so as to present the church to

himself in splendor, without a spot or wrinkle or anything of the kind—yes, so that she may be holy and without blemish.

You are aware of this concept, that Scriptures speak of the church as the bride of Christ.

I shudder when I notice how the prophet Hosea makes use of this motif. Did his wife actually become unfaithful? Did she sink so low as to sell herself as a prostitute? Did Hosea—after years of her deserting him—did he truly come across a slave auction and see his own wife for sale? Did he really have the graciousness to buy her back and bring her home, not as a slave but as his wife? Did Hosea need to go through this kind of hell to comprehend God's feelings about us?

For the church has been blotched and creased and willing to be violated. With apologies to a certain group of paperbacks, we may say the history of the church could be called, "The Case of the Dirty, Wrinkled Bride."

I

Let's take an embarrassed look at some of her stains.

In the Middle Ages, Christ's bride was the world's largest holder of land, and offices in the hierarchy—having the income from this real estate—were sold for money. Some of the lightning response to Luther's 95 theses was touched off by the people's hope that now they might be rid of the tyranny that was bleeding them blue.

But the nuptial dress of the Church of the Reformation is not without its spots.

About 200 years after Luther, there was "The Age of Rationalism," where reason was lord. As for God's becoming man, this was ridiculous, so rationalistic Lutheran preachers, noting that Jesus was born in a stable, took that as their springboard to urge farmers to keep their beasts inside during winter. This was their Christmas message. As for Christ's dying and rising to set us free from our guilt, this was further folly, so rationalistic Lutheran preachers, observing that the women came to the tomb at sunrise, would praise the advantages of early rising. This was their Easter message.

In years not too far past, Christians would storm out of their Good Friday services all afire, to hunt down the village Jew and beat him up. In our lifetime, we wince at the charge that the hour in church on Sunday is the most segregated time in the week. There are still other blotches on the bridal gown, too many to mention here.

II

Perhaps you're saying, "Preacher, you're absolutely right. The church is disgusting. I used to work for her, but I got no cooperation, and those who did nothing were the first to complain."

I have a great deal of sympathy for that attitude, because I have also seen the bride of Christ up close, and I have had several whiffs of her breath. But I can't get over the fact that Christ has loved this adulteress and given himself up for her.

This is the remarkable thing about the Gospel reading that begins with Jesus saying, "Behold, we are going up to Jerusalem." Why didn't he stay in Galilee? Yes, I remember that his hometown folks once tried to shove him off a cliff, so Galilee had its perils too, but not like Jerusalem. He'd been down there soon after his baptism and aroused so much opposition he had to return to Galilee where he did most of his work. He knew that whenever he'd go to Jerusalem, he'd be in danger, that the established church would deliver him to the Gentiles, to be mocked and shamefully treated and spit upon. Nevertheless, ". . . we are going up to Jerusalem." For Christ, reliving the experience of Hosea, "loved the church and gave himself up for her."

Now, how shall we regard this smelly, unkempt bride? They tell us that an unlovable spouse is really begging for love. Attack the monster, and it will flare back. Kiss the beast, and it becomes a lovely princess.

But we're thinking mainly about the church. Isn't it true that the uglier she gets, the more she needs our love?

Preached at Luther Seminary, St. Paul, Minnesota, and published in *The Lutheran Standard*, 17 February 1970, 3–4.

Hey Mom! Guess What Me and Jesus Did Today!

2 Corinthians 9:15

Alvin C. Rueter

When the report cards come home showing that the youngsters have done their best, is this unspeakable satisfaction God's inexpressible gift?

When there's a young fellow of whom you approve walking your daughter home—the wrens are singing, the maples are budding, your daughter's hair is shining, the lad's feet at the end of his awkward legs bounce in a special way, and they're both rather shy—is this God's inexpressible gift?

When you're playing a quiet game with the older children and the younger tykes sit and watch with saucer eyes, and you turn to look at them and they give you a little sigh and a sheepish smile, is this God's inexpressible gift?

You go for a drive. The trees hold fluffy snow on their limbs, but the road is clear and smooth and so you push down on the accelerator. Your car may not be the newest, but it's just been tuned and serviced. The power below your foot responds, the fruition of all the ages it took the oil and the metals to form in the earth and the backbreaking labor before someone tumbled onto the wheel. Every bit of this heritage is now at the command of your hand and foot. But all the conveniences of modern life can't be what Paul meant by his inexpressible gift.

There's a lake you like to sneak off to. You fry your panfish in the open air. Or you have a stereo set; you lie down on the couch and bathe yourself with the sound. Or you've been sick, and through the ministration of a kindly physician, the tender loving care of genial nurses, and the miracle-working mystery of those startling shots, you've been given merciful relief. And while you were down, your neighbors did your laundry. How can you say what you feel about hobbies, health, and friends? Yet none of these is what Paul meant by God's inexpressible gift.

Just what is it?

Is it the forgiveness of sins for Jesus' sake? Isn't that the greatest boon of all? Without a doubt. But was Paul referring to that when he burst out, "Thanks be to God for his inexpressible gift"?

This exuberance comes as the climax of two whole chapters. What was he discussing in 2 Corinthians 8 and 9? A few samples will give you the idea (I'll put what I consider to be the key words in boldface):

> And it is in God's power to provide you richly with every good gift; thus you will have ample means in yourselves to meet each and every situation **with enough and to spare for every good cause**.
>
> Now he who provides seed for sowing and bread for food will provide the seed for you to sow; he will multiply it and swell the harvest of your benevolence, **and you will always be rich enough to be generous**. 2 Cor 9:8, 10 (NEB)

Then Paul went on to explain that you and I are going to be the cause of prayers of thanksgiving rising to the throne of grace from the hearts of Christians and non-Christians in Michigan, Madagascar, and Manila:

> For through the proof which this affords, many will give honor to God when they see how humbly you obey him and how faithfully you confess the Gospel of Christ, **and will thank him for your liberal contribution to their need and to the general good**.
>
> And as they join in prayer on your behalf, their hearts will go out to you **because of the richness of the grace which God has imparted to you**.
>
> **Thanks be to God for his gift beyond words!** 2 Cor 9:13-15 (NEB)

I ask you then to consider whether God's unspeakable gift might not be the ability to give.

There may be a hint of this in what must have been the experience of a young boy long ago. I can just hear him as he runs into the house and hollers, "Hey, Mom! Can me and Joel take a hike out into the country? Joel's dad says there's a whole bunch of people out there. And Jesus is there. Can I go?"

I suppose Mother might have said, "Oh, all right, if you'll be home by dark. Here, you'd better take along some biscuits and fish; you'll get hungry walking that far."

Now when this lad came home that night, imagine how he must have swaggered: head back, chest out, arms swinging, and then yelling: "Hey, Mom! Guess what me and Jesus did today!"

Fifty years later, look at him sitting in front of his hut at sundown. See him chuckle as the youngsters run up to shout, "Hey, Grandpa! Tell us about the time you and Jesus fed 5,000 people!"

I wonder if this wasn't the kind of thing Paul had in mind when he told the Corinthians, "God loves a cheerful giver." The word he used for *cheerful* is the one from which we get *hilarious*. I can't imagine anything more hilarious for that man, refreshing his whole life, than the memory of that one spring day when he teamed up with Jesus to feed 5,000 men besides women and children. What an inexpressible gift!

Can we have it too?

Others have more beautiful homes. We're renting, and the rent is high. Or if we bought ours, we put so little down that nearly all the payment is for interest and we won't get on our feet for years. How can we afford the fun of giving?

Others have newer cars. Ours needs four tires and some work on the transmission. Others have healthy children. We're forever buying medicine. Others get wages that keep up with rising costs. We're on a fixed income. How can we afford the fun of giving?

Jesus was dealing with this very area of life when he spoke of a camel going through the eye of a needle more easily than a rich man entering heaven. It was on this very bone the disciples were gagging. Compared with us, they were miserably poor, and still they said, "Who then can be saved?" For they realized that the fingers of greed, envy, and complaining also clutched at their throats.

To dissolve this despair, Jesus then declared, "For mortals it is impossible, but for God all things are possible." (Matt 19:26) In other words, it's God's gift to be able to give! To know the hilarity of giving, to have the same fun God has. This is from him.

Sometimes we might wish God wouldn't enjoy being generous quite so much, the way he throws around the seed of dandelions, crab grass, and Chinese elms. But as I have pulled and pulled on these weeds, I've come to feel they're a sort of reverse picture of the way God throws grace around.

The Eucharist brings us that abundant grace. In the death and resurrection of Christ, there's an atonement big enough for every soul: for all the people who take baths and plenty yet for those who don't. His grace is enough for every drunk, every tyrant, every adulterer. Enough for every scoffer, every liar, every cheat. For every Pharisee, publican, and backslider. His atonement is adequate for all the billions now alive, or who have lived, or who will live. What a waste! To flood the earth with grace, enough for the many when he knows he'll get response only from the few!

But God gives hilariously. And his inexpressible gift to us is that he shares the hilarity of being able to give.

Preached at American Lutheran Church, Lincoln, Nebraska, and published in *The Lutheran Standard*, 6 June 1972, 10–11. Used by permission.

Turn on the Light for Children

Alvin C. Rueter

The preschool children are on the chancel steps, each holding up an index finger and singing, "This little light of mine, I'm going to let it shine." They get to the stanza, "Hide it under a bushel, no," covering the index finger with the other hand and shaking their heads vigorously on "No." Later they rotate the index finger above their heads for the words, "All around the neighborhood, I'm going to let it shine."

A charming scene. Parents and grandparents—indeed all grown-ups—are beaming. The little darlings are getting through to the adults with a telling reminder that Christ calls his church to reflect his light of hope. But are the children getting through to themselves?

In some churches the pastor may have a children's message during the service, one more way to encourage the little ones to be present in the assembly of believers. The preacher may have a flashlight as an "object lesson." He or she may speak of how spooky darkness can be and how comforting the light then becomes. "So, children, isn't it wonderful that Jesus is our light?"

Do Children Understand?

But to whom has the herald proclaimed this good news? No doubt to the adults, several of whom will probably comment, "I sure enjoyed that 'object lesson' today." Yet, did the children comprehend?

When pastors ask youngsters to come into the chancel for the "children's sermon," young people from age two at the youngest to ten at the oldest accept the invitation. But pastors rarely seem to realize how different this little "congregation" is.

Young children are literalists. They do not think in symbols, as adults do. I was reminded of this when I once did a flannelgraph story for a preschool department. I carelessly remarked that my character was "up a tree." Little hands went up and the question was asked, "But where's the tree?"

Well then, shall we discourage parents, teachers, and preachers from using objects in communicating the gospel to young children? Not at all. But if we're speaking to children, let's speak to children. (Not that we speak down to them. Why should we do that when our Lord has made them models for our faith?)

Using an object when speaking to children merely requires that we let the thing stand for itself. When discussing the First Commandment, we might show a small statue of Buddha or a good-luck piece (like a horseshoe). When considering the text, "Your body is a temple of the Holy Spirit," and applying that to the care of our bodies, we might show a toothbrush. The Buddha and the horseshoe and the toothbrush are simply what they are and not figures of speech.

People of all ages appreciate being able to see the good news. To turn on the light for smaller children: objects, yes; object lessons, not yet.

The Lutheran Standard, 15 April 1980, 11. Reprinted by permission.

The Fool

Luke 12:13-21

Therese Frederick

(Given 11 October 1994 in a class for aspiring permanent deacons, Archdiocese of St. Paul and Minneapolis. A three-minute exercise imitating the Black Preacher. Also following the format of a story homily. Transcribed from video cassette, used by permission.)

In Luke 12, verses 13 through 21, Luke has Jesus outside with this crowd of people and he's teaching them when all of a sudden during his teaching, this man runs up to him and interrupts him saying, "Teacher, Teacher, make my brother give me my rightful share of the inheritance." Jesus could have done that because back in those days, rabbis were often called into disputes like that and he was more than qualified, but he decided to turn this into a teaching moment. I looked again at this text in Luke and I thought to myself, "A teaching moment on what?" Well, Jesus decided it would be a teaching moment on "The Trap of Possessions and Greed." And I stopped and thought, "O my gosh, the trap of possessions. We have the house that's just been redecorated, the cars, nice clothes, good food . . . . He had my interest."

So back to Jesus. He starts telling a story. This is how the story went. There was a very rich farmer who had an incredible harvest. It was the type of season every farmer dreams of. It rained when it was supposed to rain. The sun shone when it was supposed to be warm, and the crops dried out just perfect, and when he got his harvest in, he had so much that he couldn't fit it in the silos that he had. This man was self-absorbed, so his only choice was to knock down all the granaries he had and build bigger and better ones to hold his abundance. And he said, "Now I can sit back. Now I can relax. I can make it through the droughts. I can make it for years on this harvest. It's going to be an easy life." I said, "Yeah, that's smart planning. I mean, Joe and I have our IRAs and college funds and we try to save money up and try not to get too many loans against our mortgage. Isn't that just good planning?" I thought, "This is starting to get a little personal." So, back to the story.

God says to this man, "You fool! What a fool you are!" I say to myself, "Am I a fool?" So I looked up *fool*. In those days a fool meant someone who didn't believe in God and did not believe in God's will, and usually their life-style was a detriment to society. Well, I believe in God, and I believe in his will, and I don't think I'm a detriment to society; so maybe I'm not a fool—as God called this man.

Well, back to this man. God threw him the punchline and he said, "Tonight you die. Now what are you going to do with this harvest? Bring it with you? Not! Who are you going to give it to? Are you going to let it just mold into the ground?" And then God said, "This is precisely what will happen to people who try to build riches up for themselves instead of finding riches in God."

Well, I stopped then and thought of all of us here and how different we all are from two years ago, how we are searching for God. I can think of where I was two years ago, and I'm different, and I'll never be with God the way I was two years ago because I'm so much closer to God, and I feel that we are all on that journey.

The story finishes and Jesus leaves the crowd hanging with the thought, "So what's the meaning of life?" And I, 2000 years later, I ask myself, "What's the meaning of life?" Jesus told them, "To find the meaning of life, you need to acknowledge God and give alms to the needy." So I thought about that "Urban Plunge" we did at the end of the first year, how moved I was, how much need there is out there and suffering, and yet the great programs that we can get involved in. How Steve Adrian said, "We need to be ministers in the marketplace, putting others before ourselves." I just really think that we are all on a journey walking to our God, and my prayer for us all is that we can rise to that challenge.

To Be Somebody

Luke 19:1-10

Alvin C. Rueter

A few years ago, Vance Packard wrote a book he called *The Status Seekers*. From him and others like him we learn that having an office with a window and a carpet might be more important than getting a raise.

So what encouragement is there for those who make sandwiches for a cafeteria? Or who fill mail orders at Wards? Or who make boxes at Hoerner Waldorf? Or who are retired—whose job history is in the past?

Martin Luther King Jr. coined a word that says what we all hunger for: *somebodiness*. It seems to me that's one way to describe what was driving Zaccheus, his urge to be somebody. Let's use our imaginations to see how this ambition might have been spurring him on and what his encounter with our Lord did for him and what it might do for us.

I

I'm going to call this first part *Dreams*. I'm guessing the parents of Zaccheus must have built some castles in the air. I say that because of the name they chose for him. In their language, *Zaccheus* means, "The one who is pure and just."

I'm guessing Zaccheus might also have had some dreams, flights of fancy about overcoming his handicap. Luke says he was "small of stature." We know how cruel children can be when somebody's a bit different. "Shorty" and "Runt" are just two of the names they hurl around. It wouldn't have been strange if more than once Zaccheus might have muttered to himself, "You just wait; I'll show you!" So he got into the tax business where he could show them because there was money in it. But of course he'd had to start at the bottom, say in some jerkwater village like Nazareth or Bethlehem where he served as a clerk perhaps. We can imagine he had dreams there too. "Some day I'm going to be the superintendent of taxes! And I'll have my headquarters in Jericho. Wow! With all that fertile land and all those springs of water, think of the dates I can tax. And the oil from the balsam trees, oil they make into medicine—the balm of Gilead—oil worth twice its weight in silver, oil that scents the air like perfume. (I hear that's how Jericho got its name: "the place of perfume.") Yes, that's what I want to be, superintendent of taxes. At Jericho, where I can tax all those caravans from Syria and Arabia that cross the Jordan here. At Jericho, where I'll be at the top of my profession!"

When we meet him that's where he was. Whatever in those days corresponded to an office with a window and a carpet, Zaccheus must have had it.

He was really showing them now. They weren't laughing at him any more; they were shaking in their boots. With the spears of the Roman army to back him up, he could stop any family in a donkey cart and bellow, "How much did this wagon cost you?" If they answered, "$20," he knew they were lying; it was probably closer to $40. "Don't kid me. I'm going to assess at $100 and what are you going to do about it. You owe me $30 in taxes." If they protested, "We don't have it," he'd say, "Then I'll lend it to you and the interest will be $10 a month." Zaccheus was doing all right. Not everyone will realize his or her dream but Zaccheus seems to have done it.

II

Or did he? The name-calling really hadn't stopped. And nobody dropped in at his house just to visit. No one smiled at him on the street or called out a cheery "Shalom!" Not even his family was proud of him. Yes, they accepted the good living he provided—but that's about all he was good for. They didn't care to go out in public either, because people would spit on them because of him. It must have dawned on Zaccheus that all he had was money.

Did Zaccheus ever wonder about the aspirations his parents must have had for him when they gave him his name? "The one who is pure and just"? Look at him roosting on his perch. Did he ever think he'd be sitting in a sycamore tree, one of the richest men in the financial center of Judea, squatting there on a branch like an urchin of the street? No matter how short he may have been, this was a grown man. Luke doesn't say what motivated Zaccheus, but it must have been something pretty strong. Whatever it was that pushed him to scramble up that sycamore tree, I'm calling this second part "Shattered Dreams," the dull sense that his life was empty, that for all his striving to be a somebody, he was still a nobody. Was the crowd laughing at him? Let 'em laugh. He was sick and tired of himself. He'd heard of this man who befriended sinners. He wanted a peek at him.

III

Was he surprised! Jesus stopped and looked up and said, "Zaccheus!" (Jesus knew his name!) And then he said, "Be quick and come down." What for? Did Jesus also think it was silly for the superintendent of taxes in the top district of the country to be perching in a tree? If he'd said no more, you might assume that, but he went on to say, "For I must stay with you today." Never in the world could Zaccheus have summoned up the courage to have invited Jesus—so our Lord invites himself. This is the gospel, that God comes to us. One of our hymns puts it this way:

> I sought the Lord and afterward I knew
> It was not I that found, O Savior true;
> No, I was found of thee. (*Service Book and Hymnal,* 473)

This is Christ standing at the door and knocking. This is what the prophet wrote when he was quoting God, "Before they call, I will answer" (Isa 65:24). This is like our baptism, where God claims us before we could acknowledge him.

The crowds murmured when they saw the rabbi walking home with the sinner. They shouldn't have been surprised. The God of Israel had communed with Abraham the liar. (Abraham had passed off his wife as his sister a couple of times; Sarah was good-looking and when he was in foreign territory, he was afraid they'd kill him and steal her if they knew they were married.) The God of Israel had blessed Jacob the thief, Rahab the harlot, and David the adulterer. If the crowds around the sycamore tree had only known their own history, they wouldn't have sniggered and hissed at this odd couple.

As Jesus and Zaccheus arrived at their destination, I can see the host rushing through the door and I can hear him hollering, "Mama, think of it! We have company! And guess who!"

What did they talk about? The loneliness of a publican's family? The Persian rugs bought with the bread of peasants? The dead-end nothingness of their existence?

Whatever their conversation, the love of Christ transformed this poor fellow and enabled him to declare: "Look, half of my possessions I give to the poor; and if I have defrauded anyone of anything, I will pay back four times as much" (Luke 19:8).

Jesus affirmed his break with the past, saying: "Today salvation has come to this house, because he too is a son of Abraham. For the Son of Man came to seek out and to save the lost" (Luke 19:9-10).

I'm calling this third part "The Gospel Restores His Dream." He who was lacking in height had become nine feet tall. He who'd been a nobody now felt he was somebody. He who'd been tromping on people now saw himself blessed to be a blessing. And so salvation—wholeness—had come to his house.

I'm assuming that some of us—perhaps most of us—haven't reached the top as Zaccheus had. I'm assuming some of us—perhaps most of us—still have the illusion (and I'm afraid the notion haunts me too much) that if we'd rise to the top, then we'd really be somebody. Zaccheus shows us this "ain't necessarily so." No matter on which rung we roost, would that we can find joy in knowing Christ has accepted us—that he's even willing to come to us in the Eucharist—and that's why we are somebody! We really are. Whether we solder the same connection on one piece after another, hour by hour, or make beds in a hotel day after day, or sweep floors or drive trucks or repair machinery—our status doesn't come from the window view in our office or the carpet on the floor, but from the Lord who invites himself to our house and thereby gives us dignity undreamed of.

Lord, if you could find Zaccheus and help him find himself, then you can help us be somebody too.

Alvin Rueter, *The Freedom To Be Wrong* (Lima, Ohio: CSS Publishing Co., 1985), 33–37. Reprinted by permission of CSS Publishing.

Beautiful Sinners

1 John 4:10-11

Pirkko Lehtiö

Morning Prayer, 30 January 1996
Lutheran Theological Seminary, Hong Kong

Have you ever thought how little we can see about ourselves? We sit here in our chapel looking at the backs of other people. Have you ever looked at your own back? You say, "Yes, in a mirror." But we never see our back—but even worse—we can never look at our faces—without a mirror. When we look down or to one side, we see something about our nose and cheek, but our real faces are only for others to look at. It is sometimes funny to look at somebody gazing at his or her face in a mirror without knowing that another person is watching. That person makes different faces like a mime: looks at the nose, the eyes, etc. He or she tries to find a perspective where the face would be in the best shape. That's all right. We learn to know ourselves from the outside, from that part that's hidden from us. Others have to tolerate my face. They read my facial expressions like an open book, something I could never do for myself. Am I beautiful? What do other persons think about my face? Sometimes we suddenly see our face in a mirror when we walk on the street. Immediately we correct something. We wonder: what do others really see when they look at me? What do my eyes tell them?

I remember the theme of a sermon last summer. The preacher cited a sentence as said by Luther: "A sinner is beautiful because he or she is beloved, beloved by God." We? Sinners? Beautiful? Not without the love of God. The loving relationship of God toward us is so powerful that even the ugliest person is beautiful. When we receive love abundantly, it shines on our face, on our eyes, and our whole body, in the position where we sit, in the way we give our hand to another person.

God loved the world and his creatures so much that he sent his only Son to save us, to show his love toward us. We do not have any picture of Jesus. Fortunately not. If we did have this picture, we surely would have already done a doctrine of it. More important than to know his face is to know him in his deeds and words. He came into this world because of us—to show God's love toward us, toward me. Many times we do not love ourselves. We hate to be what we are. But God loves me! When I realize that, there is no reason to hate myself. But it is no reason to love myself so that I regard myself as superior to others. My love toward myself comes out of the love I receive. To love others as myself after that is possible.

God's love toward me is without conditions. When Jesus was incarnated, he was born as a baby. He started life like everyone of us. He received the love of his mother, the caring of his father. He grew up as every other child. He was filled with wisdom (not with knowledge), and the favor of God was upon him. He lived under the same conditions as we do. He was seen by others; he lived for others. In him we see what the human life is all about. He was and is the love of God toward us. Our face can be toward him so that God's love shines to me. It is not only that he did something for me, he also looked at me. He sees in me the person for whom he came into this world. His love is not expecting anything from me. His love is only for me to receive.

I am wondering whether I indeed grasp that. The person loved by God then lives for others. Therefore we cannot see our own faces but the faces of others. It is not necessary to try to look at my own face but to look at him and the others he loves. Do I see another person as loved by God? Do I see a criminal or drug addict as his beloved one? Do I see a prostitute as loved by him? Or do I ask whether they love God? If I demand God's love from my neighbor, the gospel becomes law. Do I see a needy person as loved by God so that I am able to share what I have? When I prepared this morning prayer, I started to think about the fact that I can see my picture only as twisted in a mirror, but I am able to see in the face of others the person who is loved by God. Then I do not need to see myself at all. Through another person I see God's love and so also his love toward me.

When I look at my neighbor, I see a beautiful person because God loves him or her. A sinner, including me, is beautiful because he or she is loved by God.

And God showed his love for us by sending his only Son into the world, so that we might have life through him. This is what love is: it is not that we have loved God, but that he loved us and sent his Son to be the means by which our sins are forgiven (1 John 4:9-10 [TEV]).

Christ, I look at your loving person. You let God's love shine toward me. Let your love warm me so that I can love those you love. Let your love open myself toward your love, so that my face is beautiful because you love me, a sinner. Let me see your love on the face of my neighbor. Thank you for your abundant love. Let your face shine upon us and grant us peace. Amen.

Printed by permission.

Victims of the System: What Beards and Gray Hairs Have in Common

Alvin C. Rueter

A grown man and his family were going to visit his mother. The man—on vacation—had decided to take a rest from shaving until he reported back for work. After two days of travel and a year of not seeing his mother, he was expecting a happy reunion. But when he came through his mother's door, she saw not him but his beard. Her first words were, "You ought to have a spanking."

Thinking of all the expense of shaving and the nuisance of mowing the stubble once or twice a day—wouldn't *not* shaving make more sense? Isn't a beard more in line with nature than a naked face? Didn't this mother's grandfather likely have whiskers? Why has the beard become so distasteful to older folks?

It appears that hair on the face isn't the issue at all, but rather an underlying misunderstanding and distrust. The beard is probably just a symbol of the tension between two life-styles. The old go to bed early; the young prefer to stay up later. The old like to keep things as they were; the young want something new. The old generally respect authority; the young often ask, "Why?"

The tension is not unnoticed in a congregation. The old like the hymns they've always sung; the young want a folk song liturgy with a guitar. The old take pride in the building they sacrificed for; the young question whether the Lord's money should be invested in bricks.

Yet the old notice the young aren't backward about using their building. They accuse them of being "freeloaders" for not helping to maintain with offerings and loving care. The young point out that not every women's circle cleans up the kitchen too well either.

Seemingly Incompatible

In many a city, there will be one or more neighborhoods where these two seemingly incompatible groups are thrown together by the force of economics. The Medicare card holders—whose children have moved elsewhere—stay on in the homes they've paid for. But as some of their neighbors die, young adults move into the rooming houses carved out of former one-family dwellings.

In these communities are congregations like the one I serve: new when the homes were new, maturing with the buildings, with a constituency almost parallel to that of the vicinity. The senior citizens, having a 50-year habit of loyalty, come to their church with faithfulness and zeal. The young adults may have less commitment—if not to the Lord at least to this parish.

This means that when a newcomer young adult looks in on us, he may not find too many of his own age and may decide this is not the place to be. At least, that's what some used to tell us. Yet Bethlehem—and all other congregations like her—are called to minister to these very sections of our population which seem so disparate and discrepant.

After having lived with this situation for some time, I'm coming to believe that, although on the surface there seem to be reasons for hostility, underneath there's a great deal of unrecognized mutuality.

A Sense of Being Ridiculed

The first item on my tally of what senior citizens and young adults share is a *sense of being ridiculed.* In Psalm 71, the child of God prays: "Do not cast me off in the time of old age; forsake me not when my strength is spent."

Like used tires on a scrap heap or worn-out refrigerators that belong in the dump, many regard the old as a nuisance, ugly, and even dangerous. Instead of following the counsel of Leviticus to "rise in the presence of gray hairs," our TV commercials scream that gray hairs should be covered with dye, that wrinkles should be plastered smooth with goop.

Rather than admiring the experience and expertise of the elderly, our culture insinuates that we should adore only the young. I have some personal feelings about this, because congregations have a way of looking for a pastor who has had at least 20 years of experience but is no older than 35.

As with other forms of prejudice, we tend to deal in stereotypes. The Archie Bunkers say, "All niggers are alike." So also the youth have been heard to put all old people in the same box: "They're all cranky; they're all messy; they're all mean."

This sense of being ridiculed, which senior citizens feel so keenly, is suffered by young adults too. They also smart under the sting of being stereotyped: "They're all drug addicts; they're all dirty; they're all practicing free love."

Now some of our older ones will object: "I don't go for this business of stereotyping either, but I just don't care for the way the young people look. They wear those overalls and they go barefooted. And you can't tell the girls from the boys."

I hear voices inside me that holler the same noises. But the young respond, "Don't judge us by our appearance."

Don't we grandparents ask for the same courtesy? We gaze in the mirror and although we can't deny the marks of aging, we feel as though the same person stands there now who stood there in 1943. We want to say to the world, "Don't go by my hair or wrinkles or my fingers; I'm the same me I always was."

I understand both beards and gray hairs to be saying: "Don't cast me off for what you see on the outside. Don't lump me together with everyone else. Don't ridicule me, please; it hurts too much."

Victims of the System

The second item on my list of things common to young adults and senior citizens is that both groups are *victims of the system.*

Those who look for their Social Security checks on the third of the month—while benefiting from the system—are also its pawns. Some manipulators in Europe, afraid that Watergate weakens the president's power to regulate the economy, want to exchange their dollars for gold, driving gold up and our money down. Which means our prices keep rising. Our senior citizens with their fixed incomes have nothing to say about it, but they suffer for it.

The pills they must buy usually come from a prescription that specifies a brand name and therefore costs more. But the same medicine—without the brand name—could be delivered for just a few pennies. The senior citizens read in their journals how much the drug companies spend each year to educate physicians to specify their special products. The older folks probably use more drugs proportionately than any other group; they have nothing to say about it, but they suffer for it.

Young adults also see themselves as victims of the system. They've observed defense contractors in search of a market and heard them pleading, "Look how many breadwinners will be thrown out of work if we have to close down." Young adults have noticed the army's fear of becoming obsolete and its need for a theater of operation where nuclear armament couldn't be used, to prove it's just as important as the air force and the navy.

When we got sucked into a war, young adults had to do the fighting. They had nothing to say about it, but they suffered for it. They tried to say something, but nobody was listening. So the young men let their hair and their whiskers grow; maybe that would get our attention. They staged protests. When nothing happened, the next protest was not peaceful, and the country was outraged at those upstarts.

Whether or not we older ones agree with the young adults on this score, they're only confirmed in their conviction that they're victims of the system. But they're not alone in their frustration; if they'd look around, they'd find senior citizens are fellow sufferers.

Hunger for Personal Worth

The third item on my list of what beards and gray hairs have in common is that *both are hungering for personal worth.*

I quote from a speech by the Rev. John Mason, director of the American Lutheran Church Services for the Aging:

> We often hear it said, "I don't know what has happened to George. He can remember everything that happened 40 years ago, but he can't remember what happened five minutes ago."
>
> Actually what has happened to George has a simple explanation. Forty years ago he was a real person, a value to his family, his church, his community, and most importantly, to himself. . . . Today he lives in a world where no one cares what he thinks. . . . To live in yesterday, even in a dream world, is more pleasant than to live in the cold reality of today where he does not have value.

In the struggle for identity, the interests of young and old are particularly close. Are young adults trying to find themselves in the discovery of their proper vocation? The senior citizens had vocations, but they took them away. Are young adults testing themselves in the search for life partners? Senior citizens may have lost their spouses.

The secret of finding personal worth lies not in what is transient but mainly in what is transcendent. We find out who we are not only through what may pass away (or maybe never come to us at all) but through One who never wavers or falls. Our chief and lasting identity is as "children of the heavenly Father."

A French author, Francois Mauriac, said that no persons created by the Father, redeemed by the Son, and born again by the Holy Spirit can ever count themselves unimportant. If they take away the job that used to pay our salary, or if they don't let us have the position we'd really like—they still can't take away our major identity.

That has lots of possibilities. John says: "Everyone who believes that Jesus is the Christ is a child of God, and everyone who loves the parent loves the child" (1 John 5:1).

This suggests that we who are members of God's family have a host of brothers and sisters and that our calling is to love them all for Jesus' sake.

How do we do that? One example: in a newspaper story about the 1973 American Mother of the Year, Mrs. Ruth Nelson—her pastor said, "When she gets home from her trip, she'll probably bake an angel food cake and take it to someone who is lonely."

This vocation isn't limited to those with gray hair. The rooming houses of the young aren't always overflowing with companionship either. A kind word from someone their own age would be medicine, but cookies from a grandmother next door wouldn't be unwelcome. Nor would a faucet repair by a grandfather across the street (even though the landlord should do it).

And of course, angel food cakes or homemade bread can be baked also by younger hands and shared with the aunt or uncle across the alley. Garbage can be taken out and groceries can be bought for those whose legs won't work by those whose legs are young and strong.

I'm urging a coalition of these two groups that seem to be so much at odds. I propose an alliance to promote the kind of understanding in our society that will help dispel the ridicule suffered by both. I hope for a partnership in discovering ways to break free from the system that victimizes both. I dream of a fellowship where young and old embrace each other as though they were embracing Christ, whose sisters and brothers they are, in whose cleansing blood they have both found their personal worth.

To design a style of worship meaningful to those who like the old ways best and at the same time challenging to those who question the old ways—this isn't easy. I dare to expect increasing tolerance from both sides. I await more cross-generational groups where the old share their experience and know-how and the young contribute their freshness and enthusiasm, where new friendships and insights can blossom, where the communion of saints will be the more enriched by all the gifts with which the Holy Spirit has endowed our congregation. I anticipate with eagerness the day when I'm free to decide for myself whether to shave or not to shave.

Published in *The Lutheran Standard*, 5 February 1974, 2–5; preached previously at Bethlehem Lutheran in-the-Midway, St. Paul, Minnesota.

Everlasting Treasures

2 Corinthians 8:1-9

James Thomas

Assistant to the Bishop, Minneapolis Area Synod, ELCA

**From a sermon at Central Lutheran Church,
Minneapolis, Minnesota**
30 January 1994

Many years ago (I think it would have been about in the third grade), Matilda Belton decided one day to introduce her class to the idea of charitable giving. . . . I suspect that at some level of consciousness I knew my family was poor and that we had as many concerns as the family we were going to help, but it didn't matter that day. There was something awfully powerful at work in me on the day Mrs. Belton put that empty box in front of the class and challenged us to fill that box full. A family that was truly poor had seen its home, its collected memory, some part of its dreams, go up in flames. They needed help. I returned home. I opened up the cupboard to determine just how our household was going to get involved in this great tragedy, in this urgent drama. I looked at the can of Hunt's stewed tomatoes, but that I thought wouldn't do. I brushed aside the Carnation evaporated milk. The ubiquitous box of Martin salt would not fill the bill either. I came across a Mason jar with preserved figs. You know, I couldn't bring myself to give anyone a jar of mother's preserved figs, but I discovered I had a good choice. Standing in front of me was a can of Van Kamp's pork and beans and a can of Campbell's tomato soup. I of course went for the beans.

I know as I learned in elementary school that we give very often according to what we feel we can afford to give. Some give, of course, from the overflow. They give generously because they have it left over to give. They give not with a sense of duty or because they are moved to great pity or because they are bothered by some professional fund appeal, but they give gladly. And others give sacrificially. In 2 Corinthians 8:2-4 we read of such people when Paul writes about the Macedonians. They've been severely tested by the troubles they went through. But their joy was so great that they were extremely generous in their giving though they were very poor. "I can assure you that they gave as much as they could and even more than they could." Now try to imagine that in your minds this morning. They gave more than they could afford. They gave sacrificially. They borrowed against the future to address needs they saw today.

And then there are those who desire to give, even in our midst, who can't. And they contribute as best they can through prayer.

And sadly, there are those who can give but do not. Some people do not understand the basic plan of God, sharing. It applies to the economic life as well as to the spiritual life. Sharing, sharing with one another. The Corinthians at the moment had a surplus, and the saints in Jerusalem had a deficiency. Should positions later be reversed, their present generosity would no doubt be balanced by a generosity to them. Love is never a one-way street. The fruits of our own kindness are forever returning in fresh visions of truth. The harvest illustrates a spiritual law: "Cast thy bread upon the water for thou shalt find it after many days."

Again in the book of 2 Corinthians, Paul addresses giving. Paul addresses the responsibility all Christians have to support the ongoing work of the church in the world. He holds before the Corinthian congregation a reason for liberality which the most reluctant heart can scarcely resist. "Friends," Paul says, "there is one in the world by whom you hope." One whom you cannot be ungenerous or illiberal with. For my brothers and sisters, I will tell you something today which is an old, old, old story. To give you something that you have heard before, namely: "For you know the grace of our Lord Jesus Christ that though he was rich, yet for your sake he became poor, that you through his poverty might become rich."

Now ponder this thought. Allow it to sink into the innermost parts of your conscious mind. Force it up into your cerebral cortex. Allow it to work with the spirit of your giving, and whenever you shrink from placing the needs of the church, of the community, and of the mission of Jesus Christ in the world, whenever you are inclined to withhold the firstfruits of your labor from the church, think of Jesus. Think deeply, this morning, of Jesus and why he gave up all that he had to serve you. Think of Jesus, of his self-denial. Think of his story. And when the claims of the poor, of the church, and of the world are pressed upon you, when the needs of displaced persons are persistent, when the cries are raised, passionate cries for a threatened ecology, when the works of Christian medical workers are explained, when we hear of new missions, new congregations called into being to offer hospitality to the needs of newcomers, maybe you will hear a question such as this one:

> I gave my life for thee,
> My precious blood I shed,
> That thou might ransomed be
> And quickened from the dead.
> I gave my life for thee.
> What hast thou given for me?

Now Paul says that Jesus was rich. When I was a child growing up in a Baptist church in Louisiana—and I bet you didn't know that I had been Baptist—my pastor used highly-imaginative language to convey God's meaning. He reminded us that it was Jesus who laid claims to owning a thousand cattle on the hillside. It was Jesus who had hidden treasures of gold, pearls, and every precious thing that the earth had seen. It was Jesus who might have said, "I can stretch my scepter from the east to the west, from the north to the south, and all is mine: the world, and worlds beyond the watchful—even of the eye of the Hubble telescope—through black holes and even through worm holes and into uncharted galaxies, the whole of the world—all, all is mine."

And that's not all. He who said, "Let there be light, and light was," this one was also present in the world with love. I want to tell you something today. I would rather be poor, as poor as a streetchild in Peru today, as poor as a frightened soul in Bosnia, as poor as a black child growing up in some American city, destined it would seem for a short life filled with certain misery. I would rather be that poor and that destitute than to live rich and without love. You may bow before the god of pleasure or the god of money, but love offers a value that money cannot buy. Martin Luther King reminded us that stock markets crash, and given the fact that we can invest unwisely, money is a rather uncertain deity. This transitory god in which many people put their trust and their hopes cannot bring happiness to the human heart. Only God can do that.

Now come with me for a moment and reflect upon this: Jesus was not poor in love. He came richly endowed with the love of God.

He came richly endowed with the love of even the messengers who told lovingly of him to Mary and to some shepherds in a field taking care of their sheep. When Christ came, he identified with the poor.

When I was born, I was placed in a soft little bed in a hospital in Lafayette, Louisiana. When Jesus came into the world, he slept in a manger. He slept in a box out of which cattle fed. When he was a few days old, his mother Mary carried him to Egypt because she feared for his life. And he became a stranger in a strange world. Christ may not have been the poorest child ever born, but he was born into poverty, the reverse of the privileged child. We read in Scripture that he depended on the charity of others for food. He sat upon a well one day and asked a Samaritan woman, "Give me a drink." He looked upon the foxes as they hurried to their burrow, and the birds as they entered their nesting places, and he said, "Foxes have holes and the birds of the air have nests. But the Son of man has no place to lay his head."

Is there a message for us today? He washed the disciples' feet. He was humiliated. He died judged a criminal on what is roughly the equivalent of the modern day electric chair. Look at Jesus today, Christian friends. He left so much behind in order that we might know him. He left his manger. He left his cross. He left his thorny crown. He left his teachings, so rich, so full of love. He left all this so that we might understand better the heart of God. He was rich. Yet for our sake he became poor.

Why did he do it? The writer simply puts it, "For your sake." For your sake and for mine. I ask you today, whatever your circumstance, take this Word with you this week. Examine it and see if it does not address your life. Thank God for the influence of the Holy Spirit upon the truth, and see if this great Word does not make your heart sing with renewed hope. See if it does not lead to a confession something like this: "I may not be all that I should be, but for my sake, Christ came into the world. For my sake, he lived and he died. And I claim this. And I am rich because of it."

Some of you are sitting there looking at me as though you think that I probably don't know something about you. "I know nothing of your struggles to make ends meet." That's what you're saying. You say that you live out there on the edge. You say that you work all month long, pay rent and phone bills and utilities and when you settle the debts you are poor. You wonder how it is that you can be rich when in fact logic argues otherwise. "Silver and gold have I none." That's what you say. But let me assure you that I'm not mocking you.

Just look at what Christ has given you. You have first of all inner peace of soul with God. This peace helps overcome the insatiable greed which stifles many people as they try to live in the world today. The peace which Christ gives points you and me beyond our own confines to the community of all created beings in the world. And of course, we have the grace of God. You are rich, rich this morning with true riches.

And so we're called upon today, each of us, each in our local churches and in our home, we're called to imitate Christ, to imitate God's lovingkindness, to give our lives, to give our riches, for the life of the world. The fellowship of sharing must now be expanded to cover the largest community, which includes humanity and the totality of God's creation. The church, which has become healed through the wounds of Christ, must become an active agent in healing the wounds of all humanity. . . . We must stand before God today in a posture of worship and joyfully accept responsibility for the management of human affairs and the well-being of creation. We have everlasting treasures. Let us invest them well.

The Dog

Luke 16:19-22

Rick Witucki

(Class of 1996, Permanent Deacon Formation Program, Archdiocese of St. Paul and Minneapolis. A three-minute exercise imitating black preaching: more vivid but not less valid details. Transcribed from video cassette, used by permission.)

Do you think Jesus had a dog? I think Jesus had a dog. I was talking to Kathy last night, and I asked, "What kind of dog would Jesus have?" "A Saint Bernard. Or what about a German Shepherd, for the Good Shepherd?" Kathy and I laughed; I actually laughed more than Kathy. Kathy said, "No, Rick. Jesus would have had a mutt." And I said, "Kathy, you're right. Your wisdom comes through again. Jesus would have had a mutt. But that mutt would have heard a lot of good stories. Here's one of the stories the mutt would have heard."

Once upon a time, there was a dog that lived in a town. It was a stray dog; it was a mutt. The dog had no human master—just a Divine Master. It was very good at being a survivor. The dog knew that on Thursday morning she could go down to Jacob the Butcher, and Jake would throw her a soup bone, and that would be something to gnaw on for Thursday. The dog knew that it could go by the widow's place on Monday and get a little piece of lamb, and that would help on Monday. She knew where to get food because the dog was a beggar. The dog knew especially that if she went to the rich man's home, the rich man would have a lot of food, because the rich man had a party every night. The rich man would invite his rich friends over, have a great feast, and throw out a lot of garbage. She would go to that rich man's house, rummage through that garbage. She spent a lot of time out by the rich man's house.

One night, kind of towards midnight, after eating some of the garbage the rich man had thrown out, the dog was resting and saw a group of men coming to the rich man's house, and they had another man with them that they were half-carrying. This group of men took this other man and laid him against the wall of the rich man's house and then left. And the dog was confused by this. So she warily approached the man that had been left and saw first of all that this was a very sick man, that the man had the scent of illness on him. The man had no shoes. The man's feet were covered with blisters that had broken and then blistered up again. His breathing was very, very slow, painful. The dog knew that this was a man who was sick. So the dog said, "There's help that's needed here. Where's the rich man? The rich man can help this person; the rich man has the resources to help this poor man."

The rich man's house was dark. There was no light in the house. So the dog said, "I have to raise the alarm." The dog started to bark, and the dog was a good barker. She'd been barking for a long time, and she barked until the lights went on in the house. The rich man came out. He was dressed in a very fine robe, very fine slippers on his feet, and he looked one side to the other, saw the poor man lying against the wall of his house, looked at the dog, and yelled, "Get out. Stop making so much noise. I'm trying to sleep. Don't bother me." He went back into his house and put out the lights. And the dog said to herself, "What's this all about? Why didn't this rich man come out and help this poor man?" So the dog went up to the poor man. She wasn't too concerned that he was going to hurt her. She began licking his feet. She licked off all the mud that had been caking on his feet. She licked the sores, the old blood, until they were clean, because that's what she had learned to do with wounds, to clean them. And then she went to the poor man's head. The poor man looked at her with a faint smile and said, "Good girl. Thank you, girl." And she lay by the poor man, put her body against his body, and they slept, sharing the warmth of their bodies. Shortly before sunrise, the poor man died. The dog knew that this had happened because she felt his body grow cold, and she couldn't hear his breathing any more. The dog howled till sunrise in prayer for her friend.

Brothers and sisters, we have a choice. We can be the rich man and turn our back. When the alarm is sounded, we can say, "Go away. Don't bother me." Or we can be a dog that cleans our friend's wounds. We can be a dog that comforts. We can be a dog that prays for our fellows. That's what Jesus has called us to do.

Index